D1382721

The Glory and the Tragedy

DAN WALKER

Taylor Pensoneau & Bob Ellis

Smith Collins

WITHDRAWN

DECATUR PUBLIC LIBRARY

NOV 0 1 1993

DECATUR, ILLINOIS

Editor: Gareth Gardiner

Cover & book designer: Curt Neitzke

Copyright © 1993 by Taylor Pensoneau and Bob Ellis. All rights reserved. No part of this book may be reproduced or transmitted in any form or by any means, electronic or mechanical, including photocopying and recording, or by any information storage and retrieval system without permission in writing from the publisher. Address inquiries to The Smith-Collins Company, P.O. Box 15603, Evansville, IN 47716. Smith-Collins' 24-hour toll-free number is 1-800-345-0096.

Publisher's Cataloging-in-Publication Data

Pensoneau, Taylor.
    Dan Walker: the glory and the tragedy / Taylor Pensoneau and Bob Ellis.
Evansville, Ind.: Smith-Collins, 1993.
    p.   cm.
    Includes index.
    ISBN: 0-9623414-6-0

    1. Walker, Dan. 2. Illinois—Governors—Biography. 3. Illinois—Politics
    and government—1951—
I. Ellis, Bob.   II. Title
F546.4.W   977.3'043 [92] [B] dc20   93-71199

Printed in the United States of America

*This book is dedicated to the memory of
Marine Lieutenant Terry Pensoneau,
who was killed in action in the Vietnam
War on December 16, 1968.*

CONTENTS

Introduction

This book is a collaborative effort between two individuals who found themselves in total agreement that Dan Walker certainly was one of the most exciting figures to play a major role in the history of Illinois politics.

We felt that the time had arrived, before the passing of too many more years, to put down on paper as best we could an account of the colorful Walker era, focusing on its atmosphere and the men and women who did so much to shape the events of that fascinating period.

However, Bob and I came to the project by different paths.

Bob Ellis is the managing editor of the Daily American newspaper in West Frankfort and a widely-read columnist in newspapers throughout southern Illinois.

He was quite intrigued by the Walker saga even though he had not been on the Illinois Capital scene in Springfield to cover the governorship of Walker, which ran for four years beginning in January 1973.

While Walker was imprisoned in Duluth, Minnesota, in the late 1980s on federal financial felony charges unrelated to his governorship, Bob established a relationship with the former governor through columns on him and several visits to Walker in prison.

Out of that contact, Bob undertook the writing of a book on Walker with the cooperation of the former governor. However, because Bob had not observed firsthand the gubernatorial role of Walker, there were limits to the extent to which he could develop the book.

To the contrary, I had covered the Walker chapter in Illinois public life quite closely as the Springfield-based Illinois political writer for the St. Louis Post-Dispatch. The material for my typewriter was never more interesting than in the Walker years.

Although I left the Post-Dispatch for a position with the Illinois Coal Association in 1978, I never retreated from my belief that the Dan Walker story had all the makings of a book.

In the early part of 1991, the former governor and I had occasion to spend an evening together in San Diego, a meeting at which the book was discussed. In addition, Bob had met with me several times to seek my perspective on the book. The upshot of it all was my resulting involvement as coauthor.

Bob and I could not begin to thank enough the many persons who helped to make this book possible, not the least of which were the numerous individuals who consented to interviews essential for the telling of the story. All were very gracious with their time.

As with any book, though, some persons merit added recognition.

One is Kay Ellis, the wife of Bob and a pillar of strength for the project from beginning to end.

I benefitted in particular from the warm support for the project from Jeff Prugh of the Los Angeles Times, a lifelong confidant, and Joseph Spivey, my friend and partner at the Illinois Coal Association.

Special thanks for assistance also go to Janice Petterchak, the director of the Illinois State Historical Library; Cheryl Schnirring, curator of manuscripts at the historical library; Caroline Gherardini, editor of Illinois Issues magazine; and Stanley E. Adams, special projects consultant at the Illinois State Library.

And, of course, two other individuals deserve special mention. One is Gary Gardiner, the editor of the book, and the other is Curt Neitzke, the book's designer and typesetter.

Finally, I could not have finished this effort without the encouragement of my son Taylor Terry and my daughter Jennifer.

Taylor Pensoneau
Springfield, Illinois
March 1993

From the Mansion to Prison—
One Man's Journey

The federal prison camp at Duluth, Minnesota, seems light-years away from the rest of the United States, especially when the bitter wintry winds off Lake Superior shriek across the lofty rise shouldering the compound.

Doing their time, the inmates find it impossible to ignore the gut-wrenching isolation of the place, far from the rest of American society and the meaningful lives that many of them once led. In 1988, this was very true for one prisoner, a lanky fellow, who consumed chili and cranberry juice as he conversed with a visitor on a below-zero day in the dead of winter. Although he wore suits on occasion, the man was garbed that day in his prison uniform of khaki pants and shirt because, within a short time, he would be cleaning toilets.

Nearly a half century earlier, he had done the same thing. But then it was heads, and it was part of his shipboard routine as an apprentice seaman. The methodology of it had not changed much, he thought wryly. Everything else had, though.

Between then and now, this frozen night in Minnesota, the prisoner had scaled the heights of life beyond the wildest dreams of most of the millions of people he once led, men and women who had heeded his call for a revolutionary new chapter in American political life. No novelist could have spun a more unlikely tale.

Dirt-poor kid from San Diego and Naval Academy graduate makes it as corporate lawyer in faraway Chicago, dabbles in politics on the side but can't crack the ruling establishment in his adopted state of Illinois. So, in an all or nothing crapshoot far riskier than any Las Vegas longshot, he audaciously launches a bid for the state's highest office against the will of the last great big city political machine in the country, the monolith in Chicago run by his fellow Democrat, the legendary Mayor Richard J. Daley. And he wins, this fellow now imprisoned in Minnesota.

Defying all odds, he captures the Democratic Party's nomination for governor of Illinois by penetrating the seemingly invincible Daley machine and its candidate for the post, a celebrated political figure who had never lost an election. Then, this political outsider, bolstered by the thousands of political independents, newcomers and have-nots who flocked to his cause, goes on to wrap up his incredible odyssey to the zenith of Illinois public life by unseating the incumbent Republican governor. It all happened in 1972. Heady stuff, but true—as hard as it was to believe in looking back from a federal pen in Minnesota.

There seemed to be no way, and nobody, to stop this man as he stood in the cold of a January day in 1973 in the Illinois capital of Springfield and took the oath of office as the thirty-sixth governor of Illinois.

Governor Dan Walker.

Fifty years old at the time of his inauguration, and one of the hottest political properties in the United States.

Dan Walker, the man who beat Daley; the self-styled populist whose vows to reunite the little guy with big government had begun to capture the national political imagination.

His inaugural speech was vintage Walker, as he resolved "to sweep the arrogance of bureaucracy from the halls of power and let the voice of the people be heard once again." Faith in government had suffered, Walker averred, because "too many in government" believe that "only experts, politicians, bureaucrats or those with wealth or power can tell the people what to do."

The several thousand persons who braved the brisk weather to watch his inauguration included most of Illinois' major political figures and some of those wealthy and powerful individuals he talked about. Few had supported him, and not many liked what they heard that day. But they were not sure what to do with this new governor who had circumvented the enmeshed power structure to get elected and who now seemed intent on doing things differently.

Scandalous conduct by public officeholders already had shaken the status quo in Illinois, and now this new governor threatened to turn the state completely topsy-turvy. The old order dreaded the beginning of the Walker era, which certainly should have been the case because Dan Walker, riding high, had every intention of justifying the suspicion, hostility and, yes, the hatred aimed at him by the old guard of Illinois. They had met their match in Dan Walker, the consummate outsider who would make them regret their blackballing of him by ushering new faces and innovative programs into Illinois public life and, even more importantly, by setting a higher moral tone in Illinois government. Walker intended to show 'em. And, he did.

Political excitement, bitter confrontation, great showmanship. All were hallmarks of the Walker years. Political scientists may debate for a long time the quality of his administration,but the heavy imprints of his rise and fall will not be disputed.

The slide from the stately Illinois Executive Mansion to a Minnesota prison is a long way down. It was not a straight drop. There were slopes, plateaus and even some peaks on the way, but the end was what Walker felt in his penal days to be an ultimate and very painful bottom. He had become a lot of things, including a lawbreaker.

The unraveling of Dan Walker. Where did it start?

It might have been with an illicit love affair that Walker, married and the father of seven children, carried out secretly within the highly-visible, tightly scheduled and security-protected world, the life in a fishbowl, of an Illinois governor.

Too, it could have been his late-term frustration growing out of the unending difficulties from trying to govern as an independent-minded Democrat in a state dominated by political clubism.

Then came his defeat in the 1976 Illinois primary election contest for the Democratic gubernatorial nomination—and with that, the death of Walker's dream of a late entry into the race for the White House that year (a contest to be won by another Democrat and Naval Academy graduate, Governor Jimmy Carter of Georgia).

After leaving office, Walker did not take the well-trod path of most attorneys in his shoes by joining a large law firm. Instead, he established a multi-office, statewide legal firm. It did not pan out as he had hoped. He did succeed with a cross-country fast oil change business that he founded. However, his purchase of a small savings and loan association ended in disaster, what with the business being taken over by federal authorities and his personal financial dealings in it tied to his landing in prison.

Not many Illinoisans were aware of the problems encountered by Walker after his departure from the state's highest office. That is, until the glaring headlines on his indictment, admission of guilt and sentencing in respect to fraudulent financial activity allegations related to his Chicago area thrift. While Walker's crime did not involve his actions as governor, his conviction nonetheless heightened the cynicism held by so many in the state for their elected officials.

The state's chief executive during most of the 1960s, Democrat Otto Kerner, went to prison following his governorship after he was found guilty in a criminal trial of federal tax evasion and other charges stemming from scandalous racing track stock deals while he was governor. During the administrations of Walker and his predecessor as governor, Republican Richard Ogilvie, a seemingly endless parade of officials from all levels in the state were herded into court on charges of malfeasance. Indeed, a report by the United States Department of Justice showed Illinois way ahead of other states from 1970 through 1976 in the number of state and local officials convicted on federal charges of accepting bribes, engaging in extortion and other offenses involving corruption in office. Walker and Ogilvie always pointed out, though, that these individuals were not from their administrations.

Walker had run for office as an alternative to all this nasty stuff. He was the concerned, make it enraged, citizen who had come forward to challenge the crooks and their cronies who had made a shambles of the image of public life in the state.

So, when he stumbled, the pessimism only soared. Actually, there were other parts of Walker's life between the governorship and prison that his followers did or certainly would have found surprising.

As governor, Walker insisted on austerity in everything, including his own image. He did not flaunt his security, like some of his predecessors, and he eschewed the fancy cars and other perks normally associated with the Illinois governorship. Walker wanted to identify with the common guy, who had put him in office, not the almighty elite. The gas jockey in Vandalia was Walker's person, not the heiress in Kennilworth.

But Walker pursued a different life-style after leaving office, starting with a divorce from his wife of more than 30 years, Roberta. Walker felt at the time, to his later regret, that the former first lady of Illinois, shy and retiring to the public, was a cause of his disenchantment after leaving office.

He had no such feeling about another woman with whom he became involved after the end of his affair while governor. She was 14 years younger than Walker, beautiful and vivacious, a good businesswoman in his mind and, ironically, also named Roberta. She would become the second Mrs. Walker in a marriage that he just knew would lead to the good life that he felt had eluded him.

Roberta the second knew the world of high society, parties and balls, polo, country clubs and wealthy folks in places like Palm Beach. Admirers told them they made a dashing pair, right off a page by F. Scott Fitzgerald. It hurt to look back on it from the federal prison.

"We both opened doors to a very lovely life-style," Walker recalled. "We enjoyed each other and the glittering world we were entering. It was a life I had never tasted before. I grew up poor, learned the social graces at the Naval Academy, but never felt accepted by the glamorous side of society. I enjoyed seeing my picture, with my beautiful wife, being published on the society pages."

In time, the new Walker got into the expensive habit of buying yachts—two to be exact, each called The Governor's Lady.

"We sailed through the waterways from Chicago to Florida, entertaining the wealthy and elite on our yacht; pictures of us drinking champagne on a boat dock were published in *Town and Country* magazine. I was riding high. But like the champagne, it went to my head. It got out of hand."

Still, the good life continued. The politician who once had trudged through sun-baked fields in southern Illinois seeking votes from hardscrabble farmers now favored linen suits, Gucci jackets and tennis resort wear as he cruised to the Bahamas or flew to London for parties at the country manor of Lady Di's parents and receptions at Buckingham Palace.

Actually, to Walker, his new pursuits put him on a high comparable in a remote way to the euphoric stages of the governorship. One replaced the other.

As he saw it, "I was entitled to it. I had worked hard all my life. Nothing had come easy for me. And I had done it all honorably, to my knowledge, and except for my first wife, I had never consciously hurt anyone on the way to the top. And, by anybody's account, I had helped many."

However, Walker's fortunes were to take a disastrous yet familiar turn. While detailed attention to his businesses was ignored, his living expenses continued to mount—and so did the borrowing to keep the former governor and his new world afloat.

Walker clearly was in over his head in the management of his savings and loan, where he could not find a key to profitability. As for his oil change business, operations in St. Louis, Texas and Florida in particular were not doing well. Federal thrift regulators were clamping down on Walker's mixture of the two enterprises. Furthermore, Walker went to court twice to protect the oil change business against the vagarious conduct in the undertaking of his flamboyant business partner, Frank Butler. Wife Roberta the second was an officer of both businesses and worked with Walker in the managerial end of things.

Finally, with the conflict between Walker and Frank Butler getting out of hand, the oil change venture was sold at a bargain basement price to a large national firm. The savings and loan would slip, too, out of the hands of Walker and his wife, through the federal takeover, but not before Walker borrowed funds loaned by the institution to other individuals, including one of the former governor's sons, Dan Walker, Jr. Besides pleading guilty to federal charges of fraudulent conduct in regard to these loans, Walker also pled guilty to a charge of perjury prompted by his denial to federal authorities that he ever had benefitted financially from a loan to a member of his family by the thrift, First American Savings and Loan Association (his son had used the proceeds of a loan from the association to pay a $14,000 law firm debt on which his father Dan, several years before, was a cosigner).

In addition, Walker also entered a plea of guilty to the signing by he and his wife of false personal financial statements filed with other financial institutions. According to the federal indictment, the statements falsely exaggerated the couple's income and under-stated their liability picture.

Consequently, on Nov. 19, 1987, Walker was sentenced by United States District Court Judge Ann Williams to seven years in prison for his crimes, to be followed by five years of probation after the completion of the prison sentence. His wife, whose only direct involvement in the allegations involved her signing of the personal financial statements, escaped prosecution. Later, after Walker went to prison, she requested and was granted a divorce from him.

At the sentencing in Chicago Williams said the onetime governor had "placed himself above the law" and charged that his "fall from grace, loss of stature, embarrassment and humiliation" were of his own doing.

Walker was not about to argue. A man who 11 years earlier had been a recognized contender for his party's presidential nomination was now, at age 65, thinking only of being branded a felon for the rest of his life.

Did he blame himself? Yes, without question. Was he bitter? No doubt of it, especially in his early months in jail when he joined many of his fellow inmates in looking longingly at those on the outside who had committed the same or far worse crimes and escaped retribution.

After all, untold numbers of businessmen filed exaggerated and even false financial statements every day, didn't they? Many savings and loan executives, as events not much later were to confirm, had plundered their institutions, but were still spending their days on country club golf courses. And how many persons have told untruths in sworn depositions and not been sentenced to prison for perjury?

Walker's bitterness went a lot further, though. He felt he had been singled out unfairly for prosecution because he was a former governor, and he viewed his sentence as unnecessarily harsh. Too, he perceived in the coverage of his case a resurrection of the media hostility aimed at him, he thought, in the old days in Springfield. In his own mind, Walker also lashed out at his successor in the governor's office, Republican James Thompson, a successful political figure both envied and scorned by Walker. Envied because Thompson was thought by Walker to have benefitted from gentle treatment by the press and from extraordinary political luck. Scorned because of Walker's paranoiac belief that Thompson had conspiratorially orchestrated grand jury investigations of Walker and his administration, inquiries extending beyond Walker's years in office, in an effort to discourage a political comeback by Walker.

As the months in prison passed, though, the bitterness of Walker mellowed. His interest in the historical life of Jesus, which began with research by Walker in 1986, flowered while he was imprisoned. He even began to nurture the hope while in prison that his niche in Illinois history would take on a much more favorable light with the passing of the years.

There were even moments when Walker was able to dispel the gloom of incarceration with vivid recollections of the dramatic stages of his campaign for governor and, then, of the hope and seemingly unbridled opportunity for good created by his still implausible capture of the office.

Everything about the Walker years in Illinois politics defied orthodoxy, starting with the timing and circumstances of his surprising announcement that he even intended to run for governor.

Nothing compared, though, to the brilliant tactic that he used to draw attention to his candidacy, a 1,197-mile walk that took him in zigzag fashion from the bottom of Illinois to the Wisconsin border. The four-month trek, which began in July of 1971 at the Ohio River town of Brookport, captured the heart and imagination of the populace and catapulted Walker from a political unknown to a household name in Illinois politics.

Maybe his snickering detractors were right and the walk was corny. But it also was effective, as the early doubters grudgingly acknowledged later.

Exhaustion, sores from blisters and the elements made many days of the walk nothing short of pure misery. Yet, the daily image of the often lonely figure, trudging along in a denim shirt, khaki trousers and a red bandanna, reaped exactly what Walker wanted and needed. Very quickly, he became a magnet for thousands of Illinoisans disgusted with the political facts of life in their state. College kids, other young voters, political novices, do-gooders...they flocked to his cause.

These were the kinds of persons who bought his message that it was time for a new beginning in public life in Illinois. The civil rights movement disruptions of the 1960s, the violent opposition to the Vietnam War, the downgrading of so many cherished institutions, the coming apart of American life at its traditional seams.

All of this paved the way for Dan Walker. He was in every way a man of the hour. As it turned out, an army of countless willing recruits awaited him.

Walker himself was cast perfectly for his role. Tall and rawboned, rugged faced but handsome. The Marlboro man in person. Sincere. Also serious. Seldom was he seen as anything but serious. And, of course, that gaze. It was penetrating and mesmerizing, and nobody every forgot it.

Each day during the walk, Walker dictated to a tape recorder the day's accomplishments or disappointments, his impressions, the issues he encountered and the names and descriptions of the persons he met. These recordings would be transformed into a walk journal, which Walker consulted time and again for self-reassurance in the difficult years that followed.

The Walker portrayed in the journal was an optimist whose eyes were opened at every milepost by the dignity and simple eloquence of the people he hoped to govern. Whether in small town cafes or on big city streets, Walker listened, really listened. Later, he tried to react as governor, in both his policies and the intended character of his administration, to the concerns and aspirations voiced to him on the walk and later found in the journal.

The journal made it all so clear, and even simple. It was good reading, too.

The narrative was a compendium of Walker's daily discoveries and insights, many in the tidbit category, that only could be gleaned by somebody doing something as down to earth as walking through his or her state. The journal might have been marketed as an explorer's diary for mostly forgotten parts of Illinois away from the freeways. More salient, though, is that Walker emerged through the narrative as an individual with a lucid picture of what he was about, what he was doing and what he intended to accomplish if successful.

The Walker of the journal was not nearly as complicated as the man who later, as governor, so stubbornly defied easy analysis.

Historians may or may not come to agree with the belief of Walker—as he sat in prison—that his stewardship of Illinois would be viewed with increasing importance with the passing of time. To many political scientists, the makeup of the man, his mystique to some, overshadowed the programs and directions of Illinois government under Walker. Evaluation of the Walker governorship required penetration beyond the man himself, and that has been difficult to do.

One of the first persons to pass judgment, the late journalist and historian, Robert P. Howard, was not kind. Howard rated Walker one of the state's poorest chief executives in his book on Illinois governors, *Mostly Good and Competent Men*. To Howard, Dan Walker was a smart fellow but too sanctimonious and contentious. In the end, Howard viewed Walker as a tragic figure, a governor about whom Howard found little positive to say.

Will other opinions down the line be as damaging? Perhaps not...at least in the minds of many in the legion of men and women who comprised the growing Walker legacy in Illinois as the state moved into the last decade of the Twentieth Century.

Two of the three Democrats holding statewide constitutional offices in the wake of the 1990 election were Walker proteges. Numerous influential members of the Democratic majority in each branch of the Illinois General Assembly at the start of the 1990s were products of the Walker movement. At the same time, Walker people populated many key governmental staff slots at all levels in the state, while other Walkerites played prestigious policy roles in umpteen other segments of life in Illinois.

For a lot of these folks, the imprisonment of Walker—which ended in June of 1989—served to discourage or even make impossible fair analysis of the man and the changes he wrought. Rational discourse on Walker, they feel, has been muted.

If as some say the record will show him to be another Huey Long, then so be it. Or maybe even a pied piper.

But Walker's followers knew they were part of something special when they signed up and embarked on their improbable drive to capture Springfield from those entrenched interests. And they did it. And, for most of them, it was the time of their lives.

God, it was exciting. ❧

On Top of the World

Baur's Restaurant is a fashionable repose of artful cuisine nestled on a little brick street just south of the State Capitol complex in the middle of Springfield. Since the late 1970s, Baur's has been a gathering spot for Illinois government leaders, lobbyists and other players, a congenial atmosphere for courteous discussion of issues, a place simply to be seen.

However, earlier in the 70s, the redbrick edifice housed a nightclub, the Warehouse, a raucous bastion for rock bands and swingers.

They would jam the cabaret on weekends if the band was

good, and the one booked for Saturday night, July 7, 1973, was good. Snake and the Armpits. Squeezed into tight black leather outfits, their hair greased down, Snake and his boys looked like motorcycle toughs from the 1950s. Sweating like crazy, they belted out one pop standard after another. When band members jumped with their guitars from the stage onto nearby tables, drinks went flying and the audience screamed with delight.

At one table by the stage, though, a small party of patrons didn't budge a lick when Snake leaped from the platform to the middle of their table. Two at the table especially maintained polite but very composed smiles as Snake moved his body through frantic gyrations.

The two were Governor Dan Walker and his wife Roberta and they fully realized that every eye in the place was turned toward them. They were on top of the world that night, at the center of their universe. They knew it when one of the band members stopped the show to ask, "Is there anybody in this audience who can fix a traffic ticket?" The packed house loved that.

The late hour visit to the Warehouse by the Walkers, accompanied by several others, capped a sentimental evening for the Governor, one that had started a few hours earlier with a party at the Executive Mansion for a few reporters, Walker family members and a handful of staffers and other individuals associated with his walk throughout the state two summers before.

The event was low-keyed, a time for reminiscing by Walker and his guests interrupted only by the innocent voices of a youth choir from Bloomington brought in for the get-together.

The night marked the end of Walker's first six months in office. The man had just gotten his first Illinois legislative session under his belt, and he felt he fared a lot better during the first six-month meeting of the Seventy-eighth General Assembly than did many of the scribes and other analysts.

Actually, Walker had hesitated to deal with the Legislature on a number of matters, apparently thinking that his image would be served better by remaining aloof from the risky entanglements which can result from total involvement by a governor in every legislative matter. Also, Walker felt handicapped this first time around with the lawmakers because of the low regard for him by many Democratic legislators who had backed the regular state party organization's unsuccessful attempt the previous year to deny Walker the nomination for governor.

Inevitably, conversation during the evening at the Mansion touched on Washington, where President Richard Nixon's crew had been undergoing grilling for weeks by a congressional panel on the spreading Watergate crisis.

Walker asked several of his guests how they would handle Watergate if they were Nixon. If he was in the White House, Walker said, he would lay the whole thing out before the public as long as he believed he had done nothing wrong. Of course, the pundits already had Walker running for the White House, figuring that anybody with the astounding political success of Walker in such a short time was not about to stop with the Illinois governorship.

But Walker was not talking about the presidency, at least not openly. As Burnell Heinecke, the Springfield bureau chief for the Chicago Sun-Times later was to write about that evening at the Mansion, Walker even looked a bit uneasy when the choir sang a number suggesting that any American boy could be president.

Overall, though, that was an occasion devoted to the past, not the future. After dinner, the Governor and a few of his guests retreated for the serving of liqueur to the Lincoln Study, a small room in the Mansion used by Walker as a den. There, Walker opened a blue-covered book encompassing his day-to-day observations or, as the document came to be known, the journal of his famous walk.

With relish, Walker turned to pages on which the names of his guests were mentioned. When a reporter noted that his name was misspelled, the Governor immediately corrected it. His pride also was evident when he produced a pair of tired-looking, beaten up boots used in the walk.

Walker asked a couple of guests to stay after the rest departed. The Governor wanted to talk about his background and enthusiastically proceeded to do so during the ensuing time at the Mansion and the late evening visit to the Warehouse. His conversation dwelled on his late father—on the kind of man he had been and on the influence his father had had on Walker's mother and their two sons.

The Governor's father was Lewis Wesley Walker, a tough as leather Texan whose hard but fascinating life weighed heavily on the mind and character of young Dan.

When Walker took the oath of office as governor Jan. 8, 1973, in an extraordinary outdoor ceremony in front of the Statehouse, his father sat a few feet away behind the podium, his back rigidly straight. He was bundled up against the freezing air in a dark overcoat, with a white scarf around his neck. He was one of the few present to wear a hat, and a blanket was draped over his legs. He was almost blind, and he held a cane in his hands.

Less than two months later, on March 5, the Governor's father died back home at San Diego. He was 78 years old. Walker's mother had passed away two years earlier in San Diego at the age of 72.

Lewis Walker was a retired Navy chief petty officer who, although a son of Texas, called the area around San Diego home for most of his life.

His wife of more than half a century was the former Virginia May Lynch, and she also was from Texas. She grew up near Hutto, a small town a short hike from Galveston. Lewis Walker came off a farm close to the east Texas community of Jacksonville, which in turn was not that far from a tiny hamlet named Reklaw (which Dan Walker swore was named after Lewis Walker's family but with the name Walker spelled backwards).

The two did not meet in Texas, though. It happened after her family moved to Long Beach, Calif., and her enrollment after World War I at UCLA. As Dan Walker recalled, "They met and were married at Long Beach . . . my father was a sailor and he simply swept her off her feet."

The old man, as Walker lovingly called his father in his later years, was the model for Walker's independence and, in Walker's thinking, the inspiration for the Governor's drive to succeed.

Rough and ready, Lewis Walker came out of east Texas at a time early in the century when many men in that neck of the woods still carried guns to protect themselves. Restlessly roaming his home state, he became a telegrapher. After working for railroads, he claimed to have telegraphed in Mexico for revolutionary leader Pancho Villa.

Then, with the coming of World War I, he answered a Navy advertisement for telegraphers. In joining up, he volunteered for submarine duty. After the war, he stayed in the Navy. By the early 1920s, he was the radioman on President Warren Harding's naval yacht.

It was in Washington, D.C., on Aug. 6, 1922, while Harding was president, that Virginia Walker gave birth to her second son, Daniel. He was named after Daniel Walker, a judge in Texas and brother of Lewis Walker.

The other child of Lewis and Virginia Walker, Lewis Wesley Walker, Jr., was born two years before Daniel. Lewis Walker, Jr., went on to become a naval officer who retired as a captain.

The marriage of Lewis and Virginia Walker was dominated by the husband, who in the view of his son Daniel was an unequivocal chauvinist. "He ran everything," in the words of Walker, "but the house."

Walker's father also happened to be an alcoholic, and that

complicated family life. He did finally come to grips with his alcoholism and remained dry the last 15 years of his life, when as a member of Alcoholics Anonymous he spoke frequently on the subject throughout California.

Another predicament for the Walkers was money. After Lewis Walker took early retirement from the Navy in 1934, during the Great Depression, his family went through a severe penny-pinching period in San Diego that lasted until World War II. There were times when the father was out of work, leaving his wife and sons virtually dependent on his $60 a month naval pension for survival.

During those years, when the family lived on a small truck farm outside San Diego, Dan remembered that he and his brother raised vegetables "to sell door-to-door to get high school spending money. When there were no vegetables, we sold magazine subscriptions, hosiery and Fuller brushes. It was an experience that built character."

In no way, though, did the paucity of family dollars diminish the expectations of Lewis Walker for his two boys. He believed religiously that his line of Walkers "belonged in the top 10 percent of the population" and that this was achievable only through strict perseverance. Thus, the upbringing of Dan and his brother often smacked of a boot camp because of their father's insistence on toil, discipline and duty. He was an autocratic taskmaster.

A lot of the father was thought to be visible later in son Dan. Time and again, those crossing Lewis Walker's path were struck by his military bearing, strong self-control and emphasis on high performance by his associates and subordinates. To some, he simply was aloof, if not arrogant.

His heroes were the characters of the old West—the marshals, the gunslingers, rough and independent settlers, the winners of the Indian wars.

What about his mother? What did Virginia Walker impart to

her sons?

Idealism, above all. And religion and faith. She also taught sociability, a quality the boys did not get from their father, a loner all his life.

In the view of her son the Governor, "She was idealistic about people; she believed in the essential goodness of people and she would never say anything bad about anybody."

Although she remained in his mind "an old-fashioned lady who never worked outside the house, always standing by my father in difficult periods," the Governor also was moved in the years after he left home by "my mother's frequently strong liberal positions on issues." He got, he said, "a heavy dose of liberalism from her."

With the arrival of World War II, the life of the Walker family changed rapidly. Lewis Walker returned to active duty in the Navy and his son Lewis won admission to the Naval Academy through competitive examinations.

In the meantime, Daniel was valedictorian of the class of 1940 at San Diego High School. After that, having joined the Naval Reserve, he was mobilized as a seaman and spent most of the next two years serving on minesweepers in the Pacific.

Although saying later that it was more fun being an enlisted man than an officer, Walker proceeded to follow his brother to the Naval Academy by scoring near the top among thousands of sailors in the fleet who took competitive tests for appointment to the academy. Of the 1,250 or so members of Dan Walker's class at Annapolis, 50 were sailors from the fleet who qualified like him.

At the academy, Walker was a rebel, a sign of things to come. Unlike high school and law school later, Walker was a poor student at the academy. But he was nifty at beating the system.

When he went to the academy, he did not surrender his sailor's uniform. He had a reason for this. After classes, he liked to sneak off the academy grounds and go into town to spend nights hitting taverns with the sailors. This was against the rules, but Walker escaped detection by wearing his old sailor's uniform when making the rounds. After these forays, he would return to the academy, take off the sailor's suit, watch carefully to avoid the guards and then stealthily creep back to his room through a certain window.

If caught, he would have been kicked out of the academy and sent back to the fleet.

Decades later, as a newly elected governor at a conference at Annapolis sponsored by the National Governors Association, Walker was introduced to the then superintendent of the Naval Academy at a reception in his residence. The superintendent asked Walker if he had been to Annapolis before, and the Governor said he had. Was it for business or pleasure, the superintendent wanted to know.

When Walker replied that the question was hard to answer, the superintendent commented testily that he could not see why.

"Well, Admiral," rejoined Walker, "I am a graduate of the Naval Academy."

A dead silence followed, after which the superintendent turned with a withering look to an astonished aide and said, "You certainly didn't do your homework for me."

Later, the superintendent sent Walker a photograph of part of Bancroft Hall, where midshipmen lived. Circled in red was the window used by Walker in escaping to town for his unauthorized liberties. Under the picture was a caption that read: "Governor Dan Walker; his escape hatch." Walker never learned how the superintendent found out about the window.

As it was, Walker barely did escape the academy, finishing academically near the bottom of his class. But graduate he did in 1945.

Next, he served two years as an officer on destroyers in the Pacific, and then he resigned from the Navy to enter law school at

Northwestern University.

The law school Walker was far different from the Walker at the academy. He was ranked second in the graduating class in 1950, editor in chief of the school's law review and recipient of the Order of Coif and other honors. The Dan Walker of Northwestern law school was seen as a young man of great promise.

The years at Northwestern also nourished the growth of the new roots in Illinois being sown by Walker.

Shortly before entering law school, Walker was married in 1947 to Roberta Dowse, whom he had met three years earlier when he was a midshipman at the Naval Academy. She was raised in Kenosha, Wisconsin, but her mother's family had a long history in Lake County in Illinois.

At Northwestern, Walker became an active Democrat and helped to rejuvenate an organization called Young Democrats that had been inactive during World War II. He jumped into the successful 1948 campaign for the United States Senate by Democrat Paul Douglas, a University of Chicago professor.

Walker's days at Northwestern also left him well acquainted with a law school professor there named Walter V. Schaefer, who down the road was to give Walker his first taste of Springfield and introduce him to Governor Adlai Stevenson.

Before being appointed a justice of the Illinois Supreme Court in 1951, Schaefer was chairman of the Illinois Commission to Study State Government—the state's so-called Little Hoover Commission. When Walker graduated from law school in 1950, he planned to practice in California. However, he decided to stay a bit longer in Illinois when Schaefer tapped him for a staff position with the Little Hoover panel.

This was his first legal job. Finally, he could support his growing family. Two children were born while he was in law school; the third arrived in that first Springfield stay.

The position with the Little Hoover Commission necessitated a six-month stay by the Walkers in Springfield, and gave him his first association with the structure of Illinois government.

Twenty-three years later, when Walker was sworn in as governor, the oath of office was administered by Justice Walter Schaefer—to the surprise of nobody who had taken the time to research the background of this fellow Dan Walker who, by now, had taken Illinois by storm. ❧

The Young Turks

The first day in November of 1991 a cold rain pelted Chicago, leaving the downtown streets murky long before dusk.

From a window of an office on the fifth floor of the building at 100 North LaSalle Street, across from the gray fortress that is Chicago's City Hall, a stocky figure looked down on scurrying pedestrians trying to dodge the raindrops. Then he returned to his desk.

On it was spread the obituary page of that day's Chicago Tribune. Reading it, the man shook his head sadly when he came to a story on the death of Mrs. Dorothy Grant Arndt, a lawyer from Rock Island, Illinois, who had been active in liberal and Democratic Party politics for nearly half a century.

"She and her husband were fine people," the man behind the desk remarked to a visitor. "They were supporters of Dan, and without people like them we couldn't have done it. We could count on them."

Mrs. Arndt and her late husband Samuel, also an attorney, were helpful to Walker in the early days of his campaign for governor. He slept one night in their home when he came to the Illinois part of the Quad Cities during his walk, and Sam Arndt helped usher Walker through various stops in Rock Island.

Later, when Walker was governor, Dorothy Arndt was chairwoman of the Illinois Board of Vocational Education and Rehabilitation, which administered training and other programs for handicapped or disabled persons.

The individual that rainy day lamenting the death of Mrs. Arndt was Victor Robert de Grazia. No account of Dan Walker and his time in Illinois public life could ignore for long the presence of de Grazia.

From the mid 1950s until the end of Walker's governorship, easily two decades, few men in Illinois politics ever were more closely linked. Walker was the star of their unlikely story, but de Grazia more than merited the Oscar for best supporting actor. The Walker saga had many chapters, but few could be chronicled without getting into the numerous roles of de Grazia. Where Walker went, so went de Grazia.

As Walker led the struggle to produce a meaningful independent Democratic political movement in the 1950s, de Grazia usually was the person picked or hired to actually get things done.

When Walker was in the public spotlight in the ensuing decade, de Grazia seldom was far away. And, finally, in regard to the governorship, de Grazia successfully managed Walker's campaign for the post and, then, served as deputy to the governor while

Walker was in office.

Their relationship appeared inviolable. If Walker won praise, de Grazia also got plaudits for being a political genius. Likewise, critics of Walker seldom gave de Grazia a pass. They toiled far into the night to come up with phrases to denigrate de Grazia, whose father was an immigrant musician from Sicily.

A shadowy Machiavellian, that's what they frequently called him.

But, whatever they labeled him, the image of de Grazia became bigger than life. Whether friend or foe, nobody misunderstood the closeness of de Grazia to Walker.

Political junkies in Illinois love to pinpoint with each governor those few select individuals, usually men, who comprise the innermost circle at the pinnacle of each regime. Sometimes, this elite little group may be called the governor's palace guard.

As opposed to mere insiders, the inner circle members or palace guardsmen have daily access to a governor, can deny it to others and often largely determine what subjects reach a governor's desk for his personal attention. This can be a two-edged sword for a governor. The immensity of the job requires a necessary filtering of the paperwork and other details heading for the governor, as is the case with chief executives of most major corporations.

On the other hand, more than one Illinois governor was thought to be hurt politically by an overprotective palace guard that, in shielding a governor from the trials and tribulations of everyday Illinoisans, isolated him too much from the folks who put him in office. Losing touch can be risky for politicians.

Victor de Grazia was perceived as the main man in Walker's inner circle, and nothing leaked out from the seat of power in those days that altered that impression. The others in that special little cadre were a mystery man, a previously unsung lawyer and a former newspaper political editor.

David Green was a Walker confidant in the inner circle who

was darn near invisible to the rest of the world. Most reporters and state politicos went through the Walker years without any inkling of Green, a self-made Chicago businessman who hooked up with Walker and de Grazia in the early days of their independent Democratic political involvement.

The short, stocky Green was a classic behind-the-scenes guy— a soft-spoken and even tempered individual who shunned flamboyance, publicity and a spot on the state payroll. Only a handful of people even recognized him when he was in the company of Governor Walker, but Green was very much around, along with his close friend de Grazia, when Walker political decisions were made.

Green was an astute analyst of the ingredients needed for electoral success. He was a great numbers person or, as Walker put it, "a very close friend and adviser with a mind that is half political computer." Green was a principal strategist for Walker, and de Grazia engineered the tactics to implement Green's concepts.

Governors of Illinois always seem to find a bright young attorney for their inner team. Walker had one in William Goldberg.

When he was a practicing attorney in Chicago, Walker had gotten his law firm to hire Goldberg out of Harvard University's law school. Later, Goldberg was in charge of issue research and development for Walker in the 1972 general election campaign. After Walker took office, Goldberg was the Governor's legal counsel.

Modern Illinois chief executives also have a noticeable proclivity for including at least one former newspaperman in their ruling circles. Walker's was Norton Kay.

Kay's title was press secretary, a big enough job in itself in an administration that never attained smooth sailing with some of the heaviest hitters in the state's journalism community. However, Kay, who had built a solid reputation as political editor of the old Chicago's American, was more than a producer of press releases for Walker. Starting with the launching of Walker's candidacy and on through his governorship, Kay was very much a part of his brain trust.

Consequently, Norton H. Kay, called Norty by his friends, did his part to prolong an interesting truism of Illinois government in past decades—the almost traditional desire of each governor to have at least one or even two hard-boiled reporters at his side.

One of the first to come to mind was the late Johnson Kanady, a Chicago Tribune reporter who was a key member of Governor William G. Stratton's staff in the late 1950s. The right-hand man many years for Stratton's successor, Otto Kerner, was Christopher Vlahoplus, who joined Kerner's staff from the United Press International bureau in Springfield.

When Richard Ogilvie occupied the governor's chair, one of his top political advisers was long-standing intimate Tom Drennan, a former Sun-Times writer. The press secretary on Ogilvie's immediate staff was the irascible Fred Bird, who had worked for almost every Chicago newspaper and was nobody's fool.

After Walker, a principal figure in Jim Thompson's gubernatorial coterie from day one was David Gilbert, who also had been a Tribune scribe.

And the pattern continued with Thompson's successor, Republican Jim Edgar. In a pinch, he could go to his press secretary, former political columnist Michael Lawrence, a seasoned Statehouse war-horse with the kind of street-smart moxie not found in textbooks.

But Norton Kay, in view of Walker's troubles with the press, seemed to have more to handle than most of these individuals. Which was at least a little ironic. In looking back, Walker should have been a logical candidate for quite favorable press treatment. After all, he was the kind of underdog in politics to which many working reporters so often cotton. He should have been, and indeed was, good copy.

Walker did experience many positives with the media on the walk, when the coveted coverage necessary for the walk's success did materialize, making Walker's name well known.

Within the inner circle, Kay was pressed to improve the Governor's standing with the media. The group did not understand why the press, at least outside of Chicago, was not more hostile to the Daley machine, which could not adjust to the social dynamics reshaping the United States in the 1960s and early 1970s. Didn't the reporters and broadcasters know that Dan Walker and his followers had been fighting for a more open and responsive Democratic Party in Illinois since the 1950s?

Then there was the Walker Report, which had thrust him into the limelight for really the first time.

The report, published near the end of 1968, delved with astonishing detail into the violent disorders that turned the Democratic National Convention in Chicago earlier that year into a brawl in the city's streets and parks. Compiled through an exhaustive, crash effort by a study team directed by Walker, the report to the National Commission on the Causes and Prevention of Violence presented a vivid account of the bloody clashes between Chicago police and demonstrators against the nation's Vietnam War policies.

Called "Rights in Conflict," the report noted in its most publicized finding that club-swinging police went so overboard in reacting to dissenters in many cases that the bedlam had all the earmarks of a police riot.

Actually, blame for the turmoil was spread around by the Walker Report, but many readers did not get beyond the faulting of Chicago police. Daley and his troops were enraged. Their ire was aimed at Walker personally, even though he tried to point out that a review of the whole document would reveal numerous examples of abuses by the protesters.

Walker certainly should have known that because he and his

crew worked day and night to put the report together and he had a hand in every part of the project. For Walker, the report was to serve to rewake Americans to the need for preserving both the rights of individuals to protest and, at the same time, the rights of society to safety and civic order.

Walker's direction of the study of the violence, many persons felt, foreshadowed his entry into the main ring of Illinois politics. Those persons also noted at the time that Victor de Grazia was one of two assistant directors of the study team staff.

Walker and de Grazia, it was said, at last were coming into their own, after years of maneuvering and waiting and more waiting on the political periphery.

The real truth of the matter was that Walker's political activity had ebbed considerably during the mid 1960s. Although successful by then in establishing himself in Chicago as a civic-minded attorney widely respected, he had experienced little beyond frustration in trying to crack the political mainstream in a big-time way, either in elective or appointive office.

Too, Walker was trying to, and did, make good money for the first time in his life to support his large family. For a while in the 1960s, Walker personally lost interest in politics.

Of course, this was a decade in which, until near the end, the Chicago Democratic machine was riding high. Daley was in firm control of his city, his party, the governorship and most of the remaining political turf within his reach. Democrats held a lot of offices in those days, and the major ones, from Chicago to Springfield, were filled mainly with persons handpicked and dominated by the mayor.

In times like that, Daley could play it safe, slating for office only Democrats who could be trusted to function in accordance with the strictures of governance and party loyalty enunciated by Daley. No reason existed to accommodate the Dan Walkers, people who had raised suspicion at one point or another that they did not fit Daley's disciplined mold for model Democrats. They weren't needed because in the ideal political world of Daley, when he had it going, there really was not room for them.

A goodly number of Democrats who would flock to Walker's gubernatorial campaign had knocked earlier on the door of the Daley machine, but they were told to go home because they were unproven, unconnected, unknown. They were just nobodies.

Walker himself once tried to court the machine when he sought the regular Democratic Party endorsement for election as Illinois attorney general in 1960. He did not get it, a turndown that left him humiliated and scornful of the party's slate-making process.

To add insult to injury, his political foes later would point to that move as proof of what they saw as hypocrisy by Walker in crusading against the machine when he ran for governor.

What gave Walker reason to think that he could receive the Daley crowd's backing for attorney general? The decade of the 1950s, the period in Walker's life following Northwestern law school, was a time during which he obviously felt he had progressed far enough to ask Mayor Daley to help usher him into the state's top legal office.

For many Illinoisans, the fifties were equated with political conservatism, economic security and status quo in the social system. Under the paternalistic leadership of President Dwight Eisenhower, the nation settled down to a commonsense normality that made middle-of-the-roaders respectable again, material success desirable and corporate men in gray flannel suits the envy.

This was the calm before the storm of the 1960s. The dynasty of the New York Yankees was in full swing. Full-bosomed women still were in, as were traditional sexual mores. Innocence was not out of style, judging by the white bucks, crew cuts and Davy Crockett craze.

The scene was all so very bourgeois, too much so. Television consumed the lives of kids, who sat hypnotized by Lucy and Jack Webb's "Dragnet." L & M cigarettes were "just what the doctor ordered." Jonas Salk was testing his vaccine against polio. The United States Supreme Court declared that membership in the Communist Party was sufficient grounds for deportation of aliens.

In the middle of the decade, 1955 to be exact, Richard J. Daley was elected mayor of Chicago for the first time. He would be re-elected five times, usually in a breeze. But the first campaign in 1955 was not easy.

His opponent in that mayoral election, Robert Merriam, an independent Democratic alderman who left the party to run for mayor as a Republican, was smart, a liberal reformer and hardly lacking in supporters. In fact, two of them were Victor de Grazia and Norton Kay, who met for the first time as young workers in the Merriam campaign, perhaps the best that Daley ever faced. This was before either de Grazia or Kay knew Walker.

After Northwestern, and following his brief stint in Springfield with the state's Little Hoover Commission, Walker became a law clerk to Chief Justice Fred Vinson of the United States Supreme Court, an assignment propelled by Walker's strong showing in law school.

That experience, although cut short by the Korean War, intrigued Walker. For one thing, he recalled a special telephone on Vinson's desk in Washington for communication with President Harry Truman. When the phone rang for one of the President's frequent conversations with Vinson, Walker automatically got up and left Vinson's office, leaving him alone.

The clerkship with Vinson ended abruptly, though, when Walker was recalled to active duty with the Navy and sent to Korea to serve on a destroyer in the war zone in 1951. But that battle line role would end because of another quick change of direction for Walker, one of many for the young lawyer in the 1950s.

Through orchestration by Walker acquaintance Newton Minow, a young attorney who clerked for the Supreme Court on the heels of Walker, the post of deputy chief commissioner of the United States Court of Military Appeals in Washington was offered to Walker. Since it was a civilian review body for the military court-martial system, the Navy released Walker from active duty so he could accept the position.

In the same time frame, Minow left Washington to join the staff of Governor Stevenson of Illinois. Subsequently, when Democrat Stevenson was nominated by his party for president in 1952, his campaign tied up some of his staff.

Thus, Minow again triggered a Walker move by recommending to Stevenson that he bolster his Springfield staff by offering a slot to Walker. Stevenson did so, leading to Walker's second job in Springfield. He was an assistant to Stevenson for only a few months in 1952 because Stevenson was leaving the governorship irrespective of the outcome of the presidential election, which he lost to Republican Eisenhower.

After his short but very impressionable time with Stevenson, Walker returned briefly to Washington before moving to Chicago to pursue a law career.

He broke in there with a large firm tied to an old friend, Carl McGowan, who was on the law school faculty when Walker was at Northwestern. But it did not pan out for Walker. So when another attorney friend, Tom Mulroy, solicited Walker for his law firm, Walker made the move.

This one stuck. The firm was the one known later as Hopkins & Sutter, and Walker was a member of it from 1953 to 1966. He was a partner his last eight years with the firm, where he specialized in civil trial work.

That is, in due time. In the early days with Mulroy's organization, Walker did research and carried briefcases on big case litigation because he was sitting in only the fourth or third chair among the three or four lawyers working those cases. The first chair or lead attorney was the main participant in actual trial work. But, after two to three years, Walker got his first trial and graduated to the first chair.

For Walker, these were salad days. Fun, educational and very demanding. The firm was known as a "sweat shop," which for Walker meant working most weeknights along with every Saturday. Young men in the firm were expected to do this.

And, if the hours of his law practice were not enough to keep him occupied, Walker also became a joiner, like in law school days when he was involved heavily in extracurricular activities. Leaping from volunteer work with one organization to another, Walker was a man in continual motion as the ambitious young attorney strove to carve a niche for himself in his now adopted hometown.

If anything received short shrift, it was his family. The time away from Roberta and the kids, he came to believe, contributed to the later domestic strife in his life.

His political involvement had taken on a different flavor. During his brief time as an aid to Governor Stevenson, Walker got a taste of being an insider. That ended with the change of administration in Springfield from Stevenson to his successor as governor, Republican William Stratton.

Seeing a need for an opposition group to monitor the performance of Stratton, Walker played a leading role in the setting up of a Democratic group called the Committee on Illinois Government. Walker was its first chairman, and at the outset it was mainly comprised of young lawyers like himself who were part of the Stevenson administration.

The goals of the CIG were severalfold. One was to lay Democratic groundwork for the 1956 gubernatorial campaign. But the founders also wanted to keep alive the spirit of the Stevensonian influence on Illinois public life, something that would not interest many old-line Democratic regulars in the state who had had only minimal rapport with the unconventional Stevenson.

The agenda of the issue-oriented CIG had little appeal to veteran political professionals who lived and died on getting and keeping themselves and their allies on public payrolls. A typical night for the CIG gang was a get-together at the home of Chicago attorney Jim Clement to map out a policy paper on a pressing state issue or make a scrapbook of clippings from around the state on what Stratton was doing. The CIGers took their tasks seriously. For some, it was a stage of political euphoria, not to be experienced again even when some became very successful lawyers or held important federal or state posts.

The CIG did not think small. Many of its members wanted enactment of a state income tax, something jeered in the 1950s by many stalwarts of both major parties. The levy did come, but not until 1969. The CIG also was in the vanguard of organizations seeking governmental actions often associated with liberal reformers, such as meaningful state regulation of lobbyists.

To Walker and other leaders of the CIG, its members were to be torchbearers for the political example of Adlai Ewing Stevenson, who became the most widely respected Illinois public figure of the Twentieth Century.

Stevenson served only one term as Illinois chief executive, and he was his party's unsuccessful nominee for president in 1956 as well as in 1952. But he was articulate, witty and polished, and his handling of these political roles, along with his service as United States ambassador to the United Nations, earned him reverence around the world.

Stevenson, who died in 1965, seldom hesitated to go against the norm. He was calling attention to the problems of racial inequality, poverty and environmental pollution long before most other politicians. He was a champion of intelligence and humanity in public life, an intellectual known as a thinking person's candidate rather than a more conventional crowd pleaser. He conveyed, concluded journalist Alistair Cooke, "an impression of goodness."

Walker attributed his serious political involvement to the influence of Stevenson and, furthermore, said it was "the Stevenson experience" that made Walker an independent in Democratic circles. Of course, Walker never was an aficionado of machine politics, having grown up in a loose California political milieu alien to the tightly-controlled politics of Chicago.

The Committee on Illinois Government provided the setting for the meeting of Walker and de Grazia. After the defeat of Merriam in his race for Chicago mayor, de Grazia was manager the next year, 1956, of a successful campaign for an Illinois House seat from Chicago's south side by Abner Mikva, an independent Democratic liberal. To win, Mikva, a graduate of the University of Chicago law school, had to overcome opposition from the regular Democratic organization.

Mikva's showing drew attention to de Grazia, and he was hired that same year to be the first executive director of the CIG.

By then, Walker was no longer chairman, and he was not around enough to be very helpful to de Grazia in the two years that he served as the operating honcho of the CIG. But things between the two would change after that, and rather quickly, thanks to the growth of another organization, the Democratic Federation of Illinois, which appealed to many of the same Democrats attracted to the CIG.

Although not the first to hold the office, Walker would serve as president of the DFI and de Grazia would leave the CIG to become executive director of the DFI. There, together, the two became close, igniting the political relationship that eventually would affect so greatly the careers and lives of thousands of Illinoisans.

The Democratic Federation of Illinois also provided the

framework for Walker to get to know another young aggressive Illinois Democrat, an upstart state representative from Madison County, Paul Simon. In fact, it was Simon who was the first president of the DFI.

But this is getting a little ahead of the story. First, why was the DFI needed when an organization like the Committee on Illinois Government already was in place for Democrats not exactly in tune with the Chicago-dominated regular party leadership in the state?

The answer was that the Democratic Young Turks wanted more action; they were champing at the bit over being frozen out of both the power councils of their own party and the GOP-controlled state government in Springfield. The self-proclaimed defenders of the Stevenson legacy were restless.

For them, the CIG was too tame, too reflective of the gentlemanly calm on the surface of so much of public life in the 1950s.

Now, for the 1956 race for governor, the CIG did prepare a four-inch thick loose-leaf notebook detailing the problems of the Stratton administration in every state agency and a proposed Democratic platform for making it all better. And, the book was used extensively in the campaign of jurist Richard B. Austin, the unsuccessful Democratic candidate against Stratton's bid for election to a second term.

However, it was just obvious to the Young Turks that the CIG was little more than a study group and that the outcome of the 1956 election confirmed that something with more bite was necessary.

Enter the federation. Its origin literally could be traced to a huddle of three persons one evening in late November of 1956, not long after that year's general election, in the kitchen of the home of Carlinville attorney John W. Russell. Laying strategy that night for the establishment of the federation, besides Russell, were

Chicago lawyer and businessman Angelo Geocaris and John Forbes, a history and political science professor at little Blackburn College in Carlinville.

Geocaris was a longtime advocate of a more open Democratic Party in Illinois, a person who backed up his political convictions with his wallet. Forbes was a disciple of Stevenson who worked tirelessly in the political vineyards to preserve Stevenson's doctrine.

The idea behind the federation, germinating that evening in Russell's kitchen, called for the establishment of a network of neighborhood and community clubs in the state intended to give Democratic activists a more productive means for bringing about better government at all levels.

While the DFI was for Democrats only, its promoters contended that the federation of these clubs was not designed to supplant the regular Democratic Party. The reigning party chieftains took this with a grain of salt. To them, the DFI was another step toward mischief by the pesky Stevensonites and other party outsiders who failed to recognize the dawn of an upcoming strong era for Illinois Democrats under the umbrella of new Mayor Daley and his Chicago patronage army.

When efforts to organize the DFI were in full swing, a recruiting booklet put out by the organization outlined its objectives as the following:

To provide the means by which you can discuss the issues confronting the Democratic Party, discuss the possible candidates of the party, actually help select the candidates and work for their election.

To make politics a force in which you personally can participate—without the pressures normally associated with "machine politics."

To strengthen the Democratic Party throughout the state, and to help render it a more effective vehicle for good government.

To select and elect outstanding Democratic candidates.

To keep voters informed of the records, ideals and programs of the Democratic Party, and to inform public officials on all levels of the opinions and beliefs of the DFI.

As to the DFI's relationship with the regular party structure, the booklet noted that the DFI "recognizes the Regular Democratic Organization as the legally constituted instrument of political administration," but added that there was "room for both—and a need for both." Otherwise, it was explained, thousands of persons "who are vitally interested in politics and good government fear that they would be lost in the regular party."

In summation, the booklet came on like an ad for the Navy by urging Democrats to join the DFI "and see the world of difference between sitting on the sidelines in politics and actively participating in America's most exciting, most fascinating pastime."

Even before the DFI was set up, the independent Democratic activism to be encouraged by the organization was visible elsewhere, like in the Illinois House of Representatives. There, a small but noticeable group of young Democratic members already had shown themselves unwilling to follow the business as usual leadership line found on both sides of the aisle in the chamber. Two of these Democratic parvenus were Simon, a boyish-looking newspaper publisher from Troy, and his close friend Alan Dixon, an energetic Belleville lawyer who, like Simon, refused to kowtow to the political establishment.

Naturally, the early framers of the DFI saw someone like Simon or even Dixon, a perceived independent but already elected figure, as a logical choice to head the new organization.

And so it was that the young legislator-journalist Simon received a telephone call from Angelo Geocaris at a hotel in Cairo, Egypt, where Simon was staying during one of his stops on a freelance writing tour abroad. Geocaris asked Simon to be the first president of the DFI, and Simon agreed.

He held the post for one year, 1957, a time during which Simon would get to know fairly well the tall Chicago lawyer, six years older, who would succeed him as federation president, Daniel Walker. Through the ensuing years Simon and Walker would continue to have contact, and they would be cordial to each other but never close.

Simon felt that he saw in Walker from the beginning of their relationship a person who wanted high elective office, but Simon could not know then that their political paths would collide in a contest as dramatic as the 1972 primary race for the Democratic nomination for governor.

Walker's presidency of the DFI lasted more than a year, three at least, and it proved to be a crucible for the making of a goodly part of the Walker team that would surge a decade later to the command of Illinois government.

First, there was de Grazia. Modeled after the loose political club system then found in California and a few other states, the DFI needed a professional organizer. Consequently, in 1958, de Grazia was hired as executive director of the federation as part of the shuffle that brought Walker to the presidency.

At this point, the name of another DFI activist was an integral part of the story, Arnold Maremont. He was a Democratic millionaire industrialist and civic leader in Chicago who disliked the Daley-led party hierarchy, recognized de Grazia as sympathetic to this view and saw Walker as a potential standard-bearer for independent Democrats. As a result, Maremont was a principal catalyst in the ascendancy of Walker to head of the DFI and in the hiring of de Grazia as executive director, the salary of whom Maremont agreed to help underwrite for a while.

With Walker at the helm of the DFI, the person in charge of organization for a time and later executive vice president was Elliot S. Epstein, who would be a member of Walker's cabinet when he was governor.

By 1960, the DFI's executive committee officers and members included other names later helpful to Walker. Like Madison County attorneys Dick H. Mudge Jr. and Richard Allen, two individuals often at odds with the old-line party machine in that heavily Democratic county in the southwestern part of the state. And like David Green.

Although Walker's campaign for governor came years after the heyday of the DFI, many in the organization got an early taste of what was to come with Walker when they rallied around the unsuccessful bid of Chicago attorney Stephen Arnold Mitchell for the Democratic gubernatorial nomination in 1960. Mitchell, a Stevenson man who was chairman of the Democratic National Committee from 1952 to 1955, was sharply critical of Daley's already evident grip on the Illinois party—and he made his campaign a crusade for more openness in Democratic doings.

But, Mitchell was crushed in a three-person primary contest won by Cook County Judge Otto Kerner, a candidate handpicked by Daley. Ironically, in that primary race, Walker differed with most of his DFI mates by backing Kerner, who went on to win the governorship in the 1960 general election by ousting Republican incumbent Stratton.

For the DFI, and really all Democratic independents, the Kerner victory placed the regular Democrats of Daley firmly in the saddle in Springfield, from where they were not to be dislodged for eight years. This meant that, in the main, the 1960s were lean years for most Illinois Democrats not in step with Daley.

With so many doors of opportunity closed, and the Illinois political world seemingly doing fine without them, the independents' spirit and appeal plummeted. Some lost interest and quit politics, while others went into hibernation or read the handwriting on the wall and made up with the Daley machine.

Nobody had scurried around more in local organizing efforts for the DFI than John Forbes. So, for him and his particular brand of politics, the 1960s were fallow years.

To some, Forbes was a throwback anyway to an earlier time. His political involvement, running around the Illinois countryside pushing the Stevenson legacy, reflected his belief, in the true liberal tradition, that government could be reformed or upgraded into a much more high-minded force or instrument for the betterment of all. He wasn't in it for a patronage slot. Forbes was motivated by ideals.

But with his Democratic Party in power in Illinois through much of the 1960s, Forbes and his kind were largely irrelevant and certainly dispensable to the party professionals who equated public jobs and large contributors with political success. Satisfying the wish list of political dreamers was not a priority.

John Forbes, out of Oak Park, Illinois, and a graduate of the University of Pennsylvania, came to Blackburn in 1949. Husky and deep voiced, he was intimidating at first to freshmen in his history and political science classes at the small private school. But that usually changed. Even as he continued to exhort his students to not hesitate to swim against the current if fighting for their beliefs, most came to know Professor Forbes, a Quaker, as a soft touch beneath the surface.

Until his death in 1981, Forbes and his wife, Lydia, were fixtures on the local scene in Carlinville, which looks like a Hollywood setting for small town America. They lived in a white frame cottage, a few steps from the college campus, that had walls lined with shelves crammed with books. The home was a frequent gathering place for students and would-be political reformers. If it was fall or winter, the guests usually could count on tasting Lydia's hot, spicy apple cider.

The visitors to the Forbes home included Walker, more than once. Forbes also got to know de Grazia well in the days when they both were hustling for DFI members.

Whenever Forbes had contact with Walker, Forbes could not

help but think back to the days of the Stevenson campaign for president in 1952 when Forbes was keeping a diary on developments. In his entry for September 27, 1952, Forbes wrote that he had lunch that day with young Stevenson aid Dan Walker and that he, Walker, had voiced a desire to run someday for governor of Illinois.

When that happened, some 20 years later, Forbes worked hard for Walker in Carlinville and Macoupin County, even during the primary campaign when many of the fellow Democrats of Forbes in that area supported Paul Simon for the party's nomination for governor. But Forbes went with Walker because of Walker's link to Governor Stevenson.

And, when Walker proceeded to win it all, Forbes wrote to a friend that the new Walker administration could be "a vindication, twenty years deferred, of Stevenson's hopes for Illinois."

"It is beyond dispute," Forbes added, "that the idealism which Walker can fulfill was inspired to action by the Stevenson example. It was Stevenson who lit our lamps."

Forbes hoped that Walker would not let him down. ❧

4 Sun, Sweat and Blood

Summer days are long and lazy in those little Illinois towns down along the Ohio River at the bottom of the state. Golconda, Old Shawneetown, Cave-in-Rock, Elizabethtown, Brookport.

Brookport. That's a good one. Not as quaint as Golconda nor as historic as Cave-in-Rock, but interesting. The statue of the infantryman by the large silver bell in the middle of town is eye-catching. Miles away and hours later, visitors try to remember if the soldier was from World War I, World War II or maybe even Korea.

Another thing is the big bridge over the Ohio that carries U.S.

Highway 45 from Brookport to Paducah, Kentucky. The span is named after Irvin Cobb, a writer and humorist from Paducah, but nothing about the bridge was funny to the drivers through the years whose hands were clammy with sweat by the time they made it across the unusually narrow, two-lane structure high above the wide river. Scary, especially for unsuspecting drivers coming down from the north.

The Cobb bridge is where the walk started. The hot morning of Friday, July 9,1971, when Dan Walker and two of his sons, Charles and Dan, Jr., commenced from the foot of the bridge on the Illinois side of the river to walk through Brookport.

Although an announced candidate for the governorship for nearly eight months, the immense odds against success faced by Walker required nothing less than a dramatic and drastic turn of events if his candidacy was even to be noticed in many quarters, much less taken seriously.

Unless he did something bizarre to call attention to his quest, Walker surely was doomed to be the next Don Quixote of Illinois politics.

Walker had to come up with a humdinger, a doozy—and he and his advisors did just that. A walk the length of the state, from the Ohio all the way up to Wisconsin, an unabashed gambit to garner necessary publicity and then, through it, to capture the fancy of the public for his political long shot.

The storied city of Cairo lies at the southernmost tip of Illinois, where the Ohio meshes with the Mississippi River, and it is better known than Brookport. But Cairo was torn by racial strife at the time, and the Walker team feared that starting the walk in Cairo could pose ominous complexities that hardly were necessary on day one.

So, Brookport, a few miles back up the Ohio, was chosen for the beginning of the trek. The decision irrevocably wed the Walker campaign to the Massac County community of 1,000 or so souls. At that stage, though, not many persons in Brookport or anywhere else predicted the political significance later to be attached to that July day in 1971 when Walker and his boys trod into town.

A year and a half later, on the day before he took the oath of office as governor, Walker, Roberta and most of their children began the pre-inaugural ceremonies by attending a public brunch in the Brookport High School gymnasium. The host for the event was a committee of local residents, some of whom recalled meeting or seeing Walker during the start of the walk in the small community.

For a lot of Illinoisans, though, other things caught their attention on July 9, 1971. The death in Paris, France, of Jim Morrison, the 27-year-old lead singer of The Doors, was announced that day, and young fans from Brookport to Los Angeles went into a funk over the departure of the insolent acid rocker of "Light My Fire."

Also mourned that day was jazz trumpeter Louis (Satchmo) Armstrong, whose body was laying in repose in a National Guard armory in New York.

Walker's bid for attention even got competition that day from an Associated Press report out of Manila about the discovery of a tribe of people living in the Philippines in Stone Age fashion, a timid band isolated from the rest of the world for hundreds of years.

Still, Walker was not shut out of opening day media coverage. Enough press, including the Tribune, showed up to give the walk a look of legitimacy from the start. However, outside of the newspersons, only nine individuals were on hand to watch him begin the long hike.

Walker stood at the start by a large sign proclaiming that Governor Ogilvie welcomed visitors to Illinois. Nearby was a billboard urging motorists to "Forget Politics and Support Richard M. Nixon as Our President."

Undaunted, Walker advanced through Brookport, where he was greeted warmly by persons who did not know him from Adam. One wishing him well, Mrs. Lee Chapman, told Tribune reporter Thomas Seslar that, although she had not heard of Walker, she admired "anybody who will walk in this (96 degree) sun." And, she said, "I think we need new blood to shake things up, like to get those lazy people off the welfare rolls."

When the stories of Seslar and other reporters appeared, along with some network television attention in the first days, everybody in the Walker coterie gave a sigh of relief because Norton Kay, the campaign press secretary, had made it clear that Walker only was walking in the eyes of the public if the media said he was doing so.

After the first few days, Kay's daily chore of rounding up press coverage got tougher, giving rise to fears that the fourth estate, after all, viewed the walk as little more than a flash in the pan maneuver. Eventually, the press did come to give the walk serious attention on an almost daily basis, but coverage was disappointing in the early weeks.

On some of the early days, a lonely Walker found himself virtually talking to himself as he dreamed of escaping the searing sun that scorched the southern Illinois countryside and the miles of narrow and twisting roads that the Chicago attorney had committed to tackle.

Frankly, many of the more established politicians in the state were beginning to think he was nuts. Walker was having some second thoughts about his undertaking, too. Painful wasn't the word for what he felt. It was excruciating. That was clear to him after the first day.

Walking through Brookport with the two boys was fun. Pleasant chats with bystanders, the police chief, the operators of a lumber company and a depression-fearing man who ran a gas station. All of them expressed amazement at the thought of anybody planning to walk from their hamlet to faraway Wisconsin, a place as foreign to their world as Switzerland.

Yep, based on Brookport, Walker thought the walk might be a piece of cake. But, long before the end of the day—which came 22 miles later in the home of a farmer near tiny Bay City, where he spent the night—Walker knew differently.

Not far beyond Brookport, the heat and humidity became insufferable. Blisters on the feet popped up even quicker than expected. First on Charles, and then on Walker and the other son on the walk. For Walker, the pain in his feet soon was shooting like surges of electricity through the rest of his body. He swore that even his hair hurt.

Right then, the first day, he questioned in his own mind whether he was starting something that for himself was even physically doable.

Should he just quit? The answer, he told himself, was no. Canceling the walk now, he knew, would be sacrificing the only path to the Mansion in Springfield open to him. Walker would be setting himself up for ridicule.

But still, damn it, getting through a spirited tennis match back home in the cozy Chicago suburb of Deerfield was nothing like the grind in walking along these narrow roads in deep southern Illinois. And the sun. It never glared like this in Chicago.

Walker, a LaSalle Street lawyer, a man a few weeks shy of his forty-ninth birthday dead set on being governor of one of the most powerful states in the union, thought of little more than a cold glass of water every few steps. His continual thirst, not Mayor Daley or anything else, was now the biggest thing on his mind.

One heartwarming development for Walker the first day occurred after a brutal stretch of nearly 14 uninterrupted miles of walking when a Belleville architect named William Walker pulled up alongside the candidate in his air-conditioned car. Architect Walker had driven out of his way to find the walking Walker and wish him luck after hearing about the walk on his radio. When the architect offered to let the candidate rest for a few moments in the cool auto, the appreciative candidate was quite moved by the other Walker's effort and kindness.

Nothing was tougher for Walker the second day than putting on his boots in the morning. Perhaps the best part of that day came with the rain that began to fall as Walker and the boys tromped into the Pope County seat of Golconda. Walker's preoccupation with the ungodly pain in his feet also was broken by the driver who stopped to offer him and the boys apples and by the dog that followed them for three miles. Charles wanted to keep it for a mascot, but his dad and older brother voted against it.

The visit to Golconda went well, not only thanks to the rain, but because Walker landed a local newspaper interview and managed, along with the boys, to get a haircut. Their hair, it seemed, was coming across as a bit too long for that neck of the woods, where little tolerance existed for cultural protestors.

That evening, in the Elizabethtown area home of a hog breeder where Walker was spending the night, he received a call from a Sun-Times reporter asking about a rumor in Chicago that one of the Walker sons on the walk had been mistaken for a radical hippie. Walker replied that several members of his staff in the region of the walk had lengthy hair, but the reporter only wanted to discuss the style of the Walker boy's hair, which irritated a very tired Walker.

Walker disliked the reporter's lack of interest in the intent of the walk itself or in the insights Walker was gaining from the southern Illinoisans he was meeting. As he soaked his blistered tootsies that night, he found it tough to be a proper guest in the warm home of Ken and Harriet Jones. Walker just wanted to lay down and close his eyes. Or settle for nothing more than a cold beer.

However, by the end of the next day, a Sunday and the third

day of the walk, Walker could relax a bit in the rural Elizabethtown residence of his hosts for the night, Mr. and Mrs. M. L. Conn, and think some positive thoughts. For one thing, the 21 miles covered during the third day made a total of 62 for the trek—and the 21 more miles to be traversed the next day would put his small party near legendary Old Shawneetown.

More important though, Walker had growing reason to believe that the walk definitely was not folly.

The Tribune's headline on a story covering the first three days said: "Walker's Trek Wins Friends." In the article, Tom Seslar wrote that Walker had "achieved celebrity status" in southeastern Illinois in the initial stage of his walk.

Seslar was noticing things. Folks were talking about Walker. When a local radio station got a recorded interview with him, it announced four times within 15 minutes that the interview would be aired on the next newscast. Walker stopped briefly at a Sunday service at a small Baptist church near Golconda after being invited to attend by a member of the congregation.

But a comment from Mrs. Ferne Cox, the postmistress of Rosebud, picked up by Seslar, conveyed what Walker wanted to hear. After meeting Walker on the porch of a country general store, she remarked, "My goodness, he's just like one of us."

When that comment was read to Walker over the phone, he knew he was on the right track. He was making headway in sowing the seeds of a gubernatorial campaign on his own terms. He was unhindered down here, far from the state's population centers, in discovering what kind of candidate he really could be. He was free to measure his potential for political acceptance in an atmosphere much less structured than almost anywhere else in Illinois.

Southern Illinois was fertile ground for Walker. Long a stepchild in a state where two-thirds of the population and the bulk of the economic wealth resided in Chicago and its suburbs, southern Illinois seethed with alienation from the political mainstream, Democrat and Republican.

Any serious challenge to the ruling establishment in Illinois would strike a responsive chord in the lower part of the state—which conspicuously lacked great numbers of voters, skyscrapers, harsh winter weather, rich farms, private schools and, of course, liberals.

What voters there were, were for the most part conservative Democrats. Hardly any southern Illinoisans were aware that Walker was perceived up north as a liberal Democrat by the majority of the thousands who would join his crusade, though that impression would change in his days as governor. Also, not too many from southern Illinois knew much about the Walker Report.

However, they could not help but notice that Walker was making a special pitch to them, even sort of starting with southern Illinois, in his bid for Illinois' top office. With much of the populace turned off at the increasingly minimal contact between political officeholders and their subjects, Walker was garnering attention by actually going one-on-one with people in a most down-to-earth manner.

Here was a person really working to get elected, and in a way that made the denizens of Golconda feel as if they personally counted in his undertaking. This man Walker was restoring a modicum of dignity to the process.

Those encountering Walker along the dusty roads in the languid counties by the Ohio also saw that he wasn't making a lot of promises, hardly any. He wanted to learn what they felt about state government and what they hoped to see done or changed. He only assured the men and women he met that, through him, they could have a voice again in the governing game.

Antagonists later argued that Walker never did, as a candidate or governor, have a clearly definable or consistent plan of what he wanted to do with the governorship, apart from self-promotion.

They insisted that if he had any political philosophy at all, it was based on expediency.

At each stop on the walk, Walker was bombarded with the concerns and gripes, big and petty, of the individuals crossing his path. One person might have been aggravated about the hiring of an unqualified neighbor for a job at a nearby state hospital, while the next guy was apprehensive about the threat to the world from nuclear weapons.

Walker recorded all of it in his journal of the walk, as well as his own observations. He obviously could not miss the poverty, pollution, the decay of small town life and so on. But, also, he was surprised and then heartened by the cogency of thought and reason and by the aspirations voiced by so many individuals when afforded a chance to express themselves.

Through the walk, Walker probably learned firsthand more about the inner feelings of ordinary Illinoisans than any of the state's other modern era politicians. Many bared their souls to him, an outpouring that, Walker believed, would provide him with the spiritual fuel to prevail on their behalf if he made it to Springfield.

Before it ended, Dan Walker was convinced that the walk was establishing an almost reverent line of communication between himself and those he wished to govern. Irregardless of the way others saw it, Walker would view the walk in retrospect as an act of uncommonly eloquent humanism, something seldom found in the political or any other world.

As a unique beneficiary of a chorus of grass roots wisdom, Walker thought he grew in the walk in the manner that few men or women ever do after a fade of youthful idealism. In short, he felt it made him a better person.

Of course, the walk also served other purposes. As a candidate, Walker's campaign style left much to be desired. Formal and stiff, like the Navy officer he had been, he could not at first walk up to strangers and ask for their vote. He feared rejection. Not only was he not a backslapper, he really was a little shy.

Reporters, friends and even campaign staffers found him overly serious, too monotonous. Walker had no sense of humor, they observed. The Walker that entered the governor's race admittedly did not know how to smile when he talked.

After the first coffee reception given for him as a candidate, attended by about 20 upper middle-class individuals in their late thirties or forties, de Grazia got a call from a woman who was there. She told de Grazia, the campaign manager, that Walker "was a disaster, so cold and aloof. Everybody hated him. He can never be governor."

More than a tad uneasy, de Grazia knew that Walker's style needed more than a minor tune-up. Fundamental revamping was necessary, and the walk presented the opportunity for it.

Forced into face-to-face contact in southern Illinois with individuals considered hicks by sophisticated Chicagoans, Walker began to shed the accoutrements of the LaSalle Street lawyer's image and rediscover within himself the long buried traits of the people he knew in his days on the small farm in the San Diego hill country. Right off the bat, Walker instinctively liked southern Illinoisans, and the walk kindled a special kinship between himself and the area that persisted throughout his governorship.

When the walk started, it was almost frightening for Walker to intrude on somebody to introduce himself and explain what he was doing. But he overcame this inhibition. It took time, but he had a lot of that on the walk.

Within days, the one-on-one campaigning produced a new Walker. He no longer hesitated to approach anyone to start a conversation. Moreover, he even had the time to discuss issues with some individuals, a rarity for any candidate.

Walker also grew to understand during the walking marathon the importance of taking command of a conversation with a voter.

Or, as his friend, then United States Senator Lawton Chiles of Florida put it to Walker, the candidate had to perfect a "patter."

The idea for the walk by Walker was prompted by the success of Chiles, a surprise winner of his seat in 1970 after trudging more than 1,000 miles across Florida.

Visiting Walker in the latter part of his walk through Illinois, when Walker was up around Rockford, Chiles was impressed by the "patter" that Walker had gotten down pat.

"I'm Dan Walker, candidate for governor," the line went. "What's your name? Gee, Ed, that's a good looking tie you're wearing. Did your wife pick it out? She has great taste."

Turning to the wife, Walker continued. "What's your name? I know you're Ed's wife, Mrs. Ed Smith, but don't you have a first name? Every lady should have her own name. Margaret? That's better. I have a daughter named Margaret.

"I'm really glad I had a chance to meet you, Ed and Margaret. Have a wonderful day together, and remember that I need your help in the election."

In large crowds, the wording had to be shortened.

"Hi, I'm Dan Walker, candidate for governor. What's your name? John, I really need your help." Then, quickly, a turn to another voter. Always moving. Hitting one after another in rapid-fire fashion.

Early on, Walker mastered the strong eye contact that became one of his trademarks, like the red bandanna. He also had a way with handshakes, too.

The unblinking eye contact was for sincerity. His thumb against thumb technique in the shaking of hands was important to survive a day of that stuff. If he did not take care in putting his right hand forward to get his thumb against the other person's thumb, Walker's hand could be mangled within a short time.

The red bandanna tied around his neck turned into a logo of the walk. At first, though, he had it along to protect his hands.

Walker was a victim of vitiligo, which left the pigment spotted in the skin on the back of his hands. The problem also resulted in quick blistering from the sun.

However, not long into the walk, Walker determined that he really didn't need the large handkerchief to shield his hands. So he tied the bandanna around his neck, like a cowboy, to have it handy for wiping the sweat from his face. Sure enough, people then assumed it was a standard part of his walk outfit.

When he did not wear the bandanna at a party given for him one evening during the walk, some of the guests asked where it was. Walker knew then that he had stumbled onto another identifying characteristic for the walk, and the bandanna was not taken off again the rest of the trek—although he felt foolish at the windup striding through Chicago's Loop with a red bandanna around his neck.

But, that ending in Chicago was still more than three and a half months away from those early furnace-hot days of the walk through the Ohio River towns. Golconda, Elizabethtown, Old Shawneetown. No way would Walker forget Old Shawneetown, the remains of a place with a rip-roaring past protected from the river by a levee.

The first night in the Shawneetown area, Bill Holzman, a fast-moving advance man for the walk, failed to set the brake properly in his car when he parked it, permitting the vehicle to roll down a hill and through a fence by the home of the family giving Walker lodging that evening.

Kay had to see a doctor about a bite he received while snoozing outdoors in a sleeping bag. The doc also took a look at Walker's bloody feet. More displeasure was to follow.

A press conference was scheduled in Old Shawneetown on July 13, a day that Kay swears was the hottest of his life. After an especially arduous effort to walk into Old Shawneetown, a sweat-soaked Walker stopped to chat with the mayor, Pete Clayton, while Kay walked over to the town's historic old bank building to greet the reporters.

Nobody was there. Not a soul. Kay had made Walker trod a lot of extra miles for nothing. Drenched with perspiration himself, Kay returned to where Walker was conversing with Clayton.

When Walker asked if it was not about time to get over to the meeting with the press, Kay said that no one had shown up. Walker found that hard to take. Eventually, a reporter for a local area weekly came along and talked to Walker. Kay noted to himself that even this person was late. The candidate was not happy.

Kay did follow up by calling three television stations in the region to query them about their absence. He was told that more important events had to be covered. Depressed would not be an adequate word to describe his feelings.

This must have been about the time, as best de Grazia could remember, that Kay called him in frustration and urged that the walk be stopped. Judging by Walker's bleeding feet, Kay said that he could not envision the candidate enduring much more of it.

"But," de Grazia recalled, "I told Norty that Dan was going to keep walking. Norty thought we were going to kill him, but I said we were not going to kill him. And that was that. Still, Norty was very upset. He was there and saw what Dan looked like."

Sitting back in Chicago, de Grazia had a hunch about the walk, a good one. When the possibility of the walk first was kicked around, a group of public relations experts voluntarily advising the campaign ridiculed the notion. At least, they argued, Walker should ride between towns and only actually walk in the cities. Some even suggested that a canoe trip through Illinois waterways would be just as good.

But the brain trust calling the shots went with the walk idea, the "path of pain" as one insider dubbed it. Walker could do it. He'd have to do it. Nothing was going to come easy in this campaign for governor.

Nevertheless, self-doubt about the walk never nagged Walker more than when he stood, virtually alone, in ramshackle Old Shawneetown, his feet caked with blood and the rest of him bathed in sweat.

Within hours, his spirit would be higher. But, at that moment, under the punishing sun, Walker could not help looking at the ground as he silently asked himself if he really was sure he knew what he was doing.

The following day, in Springfield, it was revealed that Tom Owens, the Democratic chairman of Sangamon County, was going to work as a political operative for Lieutenant Governor Paul Simon.

To be paid from Simon's political fund, Owens was being hired to keep Simon's fences mended in central Illinois and to serve as a liaison with other Democratic county chairpersons in the state. Gene Callahan, the top assistant to Simon, pointed out that Owens was the first person to go on Simon's political payroll for the approaching election season.

Simon was the overwhelming favorite of most of the party's downstate leaders for the Democratic gubernatorial nomination in 1972. But they were noticing that this maverick Democrat Walker was beginning to get press ink and other attention for the first time since announcing he was going to run for the top state office.

So, the county chairmen welcomed the hiring of the popular Owens as a sign that Simon was moving to keep the situation well in hand.

They had faith in Simon. They knew they had a winner in him. ❧

Mayor Daley——A Colossal Nemesis

Leaving the first days of the walk through the Ohio River country behind him, Walker slowly inched his way up through southern Illinois.

Bloody feet or not, he no longer entertained thoughts of quitting because, with the passing of each hot summer day, he grew more confident of the wisdom of his course. A damn tough one to be sure, but smart.

He could sense it in the climbing number of people who came out of the towns and hamlets to offer him cold water or iced tea, to wish him the best and, in the case of some, to offer to help.

Many asked him to pose with them for pictures, although he noticed that local Democratic officials often took a powder when the photogs started snapping.

Another thing, he found little hesitation in those he met to voice their opinions. Walker got a real earful about disaffection with those running the show in Illinois, much more than he bargained for, even though he was an outsider challenging the state political establishment.

Granted, Walker began his trek in a long depressed part of the state, but the message he heard in the early days would change little as he gradually advanced northward along downstate corridors in ensuing months.

Get away from people like local officials, bankers and others in the comfortable column, and folks were mad. About the Vietnam War, racial hostility, the rebellion of the nation's youth, the disintegration of the traditional American values. Frustrated, they needed something or someone on which to vent their anger, at which to lash out. The most obvious target? The political elite, naturally. Especially in Illinois.

From Galena to Cairo, persons were disenchanted by the scandalous dealings of Illinois Supreme Court justices, legislators and other officials to profit, certainly unethically and often illegally, through the power of their positions.

A new wave of investigative reporting in the state, setting in about two years before Walker began his walk, had brought details of the sordid conduct home to the citizenry, and millions not sharing in the graft were sick and tired of it. Since the dark cloud tended to tinge even a lot of the honest individuals in office not tied to corruption, calls for ethical reform in government meant more if coming from somebody apart from the scene. Like Dan Walker.

Not compromised, and with really nothing to lose, Walker had a free hand to attack the ethical decay of Illinois government with the fervor of a zealot. Walker and the situation could not have been more ready made for each other.

However, outside of Chicago and Cook County, there was an even more convenient target around which the Walker campaign was coalescing—Mayor Richard J. Daley and the last truly great big city political organization in the land, his Chicago Democratic machine. Beyond anything else, Daley was Walker's political raison d'etre.

Walker capitalized on Daley to seize the governorship, Walker's time in the office was colored greatly by his vexatious relationship with Daley and, in the end, Walker was snuffed out politically by Daley. The Walker story, almost every surprising chapter of it, would not have happened but for the existence of Daley.

Not long into the walk, any doubt of the efficacy of running against Daley quickly was erased, at least away from Chicago.

Governor Ogilvie, the occupant of the seat sought by Walker, was not regarded strongly one way or the other. Tough but bland, shy to some, aloof to others, Dick Ogilvie could be had, Walker felt, if only he, Walker, could get a shot at him. That opportunity was being blocked, though, by the state Democratic boss, Daley, a figure about whom few Illinoisans had neutral feelings.

To many downstaters, the pugnacious Daley was a visible cause or root of what they bitterly viewed as their seeming lack of control over things in Illinois. His heavy-handed dominance of his world spilled over mightily into the lives of everybody else in the state. In order to ensure success in looking after his metropolis and its huge population, Daley exerted an influence in Illinois matters of state, his downstate detractors just knew, that unfairly shortchanged their part of the world and inflamed the eternal rancor between Chicago and downstate.

Something had to be wrong automatically about anything as overpowering as Chicago and its bigger than life mayor and his fabled hordes of political foot soldiers. The mere mention of

Chicago brought out the inferiority complex never far below the skin of downstate.

More and more as the walk progressed, Walker found it unnecessary to go into detail to remind his listeners that he was running to free his party from the domination of Mayor Daley and, implicit in that, to liberate downstaters from the oppression of Daley's machine. The mere mention of Daley's name usually prompted a knowing nod of the head assuring Walker that nothing more need be said.

At last, at long last, here was a guy with the guts to stand up to Daley. It mattered little that Walker once had sought Daley's endorsement for election to state office or that Walker certainly would have accepted Daley's backing for his gubernatorial bid.

But the chance of that was nil because Walker hadn't earned his political spurs under Daley's rules. By all accounts, the mayor did not even like Walker, especially after the publication of the Walker Report.

By the time Walker embarked on his walking marathon, Richard Joseph Daley had been mayor of Chicago for 16 years. He had revamped his city and machine, the former to what he felt best for it and the latter to his own political taste. If there was a better known political leader in the country, or a more despised one in some circles, only the occupant of the White House might qualify.

At national party conventions, at any gathering of political luminaries, the mere appearance of Daley attracted far more attention than the presence of United States senators or governors. Journalists from around the country hustled just to get a look at him.

After all, Daley had achieved, and relished, a role of kingmaker in the quadrennial skirmishing for the presidential nomination of the Democratic Party. He played a pivotal role in ensuring the election of Democrat John F. Kennedy as president in 1960 by driving the machine to produce a massive number of votes for

Kennedy—enough to permit him to carry Illinois just barely and pocket the state's crucial electoral votes.

When Daley died on Dec. 20, 1976, at age 74 and after 21 years as mayor of the nation's then second largest city, it was hard to picture the Illinois political world without him.

He ran Chicago like a Caesar, demonstrating in the eyes of many that a big city still could be governed. For decades, he had been both a major player and main issue, almost always with good reason, in most General Assembly showdowns and in contests for governor and other statewide offices.

The power base of Daley was extraordinary in that he wore two hats, one as mayor and the other as Democratic chairman of Cook County. Since Cook turned out Democratic vote totals far beyond any other place in Illinois, there was little mystery why Daley controlled the state party machinery.

In turn, this gave him an extraordinarily free hand to dictate the slating of major Democratic candidates in Illinois, and then to exert great influence on those elected.

Not bad for a guy who was born, raised and lived his whole life in the modest south side Chicago neighborhood of Bridgeport, a white ethnic enclave of wage earners, small houses and corner taverns near the malodorous butchering plants of the Union Stock Yards. Hardly pretentious in his personal life-style, his own home in Bridgeport was a plain bungalow at 3536 South Lowe Avenue.

Daley's showiness was found in his legacy, a big city with a dynamic physical character and other trappings of a vibrancy not found in Cleveland, Detroit and many of the nations's other older cities in the decades of Daley's mayoralty.

Judging by the rebirth of the Loop, the downtown business area bounded by elevated train tracks, as well as by the reconstruction of other well-known parts of Chicago in Daley's time, he certainly deserved his image as a builder.

In this regard, he didn't miss many bets. He literally oversaw the remaking of much of his city—from the revitalization of the skylines of downtown and the Gold Coast to the development of a large university complex, from the building of major expressways to the expansion of O'Hare airport into a world-class operation.

Daley got things done because he was a remarkable maestro, some said genius, in moving or manipulating people. Chicago is an unusually heterogeneous city, which made all the more incredible Daley's success time after time in forging coalitions of business, labor, blacks and ethnic groups to accomplish what he wanted for himself and his city.

Author Norman Mailer may have hit it on the head when he wrote that Daley in reality was "not a national politician, but a clansman—he could get 75 percent of the vote in any constituency made up of people whose ancestors were at home with rude instruments in Polish forests, Ukrainian marshes, Irish bogs . . ."

Yet, in the end, his critics argued, he did little better than most other big city mayors in combating crime, in stopping the erosion of his city's industry and the subsequent departure of jobs, and in halting the steady deterioration of many neighborhoods and the public school system. The imposing Chicago skyline could not be used as an excuse for his failure to come to grips with these problems, they insisted.

His strongest partisans, in replying to criticism about the great concentration of power in Daley's hands, often referred to *Newsweek* magazine's depiction of Chicago in 1971, a few months before Walker's walk, as a "most wondrous of exceptions, a major American city that actually works."

Still, to many of the nation's liberals, Daley was an unconscionable autocrat—and they always pointed to his conduct in the riotous days of the 1968 Democratic National Convention in Chicago as proof of their view.

Daley's reputation as a master builder would have been enhanced even further if he had realized his dream for construction of a crosstown expressway through the west part of Chicago, an undertaking which he seemed to equate in his last years with the pursuit of the Holy Grail. But Walker, as governor, would not let it happen.

Although perceived by Daley as necessary to give through traffic an alternative to the congested routes leading to downtown, the building of the crosstown highway along its proposed north-south route would have disrupted radically neighborhoods and other staples of life on the western side of the city.

Taking up the cudgel of the residential groups, businesses and other opponents of the project, Walker vowed to do everything within his power to block the expressway's construction. And he did exactly that, and the project did not happen.

In the long run, nothing may have done more damage to the Walker-Daley relationship than their standoff on this issue.

As was his manner, Daley would not let the subject go away. After the 1976 primary election in Illinois, in which Daley's machine blocked Walker's bid for renomination by the Democratic Party for governor, the mayor told the press that the suddenly lame-duck Governor Walker still was a great Democrat who'd make a dandy United States senator.

Later that day, while Walker was politicking in Indiana for a Democratic aspirant for governor, he was summoned to a phone to take what he was told was an emergency call from Daley.

Getting on the line, Walker was told by Daley that "he had just held this press conference and had said that I was a great Democrat and would make a great United States senator."

"I was flabbergasted," Walker recalled. "I told him, 'Well, I appreciate that, Mr. Mayor. Thank you very much.'"

But, then, Daley quickly added, "Now, Gov, how about the crosstown expressway?" Coming well after Walker was sure he had killed the project and ended the matter, he could not believe his ears.

For a relationship that was to have the historical impact on politics that theirs did, Walker and Daley had infrequent personal contact, little before Walker became governor and not all that much afterward.

Events in the late 1960s prompted several meetings between the two men. One came in 1968 when Walker, then president of the Chicago Crime Commission, was appointed by Daley to a task force to study the west side ghetto violence in Chicago triggered by the assassination that year of the Rev. Dr. Martin Luther King, Jr.

Walker also had periodic audiences with Daley when serving as a director of the Leadership Council for Metropolitan Open Communities, an organization set up to implement an agreement between Daley and King to bring about more open housing opportunities for blacks and other minorities in Chicago. (In addition, Walker organized and served as president of the Metropolitan Housing Development Corporation, a nonprofit undertaking tied to the King-Daley accord that was designed to come up with housing for minorities.)

During the preparation of the Walker Report, the author paid a courtesy call on Daley to hear his views of the national convention turmoil. Walker heard little from the mayor, which Walker accepted as par for the course.

Then, as in his other rare moments with Daley back in Walker's years as a lawyer and business executive, Walker sensed that Daley was quite uncomfortable with him. "In all of our meetings," Walker said, "he was not loquacious with me. He was uncommunicative."

Daley being the big man, after all, Walker surely spent more time trying to fathom Daley than the reverse. Before the release of the Walker Report, there is little to suggest that Daley regarded Walker as anything more than just another nettlesome pain in the neck, a do-gooder with an obviously inflated ego who had never gotten his hands dirty in the trenches of politics.

Walker was not an upstart who had to be accommodated like, say, Adlai Stevenson III, because Walker was a zero from out of town with no father who had been governor or other prominent relatives. In the lingo of the machine, Walker was sent by nobody.

On his part, Walker entertained no illusion that he had enough going to make any inroads with Daley. It was true. No one had sent Walker, an anomaly in the world of the Chicago machine. For one thing, he was a white Protestant, probably the rarest breed indeed among the ethnic elements contributing to the makeup of the machine and acquiescing to the then still dominant leadership of the organization by Daley and other Irish Catholics. Even more astounding, Walker was raised in southern California, a land darned near alien to the traditional societal mores of Chicago.

Walker made no secret of his espousal of reform politics, and he had tipped his hand on political independence through his leadership of Democratic maverick or borderline groups in the 1950s.

After Walker became governor, in a way that finally got Daley's attention, the Illinois political and media cognoscenti eagerly speculated about the chance for rational coexistence between the state's two political heavyweights. Surely, Walker and Daley now would bury the hatchet for the mutual benefit of each.

Following Walker's stunning victory over Daley's machine in his capture of the Democratic gubernatorial nomination, the mayor rebounded by supporting Walker in a very measurable fashion in his general election campaign against Ogilvie. Hopefully, things might now fall in place between the two.

It was not to be. One trait common to both of them was stubbornness. As the Walkerites saw it, Daley mulishly persisted in approaching the new Walker governorship with a business as usual attitude, as if nothing abnormal had occurred. The anti-machine rhetoric of the campaign would be forgiven by Daley if Walker agreed to play by the old rules that saw Illinois governors usually capitulating to Daley on what he wanted.

But Walker was not like his predecessors. He had exacted a stiff toll from himself, including the infliction of physical punishment, to establish his political independence. And that rigid streak of pride inside of him that made him do it now made any sign of obeisance to Daley impossible.

Besides, Walker was swept into office by an army of Daley antagonists, and he could not turn his back on these people, his followers, in handing out available state jobs and in dealing with issues. In politics, Walker knew, you danced with those who brung you to the shindig.

Even if he had so desired, Walker believed at the dawn of his governorship, an accommodation with Daley simply was not in the cards. Unless, Walker felt, Daley "would understand my persistent independence."

Hardly.

Right off the bat in 1973, battle lines were drawn for skirmishes between the mayor and the new Governor.

One of the first erupted over Walker's amendatory veto of a bill, passed by the General Assembly at Daley's request, that provided emergency state aid to the Chicago Transit Authority and other mass transit systems.

The gist of Walker's requested change in the bill was that he wanted Chicago and Cook County to match state aid funds to the CTA. Instead, the measure provided for $2 in state money for each local dollar.

His veto was necessary, Walker insisted, to prevent excessive use of state general revenue funds as a cure-all for each local governmental headache. However, the veto came across to many on the scene as an unnecessary challenge to Daley and other urban political leaders facing threatened shutdowns by fiscally pressed transit operations.

Consequently, the Daley Democrats in the Legislature launched a successful drive to obtain the three-fifths vote needed in each chamber to override the veto. In doing so, with the help of numerous Republican legislators, the Daley forces sent Walker an early yet decisive warning that the mayor was not about to pull out of any confrontation with Walker.

The new Governor would be getting that message in other ways, too. Climbing over the back of Daley to get elected was one thing. Trying to govern by going around him was another matter. For both Walker and Daley, there would be no truce.

Surprisingly, during Walker's four years in office, he only met Daley in private four or five times. Just one of these meetings took place in the Executive Mansion in Springfield. The rest, according to Walker, were in the Bismarck Hotel, a hangout for Daley machine pols on Randolph Street close to City Hall.

The usual setting for the Bismarck encounters was intriguing. The two of them alone in a suite. No staff members present. No other witnesses. No tape recorders. A Daley security officer always stationed at the door. "It was a very strange feeling," noted Walker. "I always felt like a conspirator."

Together, they were an odd couple. Walker, 6 feet 2 inches tall, lean and dignified, towered over his heavyset and paunchy nemesis, a man 20 years older than the Governor. The jowly Daley looked every bit as pugnacious as his manner. Walker had a fine command of the King's English. The mayor's grammar could be atrocious, and journalistic quotes of his malapropisms provoked laughter behind his back—but not to his face. Interestingly, like Walker, Daley had seven children.

In *Clout*, a 1975 book on Daley by the late Chicago newsman Len O'Connor, the author concluded that Daniel Walker was "clearly the worst of Daley's enemies."

True or not, Walker harbored tremendous respect for Daley the politician, never assuming for a minute that the mayor's linguistic bloopers and often boorish behavior detracted one iota from his political genius. Walker also recognized that Daley, who reached the top by methodically climbing a step at a time from one post to another, was one of the few powerful political figures who also understood government finance.

Daley had a marvelous talent for getting the state to funnel dollars to Chicago. Yet, although adroit at convincing others to pick up the tab for public projects in Chicago, the mayor still usually managed to win credit for himself in the process. Walker always tried to keep this in mind.

One on one, as in the secret huddles in the Bismarck, Walker and Daley could be almost cordial and dispense with the hostile posturing that their constituencies and the media almost seemed to take for granted. The two made real progress in one of these sessions on working out a unified Democratic position on the creation of a regional mass transit authority for the Chicago area, an acrimonious issue in the first meeting of the General Assembly after Walker took office.

Several of those other get-togethers, though, only served in the end to muddy further the water between them because, afterward, they would not agree on what they supposedly had agreed to in the meetings. If not for the serious import of the matters discussed, Daley and Walker could have parlayed their public lack of verbal comprehension of each other into a comedy team routine.

Really, nothing seemed too trivial to escape the relentless undercutting of one by the other.

Once, when the Governor was campaigning for a state legislative candidate in Chicago obviously not favored by the mayor, Walker was lambasted by Daley for "crashing" a bingo game night in a Catholic church to give a speech for the candidate.

Daley charged in a radio interview that the Governor "doesn't understand the rules of Catholic church bingo games. Everyone has to pay an entrance fee."

Quite to the contrary, an angry Walker retorted, he and his security personnel had paid to get in and Walker even was invited by the operator of the game to "call" a bingo card. Still, Walker feared that Daley's blast hurt the Governor in Catholic neighborhoods in the city.

Walker got more than hot under the collar when Daley, annoyed by one of the Governor's political moves, declared that Walker, back in the days of his walk through Illinois, actually rode from city to city in a car, getting out only in downtown business districts "to pose for the TV cameras."

Besides hitting the ceiling himself, Walker said that "it was all I could do to keep my sons who had walked with me from going down and personally taking on Mayor Daley." Fisticuffs in the Walker-Daley state of affairs never may have been closer at hand than that day.

A few months later, the delicate code of protocol in high-level politics was ill served as the lanky Governor and squat Mayor both stood at O'Hare airport waiting to welcome Emperor Hirohito to Illinois during a visit to the United States by the Japanese leader.

A bevy of VIPs from Tokyo, Washington and Chicago had gathered in a room to await the arrival of the Emperor's plane, which was late.

Suddenly, at a moment when the conversational noise level had died down, Daley shouted across the room, "Governor, you never responded to my invitation to the state dinner for the Emperor."

Silence immediately gripped the room as all eyes turned toward Walker.

Dumbfounded, the Governor replied, "How could I respond,

your Honor, when I never received an invitation? I know because I checked with my staff after the event was announced."

Taking no notice of Walker's response, Daley then proclaimed loudly, "My mother taught me to always respond to invitations." Those assembled were aghast.

Thinking about the incident later that day, Walker feared that he "had clearly come off second best" and that "the old pro had scored again."

"That was his frequent technique in public. Stick to the charge, ignore the response."

Early the next morning, back in the Mansion in the state capital, Walker was awakened by the security staff and told that the mayor of Chicago was on the telephone.

"Gov," said Daley, "I checked and found that an invitation to the dinner was mailed to you at 1152 Norman Lane, Deerfield, Illinois."

"But your Honor," returned Walker, "I don't live there any more. I live at the Executive Mansion in Springfield."

To which, Daley shot back testily, "Well, at least we mailed it."

As Walker saw it, this was the closest he would come to an apology from Daley. But then, Walker found little normalcy in any part of his bizarre relationship with Daley.

After leaving office, Walker was asked repeatedly, and at times even wondered to himself, if he should not have been more willing to compromise with Daley. Would Walker's life have turned out differently?

Perhaps, he admitted.

One thing for certain, Walker acknowledged later that he made a serious mistake in daring Daley publicly to run a candidate against him for their party's nomination for governor in the 1976 primary. Right off, some adjudged that to be unnecessary arrogance on Walker's part.

The feisty mayor took up Walker on his challenge, fielded a

machine-backed candidate to oppose the incumbent Governor in the primary and then provided the votes for the challenger, Secretary of State Michael Howlett, to defeat Walker.

Defeat at the polls, the ultimate price a person can pay in the practice of politics. For Walker, the nagging part was that he easily might have been spared that calamity had he reached any kind of understanding with Daley.

Yet, to have compromised with the mayor and the political establishment he so embodied, Walker insisted to the end, would have sacrificed what Walker regarded as his "stubborn adherence" to political independence on critical issues.

"I just would not play the old game so traditional in Illinois politics and government, common to both parties.

"I thought I could lead the way to a new era of open politics in Illinois, helping to end the machine rule and give downstate the share of power it deserved and was entitled to.

"My efforts in those directions were put down as tactics of confrontation and an inability to accommodate. But I called it independence."

Events following his departure from the scene, Walker later emphasized, substantiated the veracity of his course. Since things never were to be the same, Walker came to feel that his governorship, to use an old colloquial expression, was "a game well worth the candle."

By the end of 1976, Walker's bags were packed to leave the Mansion, and Mayor Daley was dead. And, for sure, nobody was arguing that Illinois politics and government would be the same. ❧

Walker's Army

Daley and Walker. Walker and Daley. de Grazia. The big names on the marquee over the Walker political chronicle. Always the stars.

Not so for Charles and Sue Kolker. Sid and Natalie Marder. Toby Olszewski. Betty Rolph. Steve McCurdy. Not even for Mary Lee and Andy Leahy, even though they were not exactly unknowns in the cast of thousands mobilized in the political insurrection that put Daniel Walker in the governor's chair.

"Sometime during the spring of 1971," recalled Sue Kolker Altman, "I became aware that Walker was running for governor of Illinois.

"My first real memory of this was an evening which I spent with two friends, East St. Louis teachers Richard Roth and Dave Bates. I was eating dinner with them, and Rich got a call asking him to meet with Dave Caravello, who was supposed to be a big Walker coordinator downstate. Rich and I had worked together in the peace movement and the Williams campaign for mayor. Rich was the most purely motivated person I'd ever met. So, when he asked me to join in the Walker effort, I indicated I would be delighted."

Several days later, when she disclosed her intention to her husband Charles, an East St. Louis attorney, she was surprised to learn that he already had been asked to run the fledgling Walker campaign throughout a good part of the state south of Springfield.

However, sensing that he could not do this without surrendering much of his law practice, Charles Kolker would agree only to play a pivotal role in handling campaign chores in the populous St. Clair-Madison county region of southwestern Illinois, a big reservoir of Democratic voters.

Walker was perfect for the Kolkers, a couple, like Walker himself, swimming against the tide at that time and place in their lives. She was spunky Sue Taksel from the nearby St. Louis County suburb of Ferguson, and he was an assertive chap from Elgin, Oklahoma, who had obtained a law degree from St. Louis University while teaching in the East St. Louis public school system—a period in which he also headed a union, Local 1220, East St. Louis Federation of Teachers.

The Kolkers were married for seven years and the parents of three children when they moved to East St. Louis early in 1968, purchasing a double story brick house at 704 North Seventy-sixth Street in the racially troubled community. He was 27 years old, she was 26. They were whites and Democrats, she a more liberal one than he. And they made East St. Louis their home during a juncture when other whites were exiting as fast as possible, many fleeing up the bluff to the fashionable west end of neighboring Belleville.

Sue Kolker Altman, although no longer married to Charles Kolker, never could forget what it was like back in those years, their salad days.

"We astounded the real estate people by saying we wanted to move to East St. Louis. Everybody else was leaving the city. We knew East St. Louis was having problems, but we wanted to help change things. We really thought we could.

"Charlie and I got very involved in reform politics in regard to city government and the East St. Louis school board. We were in the labor movement. We helped elect James Williams mayor. It was because of all this that we became identified as people who might assist Walker."

By 1971, the East St. Louis adopted by the Kolkers was well on its way toward becoming what Illinois Senator Adlai Stevenson feared might be "the first truly welfare city in America."

Slum growth and economic decline, evident in the 1950s, had accelerated in the 1960s, a decade in which the population of the Mississippi River city dropped from 81,000 to 69,000. The onetime hub of industry and transportation had become a colony of the poor and underprivileged, with a vast number of them dependent on government programs or welfare. Many of these persons were blacks, who comprised 70 percent of the city's population at the start of the 1970s.

Hope flourished anew, though, that the climate would improve with the election April 6, 1971, of a black mayor, James E. Williams, who exuded optimism that he could halt his city's slide.

The election of Williams ended the long reign in East St. Louis City Hall of the white and aging Alvin G. Fields, who while mayor also ran the St. Clair County Democratic machine, one of the party's strongest organizations in Illinois south of Chicago.

At his peak, Fields had a reputation politically as a little Daley downstate. Just as in Chicago, a seething undercurrent existed in East St. Louis against the rigid patronage control and other hallmarks of political bossism. The candidacy of Williams was a long-awaited outlet for the discontents, like Sue and Charles Kolker.

Of course, Williams' victory meant fresh faces in City Hall, one of whom was Charles Kolker. The new mayor named him city corporation counsel.

A short time later in 1971, in the Illinois River city of Peru, a good 200 miles upstate from East St. Louis, another young couple would get a phone call that would lead to a radical change of direction in their life. It was nothing that Sid and Natalie Marder could have foreseen when the diminutive Jewish pair from Brooklyn, New York, landed in Peru four years before.

To quiet Peru, a town of 12,000, from Brooklyn?

Chalk it up to the Foster Grant Corp., which brought Sid Marder, a chemical engineering graduate of New York Polytechnic Institute, to Peru in 1967 as a production engineer. His bride of two years, the former Natalie Yustman, also was a college grad, an education and history major at New York University. Yes, they were Democrats, but not active. Civic minded and looking for a niche, Natalie had focused on the League of Women Voters.

Natalie was the one who got the call that altered their life, and it came from a friend who asked her to "put Walker up for the night" and also serve as host for a reception for him at their home when the candidate's walk brought him to Peru and the twin town of LaSalle.

In the words of Sid Marder, "the call came completely out of the blue. We didn't know Walker—except for the Walker Report." The Marders had joined the ranks of those not fond of Daley after the 1968 Democratic convention, and the couple agreed with the Walker Report's partial conclusion that Chicago police had overreacted greatly in confronting the demonstrators.

"Consequently," Sid Marder said, "we agreed to help him (Walker) when he went through our town."

That came to pass Sept. 20, 1971, a day of numerous stops for Walker in LaSalle and Peru, concluding with an overnight at the Marder residence.

By that time, Walker was about 800 miles or some two-thirds of the way through his marathon, and the walk journal's coverage of that day revealed it to be typical of the venture's now almost daily ritual.

"After an early breakfast," wrote Walker, "Norty and I visited the LaSalle daily newspaper for a dull interview by a young lady reporter who took no notes. I figured it for a write-off, but when the article came out on page one it was a good one, accompanied by a large photo. It tends to underscore my theory that journalists are a little weird. At best, unpredictable."

Later, at a radio station, Walker was the guest on a talk show, the kind of which, he noted in the journal, "can sometimes become an oral mine field.

"But the questions were the usual types dealing with welfare, the racetrack scandal, parochiaid and taxes. For the first time on a talk show, the issue of gun control came up. I could just feel some of the voters turning away from me when I said that I favor gun registration, although I am a hunter myself. They demand the capacity to slay each other."

After rapping with 75 students at Illinois Valley Community College, Walker's other stops included St. Bede, a Catholic high school in Peru, where students and several priests quizzed him about his opposition to parochiaid, the name in those years for controversial proposals to provide state aid to parochial and other private schools, a course backed by many Democrats.

On the visit to St. Bede, Walker said in the journal that "my views (on parochiaid) were not too well received.

"There is a school of thought in campaigning that you should avoid areas where you know your view is unpopular. But the people seem to respect you for hitting it head on and being honest with them. And the borderline cases might be swayed to your side by the candidate's not being daunted by such obvious peril. It's also referred to as honor."

Thereafter, following a meeting with local businessmen, Walker "headed for the home of Sidney and Natalie Marder, for a dinner and reception." About 50 persons, a good cross section of individuals, showed up for the reception, pleasing Walker.

The whole visit to LaSalle-Peru went well, the journal pointed out, with Walker feeling that "everyone seemed to know me before I got there."

The journal's recording of Walker's conversations with the Marders also underlined the candidate's persistent probing for detailed background, a trait not found in most politicians around a lot longer.

For example, Walker noted that he learned from the couple, in discussing their religious faith, that "there are only about 50 Jewish families in the entire area" and that "their congregation is served by a rabbi who flies over from Cincinnati."

"I also learned from them," Walker added, "that there are no black families in the entire LaSalle-Peru-Oglesby area. Apparently, they had one black family in the area and it moved out."

After the reception, Walker and the Marders talked about a lot of other things before the candidate retired for the night. They picked up again in the morning, during breakfast, and after Sid left to go to work Walker and Natalie continued to converse.

That evening, when Sid returned home, he was informed by his wife that Walker had asked her to coordinate his campaign in the LaSalle-Peru area.

"Nat agreed to do it," he added. "And, that's how we got involved."

Unlike the Marder situation, there was nothing sudden or

overnight about the support for Dan Walker by the wife and husband team of Mary Lee and Andy Leahy. It was foreordained and couldn't have surprised anybody.

Walker's campaign was a political baptism for thousands of those who climbed aboard, but the Leahy duo, both lawyers, were veterans of the anti-machine skirmishes in Chicago before the Walker candidacy surfaced. Beginners they were not.

Political activism by the Leahys was galvanized by the assassinations in 1968 of Martin Luther King, Jr., and Robert Kennedy. The home of Mary Lee and Andy was a rented house on Lake Michigan in the South Shore part of Chicago, which along with nearby Hyde Park was troublesome territory for the Daley regime. Integration was proceeding in their area in those days, and the Leahys didn't see City Hall policies and attitudes as positives for achieving racial harmony in their neighborhood.

Anyway, as the characteristically blunt Mary Leahy put it, "I never considered myself a regular Chicago Democrat... there was no way to break in."

Serious political involvement for the Leahys began with their support for the successful 1968 drive by independent Democrat Abner Mikva for election to Congress from a south side Chicago district.

The next year, Mary Leahy beat the Daley machine in winning election as a delegate from a southeast Chicago district to the sixth Illinois Constitutional Convention, which convened Dec. 8, 1969, in Springfield.

When she took her seat in Con Con, she had all the credentials for the independent delegate bloc, of which she was an outspoken leader. Membership in the Independent Voters of Illinois, the Independent Democratic Coalition, the Committee on Illinois Government, and so on. Mikva people worked for her election. One, David Cleverdon, then an assistant to Mikva in the Congressman's district before joining the Walker campaign, introduced her to de Grazia, by that time a recognized catalyst for independent political machinations on the south side. She got and used advice from de Grazia in her race for Con Con. Their relationship endured.

At Con Con, delegate Leahy was given most of the credit for the Environment Article in the document produced by the convention—a provision specifying that Illinoisans have a right to a healthful environment and that the General Assembly was to guarantee by law the maintenance of that environment.

The other delegates found Leahy a feisty advocate of her views. But no wonder. *The Saturday Evening Post* once had said no more effective female debater than she could be found in college ranks.

Debating was an important part of her life in high school, the old Marywood Academy for Girls in Evanston, and later as an undergraduate at Chicago's Loyola University. (After getting a degree in history from Loyola, she went to the University of Manchester in England on a Fulbright scholarship and received a master's degree in political science.)

She met the man who would be her husband, Andrew Joseph Leahy, through debating activities, something to which he also was drawn.

In an earlier era, Mary and Andrew Leahy almost certainly would have been rock-ribbed stalwarts of the Chicago Democratic machine. Both from Democratic families. Both Irish Catholics. Her father a Pullman conductor; his a postman from the Bridgeport neighborhood of Mayor Daley and so many other machine biggies. Andy even went to DeLaSalle, the same Bridgeport area Catholic high school attended by Daley. Really, this couple, married Dec. 26, 1964, in St. Mary's Catholic Church in Evanston, would have been a natural for the machine at an earlier time.

However, not only did this not happen but the Leahys proved

to be among the sharpest burrs under the saddle for the machine in the period preceding Walker's election. And when he set up shop in Springfield, the Leahys were there with him as players in his administration.

After Walker's departure from Springfield, they stayed in the town to practice law together and quickly became known as attorneys to see on discrimination or sexual harassment cases, litigation frequently involving persons believing themselves to be wronged by the system. Of course, since the system then meant the Republican administration of Governor Thompson, Mary Leahy in particular became a thorn in the side of the Thompson crowd.

She reached her zenith in this role by pushing and winning a case, Rutan v. the Republican Party, in which the United States Supreme Court ruled against political patronage practices violating First Amendment rights. A disheartened Thompson called the decision a death blow to the two-party system.

Although Andrew Leahy worked with his wife on the case in its early days, the Supreme Court ruling on it did not come until four years after his death from cancer in 1986 at age 53.

Mary Leahy said the greatest day in her life came when she argued the Rutan case before the nation's highest court. Depending on an individual's view of patronage politics, one either loved or hated her for what she did.

Just like 1972, when then 32-year-old Mary Leahy, six years out of the University of Chicago law school, was in the middle of a political fire storm that burnt the rafters. In that one, baby, you really either loved her or despised her.

The summer of that year. The Democratic National Convention in Miami Beach. No bigger story than the convention's vote to fill 59 contested Chicago seats in the Illinois delegation with members of a maverick party slate tied to rebellious Chicago Alderman William Singer and the Rev. Jesse Jackson. In so doing, the convention denied the seats to a slate of Mayor Daley made up mainly of ward committeemen and other entrenched regular Democrats.

What a year for Daley. First, he fails in the Illinois primary early in 1972 to prevent Dan Walker from grabbing the party's gubernatorial nomination. Then, a few months later, his delegation is ignominiously refused seating at the party's national convention.

Mary and Andy Leahy were part of the legal team that paved the way for the success of the Singer-Jackson delegation, although neither Leahy was the chief attorney.

But, as the drama to rebuke the Daley delegates unfolded through that year from Illinois to its explosive conclusion in Miami Beach, Mary Lee Leahy was an obvious darling of the political have-nots who finally got their pound of flesh from Daley. She was a pert spitfire, always sharp-tongued, a favorite of the political writers who thrived on the constant dissension in the Illinois Democratic Party.

However, the Daley people had eyes, too, She had gone too far this time, the former little Mary Lee Cullen, originally out of the Rogers Park neighborhood, a woman who should have been one of them. They also knew she was up to her neck in the Walker campaign. They'd get her, one way or another. There was always another day in politics.

For every Mary Lee Leahy in the Walker camp, there were 100 neophytes like Steve McCurdy.

Southern Illinoisan McCurdy had the highfalutin title of chairman of the Young Democrats of Perry County as Walker hiked through the state. But Steven E. McCurdy was politically wet behind the ears, which normally would be the case for any college student just past his nineteenth birthday.

McCurdy had his hands full commuting daily from his home in Pinckneyville to Southern Illinois University at Carbondale, where he was pursuing a degree in political science.

In the early days of the walk, when Walker was in McCurdy's part of the state, McCurdy missed him. That may have been okay because McCurdy had not been sure that he wanted to meet Walker. McCurdy knew that John Rednour, a successful businessman and chairman of the party in Perry County, was a Paul Simon man. As for other Democratic leaders in the area, McCurdy was aware that hardly any gave Walker a prayer of winning.

Yet, McCurdy couldn't quite get Walker out of his mind. The more he read about Walker and what he professed to stand for, the more McCurdy was intrigued.

Of course, McCurdy recalled feeling at the time, "I realized I probably wouldn't be thought of as a very good chairman of the young Democrats if they knew I was thinking of Walker, especially when Simon was almost sure to run. And, to boot, Walker did not have a chance anyhow."

Still, McCurdy, a son of a member of the United Mine Workers employed by Consolidation Coal Co., knew inside himself that he was a liberal Democrat in a section of Illinois where conservatives dominated the party. He opposed the Vietnam War, and he would back this up with some protest marching at SIU before receiving his degree. Finally, with McCurdy, it was the thing about the party itself.

"We just did not have an open party. The Chicago machine mentality prevailed. The party was too exclusionary to new people. More of an open arms policy was needed."

Consequently, a few weeks after Walker had left southern Illinois, McCurdy called the candidate's Chicago office to find out exactly where he was on his walk. McCurdy then followed up by driving Aug. 18, 1971, with several friends to the route mentioned by the Chicago office, Highway 36 between Jacksonville and Springfield.

Sure enough, McCurdy found Walker and his two sons

accompanying him striding toward the state capital.

Pulling off the road and getting out of his car, McCurdy winced at the sight of the narrow shoulders along the heavily trafficked highway that forced the Walkers to fight to buttress themselves against the powerful blasts of air from the large semitrailers rapidly rumbling by the trio. This was more than a little dangerous, McCurdy thought.

Retreating from the edge of the highway, Walker and McCurdy sat together and talked for 20 minutes—enough time for McCurdy to decide that he had made a right move in seeking out this guy.

"From the first moment, I liked him personally," McCurdy said. "I definitely agreed with what he said he was trying to accomplish. It ended with me telling him I admired him and indicating I would do what I could to assist him."

Walker often fared well in initial encounters with individuals, many of whom, they said, felt drawn to him by a seemingly mystical magnetism that made it difficult to tell him no. One on one, at least the first few times around, Dan Walker was very tough to resist.

Toby Olszewski was an exception, kind of. She was not that impressed with Walker when she initially met him at a political gathering in 1971. Unlike many women, she was not swayed by his senatorian demeanor.

However, the then three-year resident of Kankakee did find a lot with which to agree in the Walker Report. The author of that gutsy document had to be a person of some considerable gumption, she could not help but believe.

Mrs. Olszewski, it turned out, was a south side Chicagoan, a product of the Marquette Park neighborhood. She understood, she said, "what Chicago police were like firsthand.

"They didn't deal well with youths, blacks and mouthy broads. If you weren't white, humble and shorthaired, you might have a problem with Chicago police."

She thought of herself as an independent and liberal Democrat, but not anti-Daley. After all, her father was an assistant precinct captain in the mayor's machine. She herself had gone to Maria High School when she was Susan (Toby) Reid, and she married her husband, Robert Olszewski, at St. Rita Catholic Church on the south side in 1961.

Seven years later, when her chemist husband took a job in Kankakee and they moved to that northeastern Illinois city, she lent a hand to the unsuccessful campaign to retain the governor's office by Democrat Samuel Shapiro, whose residence in Kankakee was a short way from the Olszewski home. In 1970, Toby aided the successful campaign for the United States Senate by Adlai Stevenson.

Yet, when her close friend, Betty Rolph, an early Walker backer in Kankakee, asked Toby to join the Walker effort, Toby agreed somewhat reluctantly because the candidate "simply had not swept me off my feet when I met him."

Nevertheless, Toby not only signed on with Walker but soon found herself the primary election campaign coordinator for Kankakee County, reporting to David Cleverdon, by now the statewide organization director for Walker.

Still, as opposed to so many other Walkerites, Toby never considered herself estranged from regular Democrats in her area. This was underscored by her election in the 1972 primary as committeeman for Kankakee's Sixth Ward, Second Precinct.

If they whispered anything about Toby Olszewski in those days, they said she was a women's libber, dashing around the county for Dan Walker in a short skirt and boots, her long red hair straight down the middle of her back. While she did this, hubby Bob, apolitical himself, often was the one minding their six children at night in the family's venerable frame home in the historic Riverview, old-money section of Kankakee.

Challenges always were around the corner, Toby remembered, "because women were not supposed to be as visible in leadership positions back then.

"But, I was an only child, and grew up with a lot of freedom. I never knew there was anything I wasn't supposed to do."

This became even more obvious in the early 1980s, long after the passing of Walker from her life, when she became owner and publisher of the Bourbonnais Herald, a weekly newspaper in her home area. Later, she also bought the Beverly Review in Chicago, another weekly.

After Walker, life did not end for the vast majority of those who had followed the man and his dream of a new order in the public life of Illinois.

Young McCurdy followed the 1972 campaign by serving in the Walker administration and, as with so many others, was distraught over Walker's political downfall in 1976. In the ensuing years, though, McCurdy would receive a master's degree in business administration from Lindenwood College and become an executive with Arch Mineral in St. Louis.

The Walker experience would be regarded through the years by many of the others who had heeded his call as a roller coaster of ups and downs.

Betty Rolph, the Kankakee housewife and volunteer political worker who got Toby Olszewski involved with Walker, jumped on the Walker bandwagon early because she thought he was the right person to lead Illinois in that turbulent time in its public life. New and free of corruption, and so charismatic.

Afterward, she could not disguise her deep disappointment at the way it turned out, how in her words "the Walker thing just went sour." Especially, she felt, "since he was capable of so much."

Two decades later, she still could recall with great clarity every joyous moment of the rally celebrating the conclusion of the walk on Oct. 31, 1971, at the Midland Hotel in Chicago.

Betty and her husband Robert, another worker for Walker,

went to the Midland that day with Toby and Bob Olszewski to share in the excitement of the windup of their man Walker's incredible ordeal. They took pictures of Walker at the rally, sensing that perhaps they were witnessing political history in the making.

Standing not far away from them in the crowd were Mary and Andrew Leahy. Their little daughter Brigid was perched on her father's shoulders, trying to get a glimpse of this man that mom and dad were talking so much about. ❧

The Man from Troy

Sept. 27, 1971. Two and a half months into his walk, Walker was getting a look at close range at some of America's most fertile farmland as he trooped on the edge of U.S. Highway 6 outside Geneseo, heading right along with the Illinois prairie toward the Mississippi River and the western Illinois industrial nucleus around Moline and Rock Island.

Walker had been alone for a while, noticing what he thought he recognized as sorghum growing with the corn, when it began to rain hard. He got soaked before he managed to take refuge in the motorized camper, driven by campaign workers, that usually could be found somewhere on his daily route.

The storm blew over, the sun came out blazing hot, and Walker hit the road again. But not for long.

Rich Block, a campaign aid often manning the motor home, caught up with the boss again and informed him that another interruption was necessary because Walker had to reach a phone. The media, Chicago radio reporters in particular, wanted his reaction to the big political news of the day—the formal announcement by Lieutenant Governor Paul Simon of his candidacy for the Democratic nomination for governor in 1972.

Of course, Simon's announcement was an anticlimax in that he had been campaigning for many months, four political fund-raising dinners had been held for him that year and a group calling itself the Paul Simon for Governor Committee had laid groundwork for a statewide petition drive and other steps in support of his candidacy.

The announcement did serve, though, to bring the 1972 Democratic gubernatorial scenario into much sharper focus for the political players and the writers and pundits who drool over the politicians. Simon's declaration just made everybody feel more comfortable with the situation, especially those who like things tied up in neat packages.

Although Simon naturally would be a heavy favorite to win it all in 1972, that guy out there walking the state looked like a sure bet to stay in the Democratic race through the primary election. That could be an added plus for Simon because a contested primary, one he was sure to win, would give him even more exposure. Also, of course, destruction of the Walker insurgency would be a good warm-up for Simon for the main event bout with Governor Ogilvie. Too, Walker in the race was fine with the political scribes who, even though fond of Simon, needed material for their typewriters and, besides, would not mind seeing the Lieutenant Governor squirm just a little.

At least two other individuals had said they wanted the Democratic nomination for governor in 1972. Thomas A. Foran, a former United States attorney for the northern district of Illinois who was prosecutor at the Chicago Seven riot conspiracy trial, had announced his candidacy for the nomination a week earlier. And Michael J. Howlett, then the elected state auditor of public accounts, had indicated he would ask Illinois Democratic leaders to slate him for the nomination.

However, few persons did not foresee the endorsement of Simon for the gubernatorial nomination when the Illinois Democratic Party slatemakers met in early December to put together a ticket for the 1972 primary with the imprimatur of the Mayor Daley-led party hierarchy.

Numerous polls and other soundings at the time suggested that Simon was the party's best vote-getter in the state. And he clearly was the open choice for governor of most party officials in Illinois—with the exception of regular Cook County Democrats, who would not dare make a choice publicly before the slatemaking process without the blessing of Daley.

Two weeks before the slatemakers met, Simon's campaign team released the names of 87 Democratic county chairmen in the state who were backing Simon's gubernatorial bid openly with letters of endorsement. Only 15 of the county chairmen were missing from the list, including Daley, the chairman of Cook.

Interestingly, a number of Walker partisans were among the minority maintaining that Simon probably would not receive the slatemakers' support for governor. Walker himself contended that the nod would go to Foran, with whom the Daley machine might be more comfortable than with the unpredictable Simon. Whether Walker really believed this or not was another matter.

As the Walker people professed to see it, Simon would be slated for the gubernatorial nomination only if Ogilvie appeared unbeatable in 1972. But, with Ogilvie obviously vulnerable, so this reasoning went, Daley would run a more dependable person for governor, like fellow Irish Catholic Foran.

The most logical thing for Simon, it was concluded, was being slated for the Democratic nomination for the United States Senate seat held by Republican Charles Percy, who was expected to be formidable in his bid for re-election in 1972.

However, in announcing his candidacy for governor, Simon served notice that in seeking the party slatemakers' endorsement for the office he would "not accept nomination to any other state or federal post."

Simon contended that polls showed his candidacy "preferred by more Illinois citizens than all of the other candidates mentioned, and that I run appreciably stronger against the incumbent Governor than would anyone else. Both of these factors are true in downstate Illinois, in the Cook County suburbs, and in the City of Chicago. Every authentic sampling we have seen...at county fairs and elsewhere has confirmed this."

Really, it was tough to argue with this view. Polls, surveys and other readings of the public pulse did reveal Simon to be the hottest political property in Illinois, far and away.

Results of a statewide survey by the Chicago Sun-Times, Bloomington Daily Pantagraph and several other papers, published in November 1971, showed Simon clobbering Ogilvie among voters, 50 to 34 percent (with 16 percent undecided). The same poll had Ogilvie beating Walker, Foran and Howlett—although the Governor's margin over Walker was only by 3 percentage points.

Especially upsetting for Ogilvie was the survey's finding that Simon even would top him at that point among normally Republican voters in suburban Cook County, 41 to 37 percent (with 22 percent expressing no choice). Ogilvie had run well among these suburbanites in getting elected in 1968, but many of those canvassed said they had turned against him because of the state income tax passed during his term in office.

Even the magazine *Prairie Farmer* got into the act, saying late in 1971 that an interview poll by the publication clearly identified Simon as the leading choice of Illinois farmers to be the state's next governor.

Simon seemed as unstoppable in 1971 as that year's national championship Nebraska football team, with the governorship just the next inevitable conquest in what already was a Cinderella tale in politics. To many Illinoisans, the Lieutenant Governor obviously represented the quintessence of political life; he was everything good rolled into one being.

By the time of his formal announcement for governor, the story of the then 42-year-old Simon long had been memorized by political writers throughout the state.

In almost pro forma fashion, most could bang out on their typewriters without having to resort to clips the fascinating background that made Paul Simon a ridiculously easy standout in the often dismal swamp of Illinois politics. A lot about Simon truly was idyllic.

The son of a Lutheran missionary minister, Simon had borrowed $3,600 in 1947, when he was 19, to buy a defunct newspaper in the Madison County hamlet of Troy, not far from St. Louis. Soon afterward, he was using the weekly Troy Tribune to attack gambling and prostitution in the county, vices openly tolerated by officials of heavily-Democratic Madison.

Much of the local crowd joked about Simon's exposes and editorial denunciations of the illegal activities. But not Governor Adlai Stevenson. He reacted by sending state troopers to raid some of the biggest gambling spots, a stroke that captured the attention of *Life* magazine.

Simon's role in this also caught the eye of the late Senator Estes Kefauver of Tennessee, who invited the young publisher to testify in St. Louis at the nationally televised hearings of his Senate crime investigating committee. Telling Kefauver's panel what he knew about organized crime in Madison County, Simon was labeled a "star witness" by *Newsweek* and, at the age of 22, became a bit of a national celebrity.

In 1954, Simon pulled off another stunning coup by whipping the regular Democratic organization in his county to win a seat in the Illinois House. Although he had little money, Simon waged an exhaustive house-to-house campaign in his district, knocking on doors and introducing himself. Just as many had failed to take his newspaper crusading seriously, older political hands dismissed the House bid by Simon and his volunteer helpers as a mission impossible by idealistic young amateurs.

But, he won big, and proceeded to win re-election three more times to the House before capturing a seat in the Illinois Senate in 1962.

And, just as in his eight years in the lower chamber, Simon continued during his six years in the Senate as a political avant-gardist with often independent stands on issues and outspoken views that sometimes rankled regulars in both parties. However, in so doing, Simon was able to retain an apple-pie image of righteousness in years when a number of his fellow state politicians were tainted by scandal.

In 1968, Simon became the Democratic candidate for lieutenant governor with the endorsement of the Daley-led slatemakers.

Actually, more than one cynic saw this as a calculated move to eliminate Simon from the scene by party old liners who thought of him as a political nerd, an individual whose constantly flaunted sense of political conscientiousness had worn thin. Many expected the GOP state ticket to fare well in the 1968 election, and even a lot of Simon followers feared that his widely recognized popularity would not be enough to save himself and his running mate on the ticket, Samuel Shapiro, the incumbent Governor who was slated by the Democratic leadership for retention in his post.

Once again, Simon fooled them all. Sure enough, Richard Ogilvie did topple the likable but lackluster Shapiro in the contest for governor. But, lo and behold, Simon pulled another political miracle out of the hat by defeating the Republican nominee for lieutenant governor, Winnetka businessman Robert A. Dwyer.

While it was pointed out that Dwyer never had held public office and may have been the least known of the principal candidates on either party's state ticket, Simon's victory in 1968 was unprecedented in that never before had Illinois voters picked the candidate of one party for governor and the nominee of the other major party for lieutenant governor.

Simon had proven beyond any doubt that he was a phenomenal vote-getter, and starting with the day he took office as Lieutenant Governor virtually every interested person suspected that he could be difficult to beat in the 1972 race for governor.

No longer did it matter at all whether Simon at times still irritated the old pros. By this stage, he had the bulk of the downstate regular Democratic leaders in his corner anyway, because they now believed he was incapable of being stopped. They just had not seen anything quite like Simon come down the political trail.

In early 1971, a few months after Walker had announced for governor, Norton Kay brought the candidate downstate to meet certain reporters. One was the Illinois political writer for the St. Louis Post-Dispatch, who was based in Springfield and whom Kay introduced to Walker at a private meeting in a tavern near the Capitol.

Not long into the conversation, Walker asked the reporter what he thought of Walker's chance of becoming governor. Without hesitation, the writer replied that he saw little way that anybody could block Paul Simon from the Democratic nomination for the office, adding that in the reporter's eye Simon seemed to have assumed the nimbus of more of a folk hero than successful politician in downstate Illinois.

The correspondent also reminded Walker that Simon had spent much of his adult life building a close relationship with the press, a factor, the reporter predicted, which well could come into play during a campaign to derail Simon's almost certain bid for the gubernatorial nomination.

The reporter looked across the bistro table at Kay and Walker, observed the rigidly formal manner of Walker and wondered to himself how this Chicago corporation lawyer could put much of a dent in Simon's political armor—even though the 1972 primary election still was about a year away.

Walker had a few observations of his own, though. First, he said he didn't think Simon would get the blessing of Daley for the nomination for governor. But if that did happen, Walker added, he would oppose Simon vigorously as the candidate of the party bosses and would bring out, even against Simon, a wellspring of hostility against political bossism boiling just beneath the surface in Illinois.

Walker also asked the reporter to understand that he, Walker, never had ducked a challenge in his life, including if necessary a fight with a folk hero—a depiction of Simon felt by Walker to be an overstatement.

This reporter next saw Walker in late July of that year when the scribe joined Walker for much of his walk along U.S. Route 50 in Clinton County and on into St. Clair County, and the picturesque town of Lebanon, and nearby O'Fallon.

Walker was far different now from the guy the reporter had met earlier in the year in Springfield. The stiff demeanor had given way to sweaty earthiness in a figure obviously in pain as he hustled the small town residents for votes, one by one, much like Simon first had done in 1954. But the Post-Dispatch man still did not see Dan Walker defeating Paul Simon.

Even the appearance of the bespectacled Simon set him apart.

As he entered the race for governor, he still wore the same choirboy look of his first days in Springfield 17 years earlier. To some, Simon was the everlastingly wide-eyed Illinois version of actor James Stewart in the movie "Mr. Smith Goes to Washington."

On political trademarks, Simon even had a leg up on Walker. As Walker hiked through the state, folks started calling him Bandanna Dan. With Simon, it was bow ties, often polka dot. No one could remember seeing him in anything else, at least since 1954.

That was the year when, in his first race for office, he donned a bow tie once or twice and soon found himself dubbed the bow tie candidate by the Alton Telegraph. The reporter who called attention to Simon's neck wear was the late Bill Ryan, a memorable character who covered the Madison County Courthouse in Edwardsville for the Telegraph.

Simon's rapport with the press was one of his strongest suits. Part of it was intrinsic. After all, he was one of them.

In the years after his purchase of the paper in Troy, Simon built up a chain of 14 weekly newspapers before selling his interest in them in 1966. An author of books on topics from Abraham Lincoln to world hunger, he also wrote frequent columns on issues from Springfield which he provided at no cost to more than 300 newspapers in Illinois. He called himself a writer by profession, and he was a good one, better than a number of the reporters covering him.

As part of the way the world worked, reporters sent to cover state government in Springfield knew that, if they had nothing else going, they at least had a friend in Paul Simon. Simon was helpful day or night, and many scribes, convinced that Simon alone among the major officials had nothing to hide, ignored in his case the old admonition to keep an arm's length away from those being covered.

After arriving in Springfield, few new reporters could turn down the inevitable invitation to spend a Sunday afternoon with Simon and his family in Troy, throwing a football around on the lawn of his big old home.

Of course, it did not hurt that Simon, at the heart of it all, was a true political liberal, which happened to be the bent of most working, poorly-paid reporters.

But he always seemed to go the extra mile, like in disclosing publicly the sources of all his income, since 1954, down to the last penny—a virtually unparalleled step in Illinois public life, even among the other proponents of reform and improved ethics in government.

Thus, although nobody would acknowledge it openly, the press posed a possible land mine for Dan Walker or any other person trying to step too hard on Simon in a contest for the Democratic gubernatorial nomination.

Later on, Jim Thompson, who governed Illinois from 1977 through 1990, proved to be about as good as Simon in getting consistently favorable media coverage. Like Simon, the affable Thompson engaged in an unabashedly hands-on courtship of the press that said much about their priorities. A businessperson, even one who was a contributor, might have to wait for an appointment for days, but never a reporter, whether from the Tribune or the Podunk Bugle.

The surprising thing was not that politicians as astute or successful as Simon or Thompson catered so openly to the press, but that many of their big league political contemporaries did not. Not that it was as easy as Simon and Thompson made it seem.

When it finally became clear that the 1972 primary contest for the Democratic nomination for governor would be a head-on clash between Walker and Simon, Walker began to detect, he thought, a drop-off in the fairness of media coverage of his effort. Maybe, maybe not. But, Walker sensed it, or claimed to, thereby sowing the seeds for his mind-set that he had a problem with the press, a Walker fixation that was to grow even as his campaign, covered heavily by the media, headed toward victory.

Not that Walker and his gang saw it, but a few newspeople did exist who were not sold totally on Simon. Edward T. Pound, a ferocious investigative reporter, was one. During the years Ogilvie was governor, Pound plied his trade in the Illinois Statehouse for three papers, first the Alton Telegraph, then the old Chicago Today and, finally, the Sun-Times. Pound made life miserable for plenty of people in high places in those days. He had a ruthlessly skeptical eye that gave nobody a pass, not even his mother had she been caught with her hand in the cash register.

As for Simon, Pound found him a little too sanctimonious.

More than that, though, Pound believed it interesting that, even though the Lieutenant Governor had risen as an outspoken political reformer, he was conspicuously out to lunch, Pound felt, when so many other Democrats and others finally hit the streets in protest against Daley bossism at the end of the 1960s and in the early years of the 1970s. Never one to mince words, Pound concluded that Simon had sold out to Daley so as to curry his support for Simon's lofty political goals.

A bit of background was in order here. Pound was dispatched to Springfield to cover Illinois government by the Telegraph after toiling locally for the paper in Madison County.

There, Pound had been very close to a number of individuals—like attorneys Richard Allen of Granite City and Dick Mudge of Edwardsville—who had stopped supporting Simon because they contended he no longer was the political idealist voters initially sent to Springfield.

A month after Simon announced his candidacy for governor, Pound wrote a feature on the Lieutenant Governor for Chicago Today headlined "Paul Simon: Noble Knight of Troy". The story was not as rosy for Simon as the headline insinuated because

Pound gave considerable play to the growing questions about Simon's relationship with Daley.

One quote from Mudge was specially prophetic because it painted a picture of Simon that many individuals apparently would accept in coming months in deciding to support Walker instead of Simon.

"Paul is not as independent as his public image would make you think," Mudge claimed. "I don't think every politician has his price, but Paul's price is power. It's his ambition that has caused him to rationalize that Daley's one-man rule of the Democratic Party is all right. Simon isn't dishonest financially. He won't take a bribe, but he will make whatever compromise in principle that is necessary to get Daley's support."

Simon countered to Mudge and other critics that his primary purpose in running for office was to serve the citizenry and that his fundamental objective of "looking at issues and trying to solve problems" was not going to be attained, as some simplistically seemed to think, by just denouncing Daley.

Without question, Simon had played every card in his hand as well as he could to show that he merited the party slatemakers' endorsement for the Democratic nomination for governor in 1972. However, as with any matter involving Daley, nothing was assured until the deed was done.

The waiting finally neared an end in early December of 1971 when Illinois Democratic leaders sat down behind closed doors in Chicago for the climactic session of the slatemaking rite for the 1972 election.

Illinois Democratic slatemaking—a target of Walker's scorn—was a great equalizer. It was one of the rare times when governors and congressmen stood, hat in hand, on the outside with the reporters. Only top party officers were privy to the ticket-making deliberation carried out in a ritual as secretive as that of the most tightly controlled fraternal organization.

The intent was to save the party money and trouble, said slatemaking advocates. By convening on the eve of an election year to endorse candidates for major offices, the ruling clique of the Democrats headed off the chance of an open primary fight and the disunity it brought.

As the critics viewed it, though, the process virtually excluded Democratic rank and file from a voice in the party's business. Little debate on issues occurred because candidates had to convince nobody but a handful of men about their capability, the detractors pointed out.

Clearly, the process was a biennial reminder that the Chicago Democratic organization had not died like so many other big city machines.

The decisive Chicago windup of slatemaking in 1971 was good political theater as Mayor Daley and other party elders (members of the Democratic State Central Committee along with Democratic officials from Cook County) strode through the halls of the Sherman House to their guarded meeting place, the Emerald Room.

After that, aspirants for major spots on the 1972 Illinois Democratic ticket were called in, one at a time, for private chats with Daley and others. The supplicants were questioned mainly about financial backing and party loyalty, especially whether the hopefuls agreed to abide by the decision of the slatermakers.

Had Simon not been selected for the gubernatorial slot on the slated ticket, he was prepared to challenge the slatemakers' choice through an open fight in the state primary election the following March. Still, by participating in the slatemaking, Simon was blasted by Walker for capitulating to a demeaning relic of dictatorial politics.

Naturally, Simon reckoned that Walker would have gone into the Emerald Room too if he had thought he had a chance of being slated for governor. After all, Walker had tried his luck with the slatemakers once a little more than a decade back, but nothing came of it.

In the end, to the surprise of nobody, Simon was slated to be the Democratic candidate for governor.

Endorsed by the slatemakers for the nomination for lieutenant governor was Neil F. Hartigan, a former administrative aid to Daley and attorney for the Chicago Park District.

A veteran member of Congress from Chicago, Representative Roman Pucinski, was slated to run against Percy, and Howlett, a popular figure in the party, got the nod for the nomination for Illinois secretary of state.

So, at last, Simon had jumped this hurdle, one viewed by more than a few analysts as perhaps the trickiest square to be leaped by Simon on the checkerboard to the governorship.

In that he had done what he felt he had to do, Simon would find comfort in the words of political writer Michael Kilian in a flattering portrait of Simon distributed by the Chicago Tribune Service in January 1972.

Giving Simon credit for getting the backing of Daley, Kilian opined that, in the end, "unless one wants to bloody his head in a party primary fight, and undoubtedly lose, the Democratic nomination for governor must come with the blessing of Richard J. Daley."

Next, Simon would have to handle Walker, which Simon certainly had every reason to believe he would do. Adding the weight of the Daley machine support to Simon's already demonstrated statewide popularity would make any person appear unbeatable in a Democratic primary fight. ❧

The Stevenson Campaign
—Dan's Warm-up

On the surface, Illinois Treasurer Adlai E. Stevenson III cruised as smooth as silk into his United State Senate seat in the 1970 election. He demolished his Republican opponent, incumbent Ralph Tyler Smith, in a cakewalk. The Stevenson campaign rolled over Smith like a well-oiled tank. Adlai and his campaign crew made it look easy.

However, appearances can be deceiving.

Stevenson certainly took care of Smith well enough. But Adlai's campaign team? That was another story, a script with more back stabbing in it than a soap opera.

Not until after the election did it begin to look as if much of the really interesting stuff about Stevenson's race went on behind the scene, where the Machiavellian differences among his campaign staffers provided a hell of a lot more juicy tidbits than Stevenson's public dispatching of Smith, a hapless underdog in the contest from the start.

Early on, Stevenson asked his Chicago attorney friend Dan Walker to chair his Senate campaign. The two had known each other since the early 1950s, when Walker was an aid to Stevenson's father, the late Governor Adlai E. Stevenson. They were not social pals, but they shared a distaste for machine politics— although Stevenson had received the endorsement of the Daley slatemakers for the Senate race. The younger Stevenson was very impressed with Walker's organizational skills.

Stevenson did not know that, since early in 1970, Walker, de Grazia and David Green had been discussing privately but earnestly a Walker candidacy in two years for either governor or United States senator.

Walker still had not committed to run in 1972, but the talk had progressed to the point where the trio brought into their huddle Mort Kaplan, a Chicago public relations man who would be a Walker political strategist from that time on through the end of his governorship.

But, just as the four individuals, the "planning group" as Walker called them, neared a decision on Walker's political future, Stevenson asked for Walker's help, creating what Walker felt initially to be "a major problem." Now what?

Well, after further deliberation, Walker later related, "the (planning) group determined that handling Adlai would be a good step for me.

"I would get some good exposure around the state with Democrats in setting up the campaign, attending meetings and things like that. Adlai was almost surely a winner, and that would do me no harm.

"So, I accepted Adlai's request."

In getting a yes from Walker, though, Stevenson was not told that the Walker group would use the Stevenson campaign as a training ground for a projected bid for a major state office by Walker in the not too distant future.

"I never knew," Stevenson was to tell the Post-Dispatch. "I was like a babe in the woods about the Walker candidacy brewing right under my nose."

The night of Nov. 3, 1970, election day, some friends did tell Stevenson that Walker seemed to be trying to steal the show at a gathering of Stevenson supporters in Chicago to celebrate his landslide over Smith by a statewide plurality of 545,000 votes.

When the television cameras focused on Stevenson and his wife Nancy on the podium, Walker was quite visible in the picture behind the Stevensons even though the couple stood on a raised platform.

This was possible because Bill Holzman, then a Stevenson campaign aid before joining Walker, had gotten down on his hands and knees behind the Stevensons and motioned for Walker to stand on his back, which Walker was able to do with a little balancing help from others in back of Adlai and Nancy. By then, Walker definitely had decided to run for governor, but nobody outside his little group knew it.

Again, the Walker brain trust saw nothing wrong in getting extra mileage out of the Stevenson campaign as long as the candidate won. Little doubt of that ever appeared to exist.

Stevenson, a bearer of one of the best known names in Illinois history, already was a proven winner in statewide balloting. Alton lawyer Smith was speaker of the Illinois House when Governor Ogilvie named him to the Senate seat vacated by the death in 1969 of Republican Everett Dirksen. However, Smith was not widely known by the state electorate.

Bill Holzman was an initial Walker recruit to the Stevenson campaign staff. Thin and redheaded, Californian Holzman had been a Democratic activist on the West Coast. He was assigned scheduling and advance duties for the Stevenson effort. Holzman also was at home on a tennis court, like Walker, and the pair played frequently in the years to come.

Walker also got Norton Kay to join the campaign as press secretary, signaling the start of their working relationship. Kay came to the Stevenson campaign from Chicago Today, where he served briefly as political editor after Chicago's American was revamped and became the tabloid Chicago Today in 1969.

Instrumental in the operation of the Stevenson campaign's Chicago office would be Nancy Shlaes, an attractive University of Chicago graduate from New Jersey who had worked closely with de Grazia at the Democratic Federation of Illinois and in other independent Democratic undertakings. Later, she would be a paid administrative director of the Walker gubernatorial campaign, assisting de Grazia in his management of it. In 1977, after the death of the Walker governorship, she and de Grazia were married.

Still another Walker person on the Stevenson team was a 27-year-old Chicagoan named James Houlihan who was to go on to get elected as a state representative and serve as a floor leader in the Illinois House for Walker when he was governor.

As for de Grazia, his mere presence via the campaign sparked much of the friction below the surface. Friends for many years, Stevenson and de Grazia often conferred when Adlai was state treasurer. By the time the 1970 campaign arrived, though, their relationship had cooled because Stevenson suspected that Vic was tipping columnists and others to things that nettled Stevenson.

Walker was told by Stevenson that he didn't want de Grazia to have any position in the campaign. Stevenson's insistence on this, he felt, was a reason for the tension that arose in the campaign between himself and Walker. Back then, Stevenson contended later, he did not grasp fully the tightness between Dan and Vic.

In spite of Stevenson's dislike for de Grazia, Walker still consulted his friend on campaign matters. The influence of de Grazia was perceived, for instance, in the urging of Stevenson by the Walker people to needle Daley whenever possible.

However, Stevenson, although not afraid to criticize Daley when he thought it appropriate, was hesitant to irritate the mayor more than he already had done by choosing Walker, whom Daley hated, to run his campaign. If anything, the liberal Stevenson believed his candidacy could use a stronger image on law and order issues, which were increasingly popular with voters at the time.

For that reason, Stevenson brought Thomas Foran, the Chicago conspiracy trial prosecutor, into the campaign as co-chairman a few months before the election. Foran also was a guy on good paper with the Daley machine.

Actually, at the end of 1969, Stevenson named Lieutenant Governor Simon, another old friend, downstate chairman of the campaign, but many viewed Simon's role as largely ceremonial.

However, in the eyes of Walker, bringing in Foran diminished his role as chairman and exacerbated the backbiting between campaign staffers identified with Walker and those close to Stevenson. Ironically, when Walker later faced prosecution by federal authorities in Chicago, he hired Foran to defend himself.

Walker saw another development as quite damaging to his rapport with Stevenson. It concerned Anthony T. Dean, a young Kansan and Yale University graduate working as a campaign organizer in the Chicago suburbs. Dean also was a conscientious objector to war who during the Vietnam hostilities had performed alternative duty to military service as required.

Walker said that Stevenson wanted Dean fired from the campaign, but Walker refused in saying that he told Stevenson that Dean should be respected as a bona fide objector.

As Walker reconstructed the exchange, "I told Adlai it was his right to get rid of Tony. But, if he persevered on it, I and I believed many other staff members would resign in protest. Adlai finally gave in to my point of view, but it was downhill between Adlai and me after that.

"He made it clear that he wanted to run his own campaign, even to picking the photographs he would use in brochures and overruling the experts on matters pertaining to commercials. Since it was clearly his right to make his own decisions, I gradually withdrew from all duties except those relating to organization and administrative operation of the staff. Besides, it was clear Adlai was a shoo-in."

Walker had other subjects on his mind anyhow. As the Stevenson-Smith race unfolded, Dan's private little group continued to meet. Finally, in the summer of 1970, the members of the group congregated in the Pheasant Run resort at St. Charles, where a suite for them was booked for a night. It was decision time in regard to 1972.

Should Walker run against Percy or for governor? Senator Percy undoubtedly was popular and would be tough. It might be possible, though, to get the regular Democratic leaders' endorsement for a race against Percy. That surely was out of the question in the event Walker sought the governorship, the position loaded with meat and potatoes power, the kind you could hold in your hands.

"We finally decided on governor," Walker recalled, "because that was what we all really wanted. It was the tougher choice, but I didn't really want, in my gut, to be a U.S. senator. Furthermore, tough jobs have never frightened me away."

The next item to be determined was timing. When to announce for governor? Predicting accurately that Walker's candidacy would be opposed strongly by the Chicago machine, de Grazia argued that a very early announcement was needed, as much as two years before the 1972 election, to give Walker a long period to get known.

However, announcing that early left Walker worried at first "about the impact this would have on Adlai because he would know that, while chairing his campaign, I was plotting my own political future."

But, Walker quoted de Grazia as retorting, "So what? Adlai's sure to win. He can easily live with our announcement after his initial pique dies down."

So, before the night was out at Pheasant Run, Walker and his confidants decided to spring the gubernatorial announcement in November of 1970, several weeks after the election. They were confident it would be a political bombshell. Until then, secrecy was the watchword.

Before leaving Pheasant Run, the group also decided to ask Norton Kay, Holzman and Nancy Shlaes to join the Walker campaign as soon as Stevenson's ended.

The day picked for Walker to announce his candidacy was Nov., 18, 1970. With that decision out of the way, Walker, de Grazia and Green began debating how hard to hit Daley on announcement day.

Right away, however, up popped one of those little things that keep the pot boiling. After setting the date for Walker's announcement, his group learned that the swearing in of Stevenson to the Senate had been set for the same day, earlier than observers had expected. What else would happen? As if Adlai would not be upset enough just at learning of Walker's candidacy.

On the other hand, that would pass, unlike a million other things that now confronted Walker as he prepared to seek the governor's chair in his adopted state.

The first thing he wanted to get to work on was making arrangements for his departure from Montgomery Ward & Co. In 1966, Walker had left his partnership in his Chicago law firm, then known as Hopkins, Sutter, Owen, Mulroy, Wentz and Davis, to join Montgomery Ward.

When he decided to announce for governor, he held a $118,000-a-year position as a vice president, general counsel and director of Montgomery Ward. He also was vice president and general counsel of Marcor, Inc., the parent firm of Montgomery Ward.

In announcing his candidacy, Walker said that he was taking a leave of absence from Montgomery Ward in order to campaign. The following spring he resigned from the operation.

At the time of his resignation, he publicly disclosed his latest income tax returns—as well as other information which showed Walker to have an estimated net worth of $355,000. Much of that, though, came from his stock holdings in Marcor, which he valued at $327,000 in April 1971.

Prior to entering the political arena, Walker had started toning down a number of his civic activities.

Most noticeably, late in 1969 he turned down a third term as president of the Chicago Crime Commission to accept his leadership role in the Stevenson campaign.

As president of the private citizens' organization, Walker had called attention to himself by overseeing the publication of detailed reports on the crime syndicate's invasion of legitimate businesses. Because the reports named firms and individuals allegedly connected to the syndicate, eyebrows inevitably went up in certain circles in the Windy City.

The media also saw this as pretty gutsy on Walker's part. Like the New York Times, which said in December 1968 that "Daniel Walker does not lose any sleep over it, but his name surely stands near the top of any list of candidates for elimination by the Chicago Mafia."

Walker also now had to face seriously for the first time the political money game. He winced at the thought of trying to raise quickly needed up-front dough for the campaign from close friends. He already had a distaste for political fund-raising at the start of his campaign, and his opinion of this necessary task only would get worse from that point on. To Walker, coming up with dollars was the bane of politics, and it would haunt him through the moment of his final political breath.

Looking back, he said later, "I am amazed at our audacity in overlooking the problem of how we could possibly raise the money for a major statewide campaign."

Beyond that, he later philosophized, "I don't think any of us appreciated the magnitude of what we were commencing when we announced for governor.

"Always the optimist, I thought surely that some of the Chicago establishment and most of downstate would immediately welcome my candidacy against the Chicago machine. Perhaps Vic, Dave and Mort were more realistic than I. If so, they kept their fears quiet."

Walker's statement of candidacy certainly did turn out to be geared to stir anti-Daley feelings.

Announcing as scheduled on Nov. 18 his intent to run for governor in 1972, Walker asked Illinoisans to join him in a "political adventure" to overcome two political machines and incumbent Governor Ogilvie in order to put governing control of the state in the hands of the many millions "who know political exclusion."

Stating that a new agenda for Illinois was essential for getting state government working again, Walker declared war on "the old politics...that have straitjacketed both parties for years."

Consequently, he emphasized, he would not seek the endorsement of the Daley slatemakers for the Democratic nomination for governor.

In the wording that constituted the manifesto of his candidacy, Walker pledged to take his candidacy "to the people rather than court the kingmakers in the Democratic Party." He would take his candidacy directly to residents of every one of the 102 counties in Illinois, he said.

"I shall run for governor in the 1972 Democratic primary regardless of who else enters the race and regardless of what the Democratic State Central Committee does. I shall not seek the endorsement of the Democratic Party slatemaking committee.

"This small group of politicians, meeting in secret, has no power in law to endorse candidates. Only the voters of Illinois, casting their ballots in a primary election, have the legal right to choose who runs on their behalf."

Walker noted that his party had been opening its doors across the country, but not in Illinois. Here, he continued, the party "is still controlled by an antiquated machine dedicated to special privilege politics and performing a discredited function: the exchange of jobs for blocs of votes."

By ending Daley slatemaking, Walker concluded, "we will eliminate the patronage system and the political prostitution of our courts. We will construct a political system that will not tolerate politicians who have persistent ties to organized crime and those who use party position to acquire personal wealth."

In a debate within the Walker group on how far to go in the announcement on Daley, de Grazia argued for an outright assault with no fudging. As often happened, he prevailed.

"As the English peasants used to say, 'If you are going to be hanged for stealing a goose, you might as well be hanged for stealing a gander,'" Walker would say afterward.

"Thus, we opted to make no placative move toward the boss. We attacked."

Of course, lest he be accused of blaming everything wrong on just one political enemy, Walker also lashed out at Ogilvie and the GOP.

Pointing out that Democrats "have no monopoly on machine

politics," Walker averred that he also was running "to oppose Richard Ogilvie's Republican machine, which is just as destructive of the public's rights.

"It is said that government is too important to be left to politicians. But politics itself is too important to be left to politicians."

Nevertheless, Walker added, "I have no illusions about the difficulty of the task ahead. Machine politicians do not lightly relinquish the gears and levers of special privilege."

Indeed, Walker held, he himself was not even a politician at all, only "a citizen deeply concerned about politics and government in Illinois."

Walker ended his statement of candidacy on a high note, saying in language almost obligatory for Illinois political speeches that the state had "all the requisites for greatness—the geography, the resources, the traditions.

"Most important, we have the people. This is the national heartland. Working together with a new agenda for Illinois we can build a model for a just, humane, exciting America."

Walker's formal announcement did not ignite an overnight uprising in the streets of Illinois cities. Many news editors gave a bigger play to the announcement by the Soviet Union that it had landed an operating, self-propelled eight-wheel vehicle on the moon called Lunokhod I.

Also upstaging Walker was a story down at Fort Benning, Georgia, where an Army prosecutor had begun the court-martial of Lt. William Calley, Jr., for his role in the alleged My Lai massacre in Vietnam of more than 100 civilians in 1968.

Still, Walker's action hardly could be ignored. It did come as a real surprise to the Illinois political world, where secrets live about as long as it takes a pol to reach the nearest phone. Walker's little cadre had its bombshell.

The initial reaction centered not so much on whether Walker

could win, since nobody gave him much of a chance, but on the relationship of the Walker candidacy to the Stevenson campaign. That was the intriguing part, the thing that triggered frantic scurrying for a few days.

Political writers found it hard to swallow at first that the Walker undertaking was not an extension of the Stevenson campaign, an initiative sanctioned by Stevenson. If true, that meant that Stevenson, now ensconced safely in the United States Senate, was part of a political conspiracy to keep the heat on the Daley machine issue and, in the process, create a pothole on the road to the governorship for Simon, who was thought to be close to Stevenson.

Recognizing this, the Stevenson camp retaliated with a full court press by its first team to repudiate any appearance of Stevenson fostering the Walker candidacy. Called damage control, it involved a flood of phone calls to key Illinois political players, along with influential media types, disavowing any role by Stevenson in the Walker campaign.

On the phone were top Stevenson emissaries Thomas J. Wagner, Adlai's closest assistant, and John Taylor of Cass County, Stevenson's best known downstate operative. Chicagoan William Flanagan, a veteran political flack for Stevenson, quickly got hold of certain reporters. Even Milton Fisher, a leading Chicago bankruptcy lawyer and the treasurer of Stevenson's campaigns, got into the act.

The gist of the message from the Stevenson men was that Adlai knew nothing beyond vague rumors of Walker's intent to announce for governor until it was confirmed in a telephone conversation between Walker and Stevenson shortly before Walker went public.

By then, Stevenson already was in Washington, where his swearing into the Senate, although intended on Nov. 18, actually occurred the day before at the request of Stevenson so he could vote on job safety legislation.

Later, Simon recalled that he was asked by Stevenson to join him in Washington for his Senate induction activities. The request came a day or two ahead of time, Simon remembered, and he told Stevenson he couldn't come to Washington unless it was necessary. Stevenson replied that Walker apparently was going to announce for governor in a day or so and that Adlai felt it important for Simon to be by Stevenson's side. Simon went to Washington.

A witness to the reaction in Washington to Walker's announcement was James Bagley, a young political science graduate of North Park College and a son of the chief engineer of the Chicago Park District. Bagley was one of a handful of Stevenson campaign workers taken to Washington by Stevenson for a staff slot.

Years later, Bagley still recalled vividly "the shock, and then the setting in of some anger, that followed our learning of Walker's announcement in Chicago.

"We were all naturally feeling great about Adlai entering the Senate, but suddenly here were all these reporters wanting comments from Adlai on the Walker development...and from Paul Simon, too. At first, myself and others didn't know what was going on, what the reporters were talking about."

Many in the Stevenson coterie, Bagley recollected, "would think of Walker's running as a joke."

In the words of Bagley, "We didn't see how he could ever beat Paul Simon in the primary. In the opinion of many who worked with or under Dan in the campaign, he was not cut out for campaigning. He was just too militaristic, too severe. Just a cold fish. Really, some back in Washington thought that Dan had gone off the deep end in announcing for governor."

Anticipating a negative reaction from Stevenson, but surprised at the extent of its bitterness, the Walker team had to play its own game of spin control to try to get the best possible interpretation of the situation out to the public. The press had to be dealt with, a job for Kay.

In his own whirlwind round of calls to reporters, Kay insisted that Walker's candidacy was not an outgrowth of the Stevenson campaign in the mind of either one of the men. Instead, Walker's effort was a continuation of the Illinois Democratic Party reform movement that had been brewing for a long time, Kay said, and that had included Stevenson as a key early supporter.

"Dan just feels a more direct assault on the bossism stranglehold is necessary," Kay told reporter after reporter. Party revamping, he added, "is bigger than Adlai or any other single person."

More than a skirmish, this may have been the first pitched battle of the Walker candidacy, even though it was only hours old. Kay came out of it pretty well, if only in part because reporters by nature are sympathetic to underdogs. Members of the fourth estate have got to have stories, too.

Typical of the follow-up coverage was a column penned by John Dreiske, the crusty political editor of the Sun-Times, two days after Walker revealed his intent to run.

Under a headline proclaiming "Dan's the man, idealists," Dreiske wrote that Walker was "opening up a vista that may be very appealing indeed to those many youngsters who wanted Adlai to get in the ring with Daley and slug instead of joining him."

"Now those young people," Dreiske continued, "are being shown a new battlefield on which they may die gloriously, oblivious to all but a belief that it's the battle for principle that counts—not victory."

On the whole, Kay couldn't have written it much better. ❧

Walker v. Simon

Sure enough, the 1972 primary race between Dan Walker and Paul
Simon had it all. Especially drama.

Modern Illinois political history has seen closer contests, like
Big Jim Thompson's victory over Adlai Stevenson III in the 1982
gubernatorial fight by the razor thin margin of 5,074 votes.

Also, the 1972 primary was not the first time the Chicago
Democratic machine was beaten in a battle for the party's nomination for governor.

Take 1936, for instance, when the machine, then under Kelly-
Nash leadership, tried without success to deny Democratic Gov-

ernor Henry Horner nomination in the primary for a second term. Horner topped his machine opponent, Dr. Herman Bundesen, Chicago's health commissioner, in a rancorous primary tussle, after which Horner went on to retain his office with a victory in the general election.

Horner was an incumbent, though, not a political outsider like Walker seeking statewide elective office for the first time.

Really, the Simon-Walker primary contest outcome, 36 years after Horner's primary win, qualified more readily for that magical category of once in a lifetime happenings. Joe Namath and the Jets victorious in the Super Bowl. Miniature Hebron capturing the Illinois high school basketball crown. No way should stuff like this occur. Only in Disney films.

Of course, Walker's bid for the governorship was more than a little make-believe from the start. At least to those normally well versed on such matters. Political pros and junkies, reporters and the rest. Amusing, yes. Even entertaining. But not taken seriously, not really, until the night of March 21, 1972, when the incoming results of the day's primary election showed the impossible was happening.

Six days before the primary, Walker surfaced in the State-house press quarters to predict "the biggest upset in recent Illinois political history."

"I can tell at every factory gate," he added, "that my candidacy is getting across. We're going to win."

Candidate after candidate troops through the press room in the Capitol, none of them ever predicting they are going to lose. It was not that Walker's prediction fell on deaf ears among those Statehouse journalists, many of them very skilled and hardened performers. They just couldn't believe him because under no circumstances did they see Walker stopping Simon.

In later years, perhaps on one of his yachts or certainly in prison afterward, Walker would reflect warmly on his 1972 primary campaign and conclude that historians would consider both it and his subsequent general election race veritable models of success. The same could not be thought about 1976, his year of defeat.

"Every campaign, to be successful, should have a good, hardworking candidate, a solid structure and a vivid spirit," said Walker. "Each was totally in place for us, I believe, in 1972.

"Unfortunately, all were lacking, at least to some degree, in 1976.

"First, my spirit in 1976 was not up to the 1972 level for a lot of reasons. I had lost some of my enthusiasm. I encountered more negative persons. I had marital problems, and the business of government interfered, both in time and mental concentration.

"I was simply not as good a candidate during the second campaign as I was in 1972. I'm better as the outsider battling the odds than I am as a defender, even given the political advantages of incumbency."

Everything fell into place for Walker in 1972, particularly in the primary. Besides a hardworking candidate, a supportive structure and unyielding spirit, the Walker campaign had its army of thousands, political ragtags perhaps, but also remarkably zealous.

Furthermore, Walker had a primary foe who broke with his tradition by trying to play it safe with a low-key campaign designed to discourage boat rocking. Folks never saw the fighting Paul Simon of old in the primary race. The Lieutenant Governor, understandably confident because of a string of successes that made him appear politically invincible, attempted to ignore Walker.

Simon, who had left few stones unturned in past campaigns, left plenty this time as he sleepwalked through the primary seemingly oblivious to the tenacity of his challenger. Simon simply couldn't fathom how his political standing, built up over so many years, could be threatened seriously by a Johnny-come-lately like Walker. Illinois politics had too much substance for that.

Simon came across as a man who felt he had it in the bag. Far from acting like they were hungry for the state's top prize, Simon's followers were smug. It fit into Walker's game plan perfectly.

To Daniel Walker, his pursuit of the governorship was a crusade. He rode the horse out front, leading his volunteer soldiers on a mission to capture the Holy Land from the infidels. Not as visible was the person running the campaign, de Grazia.

"Vic's job," Walker recited, "was to get me elected. Mine was to govern after I was in office. Hopefully, one wouldn't get in the way of the other."

Added Walker, "It's very hard to govern effectively if you've run a bad campaign."

As manager of the campaign, de Grazia, a onetime student at the Chicago Conservatory of Music who had wanted to be a musician like his father, orchestrated everything and everybody. Walker retained a strong voice in policy decisions, but just about all else was delegated to de Grazia—a seasoned taskmaster in campaigns against the machine, against heavy odds.

In years following, critics placed a good part of the blame for Walker's problems at the doorstep of de Grazia. Walker never agreed, nor did he ever hesitate to defend de Grazia, an individual who demanded more of Walker than any person since Walker's father.

The conduct of de Grazia in the campaign and afterward, Walker believed, "generally belied the view of Vic held by some people that he was a tough, vindictive, power hungry, macho villainous personage.

"Not that he didn't have some of these characteristics to some degree, especially when it came to dealing with people who tried to hurt us, or were unfair to us during the campaign. But, those traits were never dominant."

Throughout the campaign, de Grazia was a man constantly in

motion—a whirling dervish often impatient, frequently jocular, always bitching about the paucity of funds, demanding impossible results from Walker and the others.

Still, de Grazia made few campaign decisions without consulting David Green, who always was around when it counted even if he remained unobtrusive to the regular Illinois political world.

To Walker, the plain-speaking, publicity shy Green complemented de Grazia because "he (Green) was even more of a thinker."

In Walker's eyes, Green had "a brilliant mind, much of it computer and the rest sound instinct." Green was the person with a nose for sniffing out votes in unforeseen places, and he had a knack for then tabulating those votes, with uncanny accuracy, before they were cast.

Not many politicians had Green's "counting mind," Walker felt, including himself.

Tallying votes ahead of time, Walker said he learned, "is not as easy as it sounds. A book could be written on the subject. It can be as difficult as understanding politics."

Dan, David and Vic. Invariably the bottom line. Walker thought of them as partners. He recalled "making no major political-government decision whatever without consulting and listening closely to Vic and Dave."

Victor and Dave did more than stay in touch after the end of Walker's political career. Later on, Green's successful business operations included the D.G. Group, Inc., in Chicago, a litigation consulting firm. Green was the board chairman of D.G. Group and de Grazia its president.

Rounding out the circle of top Walker advisors were Kay and Goldberg, the latter starting out part-time on the campaign but rapidly moving into the middle of things on a night and day basis. Very close to Walker since their days as trial court partners at the

Hopkins-Sutter law firm, Goldberg became, as Walker put it, "my conscience." Whenever there was a close call, Walker sought Goldberg's advice.

After Walker won and took office, the Governor and these four individuals comprised a solid ring around the pinnacle of power in Illinois, permitting the rest of the world little insight into their strategic deliberations.

It could be tough to get a hearing from this little ruling circle, even for other Walker team members whose perceptions and advice had counted in the struggle to capture control of Illinois government. If there were differences among those in the top Walker echelon during its glory days, the disagreements, and everything else, were hidden from view.

For instance, not until after his departure from the Statehouse was it learned that Walker sometimes felt while he was in office that Kay might have done more to offset the often unfavorable press coverage of the Governor's office and its policies.

Although describing Kay as "an indefatigable worker and fine writer," Walker would say later that he "wished Norty could have persuaded me to work harder at developing better relations with the press.

"But, in fairness, that's hindsight. Vic dominated Norty totally, and I think Norty was always a little afraid of him."

Looking back, Walker also noted that three of his top four advisors—Green, Kay and Goldberg—were Jewish. Raised by Texans in the poor hinterland of San Diego, where many of his neighbors were Dust Bowl fugitives out of *The Grapes of Wrath*, Protestant Walker had little contact with ethnic diversity in his early years, except for the Japanese farmers and Mexican farm workers.

He had no idea of a bar or bat mitzvah. Nor of much of anything about first or second generation Europeans, so many of whom he would encounter later, at times with difficulty, in

Chicago politics. This was the reason why, in the early months of his gubernatorial quest, Walker was more comfortable downstate than in visits to Chicago ethnic neighborhoods.

Reflecting on his Jewish advisors, and on the numerous Jews in his political following, Walker remembered his father saying that Jews "understand politics with a different and important perception.

"I never figured out how Dad, a man who was raised in backwoods Texas, barely graduated from high school and who spent his adult life as an enlisted person in the Navy, notoriously anti-Semitic in those years, acquired such a deep respect for Jewish thinking. I can only guess that it came from reading the Old Testament. He was an avid reader of the Bible. But, to my knowledge, he had only one Jewish friend, a San Diego men's wear retailer.

My lack of knowledge of Jewish customs and expressions was a real campaign handicap. It just wasn't my shtick, as I learned to say. The staff kidded me about it unmercifully. I think Vic deliberately did it so I would learn."

Lacking support from precinct captains and other Democratic regulars, the Walker campaign had to recruit and organize thousands of volunteers. This job fell to David Cleverdon, the top person in the campaign structure under de Grazia.

Like numerous other Walkerites, Louisiana native Cleverdon joined the Walker effort at the request of de Grazia and had a link to the University of Chicago, where Cleverdon had been a theology student.

Living on the road and out of truck stops, the 31-year-old Cleverdon, a veteran worker for liberal Democrats and their causes, put together with missionary fervor for the primary a network of volunteers who were to run circles around the party regulars in county after county.

Many in Cleverdon's battalions were recruited by Walker

himself, especially in the Chicago area where Walker's time in the months after the walk was consumed by coffee hours in the living rooms of supporters. There may have been as many as 400 of these informal gatherings, all of which were, in Walker's memory, kind of the same.

"The coffees were arranged by our organizers at the homes of friends throughout the Chicago area. The purpose, of course, was to recruit more organizers and workers.

"Five to 10 times a day, groups from as few as three on up to 25 or 30 would hear my pitch. I'd walk around the living room or dining room, introducing myself and asking for names, which I memorized. Then coffee or tea and small talk. Introduction by the hostess. I give the pitch and take questions. Look at my watch and express regrets. Go around the room, thanking each person, hopefully by her or his name, and asking for help.

"After I leave, the organizer does the hard sell and gets potential workers to fill out information cards."

Effective? Through these frequent stops, a bunch of them in the Chicago suburbs, Walker figured he picked up as many as 2,000 enlistees. This was an astonishingly large number of workers to recruit in a primary election campaign.

The Walker circulating through these gatherings, by this stage, was an accomplished one-on-one campaigner, a person now in his element. The stiff clumsiness of an earlier time had been replaced long before by a much more relaxed and easygoing approach, good for the face-to-face encounters that Walker sought in the primary campaign in stores and banks, on busy streets, anywhere people could be found. Shopping centers could be fertile grounds, in spite of the disapproval of campaigning in the malls by many of their managers.

During evenings in the sprawling Chicago burbs, home to about a third of the Illinois electorate, Walker got a good reception in bowling alleys. But there was no serious issue discussion in these places, just small talk.

"How's your game tonight? Let me watch your form. It is sure hot in here. How about a sip of your beer?" But never accept an invitation from a kegler to roll a ball.

In the primary in particular, Walker tried to avoid speeches at large meetings or rallies. He usually could not command big audiences anyway. When he did, the hall normally would be populated by individuals already backing him.

While Walker hustled for votes, Kay and the headquarters crew pumped out the press releases and other campaign materials stressing the themes and issues of Walker's candidacy. Nothing that complicated. Just daily assaults like a jackhammer against the obviously soft underbelly of Illinois politics.

No Republican ever swung harder, without letup, against the Daley machine. Its power, its abuse of that power, its refusal to purge many of its stalwarts caught up in the Illinois political corruption revealed almost incessantly in the early years of the 1970s.

Paul Simon was fair game now, too, as the person who'd requested and received the machine's backing for the Democratic gubernatorial nomination.

Naturally, Walker seldom failed to lambast the machine downstate, where the machine was an easy patsy, where the ingrained hostility against Daley made it easy to fan the flames of opposition to the machine.

Much more was involved, though. Walker was at war with just about the entire body politic of the state in the climactic months of the 1972 primary campaign as he militantly reminded the populace of the scandals that had debased Illinois officialdom.

Walker was appealing to a sense of moral outrage among the voters. In doing so, he had more to draw on than he ever could use.

As 1971 was ending, the public was hit with the indictment of former Governor Otto Kerner for allegedly unlawful activities in connection with profitable racing stock manipulations while he was chief executive of Illinois.

That bombshell concluded a year that began with the startling news of the discovery of a cache of more than $800,000 in shoe boxes hidden by the late Illinois Secretary of State Paul Powell, another Democrat.

Follow-up investigations of Powell's financial dealings cast a cloud over many of his political cronies, most of them Democrats. For one thing, the probing confirmed the often rumored ties, through stock or other holdings, between many of Illinois' leading politicians and the state-regulated horse racing industry. In many cases, the financial interests of the politicos were well hidden or cleverly camouflaged.

A year or so before all of this, Chief Justice Roy J. Solfisburg, Jr., and Justice Ray I. Klingbiel of the Illinois Supreme Court were forced to resign after it was shown that they had received and retained stock in a Chicago bank when a case involving an officer of the bank, Theodore J. Isaacs, was before the court.

In the case, the court went on to rule in favor of Isaacs— ironically the same Theodore Isaacs who had been state revenue director under his close friend Kerner and who would be implicated and convicted later with Kerner in the racetrack stock dealings that ensnared Kerner.

A few years earlier, another former governor, Republican William Stratton, was acquitted in a trial of federal charges that he had evaded $46,676 in taxes on unreported income during his second term in office.

Even Ogilvie, the incumbent awaiting the winner of the Simon-Walker contest, had not been immune from allegations or, at least, innuendos.

As an example, the Wall Street Journal revealed in 1971 that the late Philip J. Levin, who headed a firm that controlled two racetracks in the Chicago area, contributed $100,000 to Illinois

Republicans in the summer of 1970. At the time, the Illinois Racing Board was questioning Levin's fitness for participating in the racing industry in the state. He eventually was permitted to pursue his interests by the Republican-dominated board.

Pointing his finger at all this stuff, Walker preached throughout the primary campaign for stronger laws mandating strict ethical standards of conduct for public officials and candidates for office.

What Walker wanted was complete public disclosure of all campaign contributions by candidates and officeholders, as well as detailed revelations of their personal income—something which Simon of course had been doing for years.

Walker also wanted to enact stiff penalties, including imprisonment, for officials benefiting illegally from public office and for persons offering or accepting illegal campaign contributions. He also desired the imposition of a ceiling on permissible campaign expenditures.

He insisted that state ethical strictures apply to political parties as well as to individuals and that officeholders be banned from double-dipping: the receipt of more than one public salary at the same time. The latter proposal was aimed mainly at the Chicago machine, the political base of most of the state's double-dippers.

In pushing for disclosure, Walker charged that "for way too long there has been a curtain of secrecy between the people of Illinois and their government, a curtain that has permitted public officials to amass fortunes, to take what can only be called bribes without even facing—until it was too late—difficult or embarrassing questions.

"Only the cold glare of publicity can prevent many offenses. An official who knows that all his financial dealings will be public will keep them from being interesting."

On the other side, Simon's publicity mill churned out just

enough press releases to keep the media from concentrating exclusively on Walker. Not much new or gripping was forthcoming from the Simon camp, though, because the Lieutenant Governor's stands on many issues were old hat by that point.

Simon had sermonized on the need for ethical reform in government for years, and already had tried to put into practice, or at least had recommended, a number of steps Walker was proposing.

But while Walker played with fire by naming public officials whose allegedly improper conduct necessitated tougher ethical mandates, and tried to goad Simon into doing the same, Simon blandly refused to get personal. About the only individual criticized by Simon by name was Ogilvie.

Simon didn't want to waste campaign ammunition against Walker, issue or resource-wise. Too, by not retaliating against Walker's personal attacks on him, Simon figured that he would have a much easier time uniting the regular party with the Walker partisans after the primary.

Two years later, while running successfully for election to Congress in 1974 from the state's southernmost region, Simon acknowledged in an interview with the St. Louis Post-Dispatch that his confidence of victory in the race with Walker prompted an intentionally low-key campaign by the Lieutenant Governor.

"I wasn't campaigning hard day after day. We weren't really encouraging a lot of media coverage We were saving all of that for the general election," Simon said.

"Certainly, we could have spent more money to answer Walker's charges.

"But, in a primary, if you believe you're ahead, you don't want to make your opponents and their followers angry. In a general election, it's a totally different situation. You don't think about making opponents angry."

Key advisors to Simon in the primary contest were William P.

Colson, a Chicago lawyer who was Simon campaign manager; Eugene Callahan, the top assistant to Simon in the Lieutenat Governor's office; and close Simon friend Richard J. Durbin, an attorney who later would be elected to a central Illinois seat in Congress while residing in Springfield.

Simon also had an inner circle asset that many officeholders lack, a politically savvy wife. Jeanne Simon was State Representative Jeanne Hurley, a Democrat from Wilmette, when she and fellow House member Simon married in 1960, a union that created an extraordinary husband-wife legislative team. Although Mrs. Simon, an attorney, did not seek re-election after her marriage, her grasp of Illinois politics gave her husband an unusually potent ally by his side.

The competition in the primary for the Democratic nomination for lieutenant governor also seemed to be a positive for Simon.

The person slated by Daley as Simon's running mate, Neil Hartigan, may not have been a household name south of his hometown of Chicago, but he bore the party regulars' stamp of approval.

Running against Hartigan at the request of Walker was Mayor Neal E. Eckert of Carbondale, a guy with a nice pedigree but a complete newcomer in state politics.

The 33-year-old Eckert, who met Walker during the southern Illinois leg of Dan's walk, was a businessman-farmer and a part-time teacher at Southern Illinois University as well as the occupant of an elective municipal office.

Along with an attractive wife, Eckert brought a recognizable name to the Walker campaign, at least in the lower part of the state. Neal was a member of the family that operated Eckert Orchards, Inc., of Belleville, the largest apple grower at the time in Illinois.

Walker said that Eckert was exactly what he wanted in a

running mate, a fresh faced political novice carrying around no state government baggage.

Back to Simon, though. Aside from the Lieutenant Governor's wife, the most respected Simon operative was Callahan, an individual of unlimited energy. A farm boy from Milford in Iroquois County, Callahan was a widely read political columnist for the old Illinois State Register in Springfield before undertaking a state government career in 1967 that included service in several other posts before he joined Simon's staff in 1969.

As Simon's man Friday, the forthright Callahan was adept at handling the press, schooled well enough in state government to deal with the bureaucrats, and highly respected by rank and file Democrats—many of whom in middle Illinois had depended on his column, "Callagrams," for inside political dope. Callahan did not mince words, be it with a janitor in the Statehouse or Paul Simon. It also was not Callahan's nature to turn the other cheek.

As the primary campaign rolled on, Callahan, then 38 and already white-haired, became increasingly uneasy with the restrained tone of his boss's approach, most notably in Simon's refusal to reply to Walker's daily charge that the Lieutenant Governor had allowed himself to become a dupe of the Daley machine. Callahan's concern was not heeded, though, by either Simon or Colson, who himself had close ties to the machine.

Finally, things came to a head. On the Saturday before the primary election, the Sun-Times contacted Callahan about a Walker criticism of Simon that Callahan considered ridiculous. Callahan retorted that Walker's remarks were a diatribe amounting to a "deathbed confession" by a candidate knowing he was doomed to defeat, an assessment that got into print quickly.

"When Paul saw my quote," Callahan recalled, "he came to me in an very angry manner and said that my language was the worst thing he had ever read.

"I told him I disagreed with him and would keep talking back to Walker because I just could no longer see Paul's refusal to do so.

"He was quite angry with me over this. But, that time I was right and Paul was wrong. Only one other time was Paul upset with me, and that time he was right."

In the interview with the Post-Dispatch two years later, Simon conceded that "Gene did want me to answer Walker's charges, and I should have done it. Some advised me not to reply to Walker, to avoid further muddying the waters, but I should have countered."

To capture the governorship, the Simon team budgeted for a campaign in the neighborhood of $2,000,000, with as little of that as possible being spent in the primary. As it turned out, Simon's primary campaign cost about $500,000, and many of the bills remained to be paid after it was over, a factor compounding his disappointment in the outcome.

Walker's campaign spent something between $750,000 and $1,000,000 in the primary race, one of the last before state law required public disclosure of campaign expenditures and identification of contributors.

At best, the financing of the Walker effort was an uneven affair, a tortuous endeavor that he himself called a sorry tale.

Initially raising $50,000 from close friends to launch his candidacy, Walker spent the money quickly on campaign staff salaries and headquarters rent, supplies and newspaper advertising, an outlay Walker later regretted. Political ads in papers, he came to conclude, had little of the impact of television and, to a lesser extent, radio commercials.

With staff paychecks seldom being handed out on time, printing bills going unpaid and other monetary requirements unmet, Walker was forced to spend hours begging for money by phone. "Such pauperizing," he complained, "was humiliating."

A lot of ballyhoo noticeably surrounded one particularly generic solicitation, a dubious effort dubbed "Dollars for Dan" that involved chain letters, special buttons, a new wave of volunteers and special appearances by the candidate himself. It flopped, bringing in only about $5,000.

The fund-raising crunch became acute at the start of 1972 when the Walker strategists realized it was imperative to run expensive commercials on television if Walker was to have a shot at winning. To get the needed infusion of dough, though, Walker had nowhere to look but in the mirror.

"At the time, I had stock options on a substantial amount of Montgomery Ward stock that had risen in price considerably over the option price," related Walker.

"I borrowed about $100,000, exercised the options, and immediately sold the stock for a profit. I loaned the campaign about $250,000, which I later recovered."

The maneuver caused a bummer for Walker, though. "The bad news," in his words, "was that, much to the delight of the IRS (Internal Revenue Service), I didn't hold it for the capital gains period, meaning that I would have to pay regular income tax on the gain. With this and other stock similarly sold in the fall, my tax bill for 1972 came to $243,000.

"In any event, I loaned the bottom line proceeds to the campaign, and we went on television. It wasn't Ringling Brothers, but we had ourselves a show—commercials that mostly featured the walk."

In the end, a goodly amount of the $750,000 to $1,000,000 spent to defeat Simon came from Walker and David Green, who also had loaned the campaign a sizable figure.

"Dave and I used to kid each other," Walker said in later years, "that if we had lost we would have had to declare bankruptcy and head for South America. If we had lost, there would have been no prospect whatsoever of raising money to cover the deficit. I literally would have been broken.

"The vista would have been no assets, no job and an overwhelming debt. Out of concern for her, I did not even inform my wife, Roberta, about the extent of my financial involvement. I just worried a lot. I don't know what I would have done if I had lost the primary."

But that was one bullet in the course of his life that the high-rolling Walker dodged. He would not be so fortunate later on.

One of the few nationally known persons associated with the Walker effort was David Garth, a political campaign media specialist from New York and an old friend of de Grazia and Green. Garth was especially valuable in plotting the role of television in the campaign.

After the dust settled, Walker concluded that his television commercials were a big reason for his primary victory. For the most part, he felt, "the public got its information and feel for the candidates mainly from TV."

"In those days," opined Walker, "political reporters paid little attention to the TV ad wars waged by candidates, and my opponent seemed largely unaware of my blitz of TV commercials."

Historians may have other notions about the main factors that propelled Walker's upset of Simon. Walker himself listed, along with the marketing of his candidacy on television, the carrying out of the walk and the almost frenetic support of its man by the politically makeshift army of volunteer recruits to the Walker cause, thousand of whom were immersing themselves in politics for the first time.

There were other things, too. The uproarious flap over Simon's injection of the state income tax into the primary battle. Walker debating an absent Simon. And a federal court decision that permitted an extensive crossover by Republicans to the Democratic side of the primary, many to vote for Walker.

No question, the income tax and crossover developments were major happenings that affected the primary outcome, obviously not to the liking of Simon. As for Walker's debate with an opponent not present, that was another matter. It certainly was ingenious, if not downright weird. Just another ploy from the same production company that staged the statewide walk.

The background for this tricky little maneuver was predictable enough.

Naturally, Walker wanted to debate Simon around the state face-to-face, just like every other political underdog seeks to debate a favored opponent so as to garner exposure that invariably boosts the underdog. Naturally, Simon really did not want to be drawn into a string of debates, believing in his own mind he had nothing to gain by facing Walker publicly.

Naturally, representatives of Walker and Simon pretentiously went through the motions of trying to negotiate a format for debates acceptable to each side. And, naturally, no agreement was reached, to the surprise of absolutely nobody.

End of the debate story? Not at all.

Never daunted by business as usual, Walker did engage in a series of debates in Illinois cities in the weeks leading up to the election. Of course, Simon never showed up. However, a big picture of a smiling Simon was always present, along with tape recordings of Simon talking about issues in the campaign. Walker in the flesh versus Simon's disembodied voice. Another one for the books.

At each stop on this road show's schedule, Simon's voice coming out of the tape on this or that point of contention would be followed by strong rebuttals from Walker as he addressed an empty chair holding the recorder. Walker always had the last word. It was safe to say he didn't lose any of these strange encounters.

The Walker campaign repertoire also featured other devices designed to needle Simon. One came into play several weeks before the primary when a so-called truth squad of three individuals from Simon's home territory, persons seeking his defeat, began to trail him.

Led by onetime Simon supporter turned antagonist Dick Mudge, the trio said it wanted to convey to anybody who would listen a belief that Simon no longer was an independent political reformer but a manipulator skilled in playing regular Democratic organization elements against other party factions.

In this effort, Mudge, a former state's attorney of Madison County, was joined by his old pal, Granite City's Richard Allen, a veteran player in independent Democratic politics in Illinois, and William Thomas, another Granite Citian and a former leader of the young Democrats of Madison County. Like Mudge and Allen, Thomas once had been a Simon backer.

Coming along as it did in the final stage of the primary race, Mudge's truth squad largely was dismissed by all but the Walker crowd as too gimmickry to be taken seriously by sophisticated voters. If Mudge and the other two "were friends of Paul Simon," Colson said in a prepared statement, "spare him his enemies." That was that.

By this time, to be sure, the schemes of the Walker campaign to damage Simon were wearing thin with more than the state's political establishment.

Throughout Illinois, newspapers were endorsing the election of Simon over Walker in droves. The pro-Simon editorials complained that Walker's campaign tactics were unfair or unworthy of an aspirant for governor.

Labeling Walker a mudslinger in an editorial 11 days before the primary, the Galesburg Register-Mail castigated Walker for "below-the-belt swings" that showed he "can't even conduct a clean campaign."

"If he (Walker) is demonstrating to us the type of government he is going to hand the citizens of Illinois," the editorial declared, "then we'll stick with the corruption of machine politics and thank

Dan Walker just the same."

But the Register-Mail was missing something. Thousands and thousands of Illinoisans were not about to stick with the corruption of machine politics, and they at last had found an outlet for their discontent in the candidacy—gimmickry or not—of Walker.

The intensity of their feeling, and its translation into political action, was misread sorely or badly underestimated or just plain ignored by those who should have caught on or picked up on such things.

True, the result of the Walker-Simon race was not determined by Walker debating a no-show Simon or by truth squads.

The key to the outcome lay in hundreds of places around Illinois like Clarence Rasmussen's gas station-garage in Rochelle, where Alice Marks and other Walker volunteers had free use of space formerly used for tire storage to work night and day for their man's election.

To understand the real gist of the 1972 primary race for the Democratic nomination for governor, the people who run Illinois should have been aware of Rasmussen's garage—and of what was going on there. ❧

The Real Battlefield

Alice Josephine Marks fit the mold perfectly. An elementary school reading and art teacher in the 1960s, a political liberal with a strong dislike for, besides the Daley machine, corporate management types and other big shots in general who in her view of life exploited little guys and gals.

She had not been active politically—not until she and her husband, Henry, threw themselves into the bitter fight at the start of the 1970s to block construction of a proposed east-west extension of the Illinois toll highway system from Highway 47 to Sterling-Rock Falls.

Opposition to the project was spread across northern Illinois counties Kane, DeKalb, Ogle, Lee and Whiteside, but seemed especially focused in the rich farming area in which Alice and Henry resided. Like other opponents, the couple, whose home was by a small airport a short distance from Rochelle near the Ogle-Lee county line, felt strongly that they could live without the environmental damage and commercial development certain to be linked to the tollway extension.

Alice Marks and her cohorts tried to get Lieutenant Governor Simon involved in their battle, but felt they received from him little more than a sympathetic ear.

So, at the suggestion of her aviation mechanic husband, Alice decided to try in 1971 to bring the candidate walking the state into the fray. Making contact with Walker through Mary Parrilli, his longtime secretary at Montgomery Ward, Alice Marks persuaded Walker to attend a meeting of extension opponents at the farm home of Alice's friends Paul and Hazel Swartz near Dixon.

"I didn't like it that Walker was a big business executive and probably rich," Mrs. Marks recounted, "but he had declared his independence from Daley...and he certainly turned out to be an opponent of the tollway extension.

"I joined him the night of that meeting. And a lot of the other tollway fighters were soon joining him, even though many were Republicans."

That northern stretch of the state proposed for the tollway extension was rock-ribbed GOP terrain. The identifiable Democrats who could be found were not for Walker, making it tough for Alice Marks and the other tollway battlers now suddenly embracing Walker's candidacy.

Nevertheless, in order to make the most of what Alice Marks and the other new Walkerites sensed might be a once around political experience, they "talked to everybody to vote for Dan in what mainly was a crash effort by word of mouth," she said.

A shoestring operation to put it mildly, the Walker primary campaign in Ogle County raised only $400 in local contributions. The Walker state headquarters provided precious little literature. It was even tough to get the candidate to come through the region.

But, operating out of free space at Rasmussen's service station in Rochelle, Alice Marks and the other Walker supporters, many of them also teachers, made their own campaign materials. And they got them displayed in every diner, barbershop, beauty parlor and store in Rochelle, Oregon, Mount Morris and the other places in quiet Ogle.

Part of this undertaking, Mrs. Marks noted, "involved the use of my own little printing press, made many years before, to print campaign brochures and posters. We did the posters in black and red and edged them with a bandanna print design.

"It was challenging and exhaustive. Yet, it was a great thing because Dan's candidacy made those of us backing him in our little area feel at least like we for once were part of what was going on."

That feeling was contagious for others in the Walker volunteer army throughout the state. With their pace gaining momentum in the last weeks before the primary, not many really needed the final call to action by de Grazia a week before the election.

"More than 7,000 volunteer workers for Dan Walker are plunging into a final week of special activities that has been designated Walker Week," de Grazia trumpeted. "We're going to buttonhole voters in the fields, in the streets and in the stores. We're working for an overwhelming turnout to insure the biggest upset in the political history of the state."

Sure enough, the Walker people were in motion everywhere, from the Illinois River backwoods town of Goofy Ridge to the Polish enclaves hugging Milwaukee Avenue in Chicago.

In Macoupin County, the Quaker professor from Blackburn, John Forbes, was kicking in his aggressive networking for Walker, straining his relationship in the process with many of the numerous Democrats in the county backing Simon.

The vibrancy of Toby Olszewski and her Walker crew in Kankakee County was giving local Simon followers a wrong impression. The Simonites did not know that Olszewski only had "13 really good volunteers" in her band nor that she got the job done in the primary even though she could not stand David Cleverdon, the Walker campaign official to whom she was supposed to report.

Simon did not defeat Walker by nearly as many votes as expected in Kankakee County. In LaSalle County, where the Marders were cutting their political teeth on the Walker campaign, Walker whomped Simon by a nearly 2 to 1 margin.

For a long time, the Simon-supporting Democratic regulars in LaSalle County simply were amused at the street by street canvassing by the Marder-led Walker volunteers and by the fundraising dinners that Sid and Natalie put on at the Hotel Kaskaskia. As life goes, though, the Marder family was too sick with the flu primary night to appreciate Walker's victory.

Up and down the line, Walker partisans dutifully blanketed their assigned areas like Mormon missionaries. In Perry County, young McCurdy missed few doors in handing out literature and bumper stickers in Pinckneyville, in DuQuoin and in the hamlets in between. When the primary results were tabulated, he was amazed to be part of a victory that wiser heads said could not happen.

Populous Madison County obviously posed special problems for the Walker campaign in regard to organizing and other tasks. Consequently, several weeks before the primary, a 23-year-old Chicagoan who had become a top troubleshooter for the campaign, Patrick Quinn, was dispatched to Madison. Almost overnight, the tireless Quinn pulled off a headquarters opening and galvanized scores of impressionable college students to go to bat for Walker.

The key neighboring county of St. Clair also was a challenge for Walker, although his organization was better in St. Clair than in Madison. Hoping to dilute the potentially major vote bloc for Simon in St. Clair, Walker did get into the county numerous times before the primary.

East St. Louisan Sue Kolker Altman recalled that, for a while, "Walker almost seemed like a member of our family. He didn't actually stay at our house, but he was there a lot for meetings and coffees."

"One night," she noted, "the PTA group of which I was vice president had a chili supper. And, yes, Walker went to the event with us."

Still, she added, "even with all the contact, I'm really not sure I got to know him as a person. That was not easy to do. Of course, he made a wonderful impression the first time you met him. The eye contact. The great sincerity. But, when this went on for the fiftieth time, you started to wonder."

Few younger Walker workers in the state could be found than the three children of Sue and Charles Kolker. Jay, 8 years old; Cindy, 7, and Chris, 5, accompanied their mother in passing out pamphlets in racially-mixed precincts in their section of East St. Louis.

After the primary, Sue recalled proudly, "I could say that my kids worked the only two precincts in the city that went for Walker over Simon."

The fire, the hunger so evident in many Walker troopers was much less visible in the Simon ranks, which were dominated by seasoned politicians confident that the mere presence of Paul Simon on the ballot would be enough in itself to deter the Walker insurgency.

Simon's backers just could not bring themselves to view it as a real race.

To them, it was not much more complicated than the way it

was remembered by Jim Rea of Christopher in the heavily-Democratic county of Franklin in southern Illinois.

Rea, then a community development official for Southern Illinois University, met Walker when he walked through Johnston City and was suitably impressed. But, added Rea, "I was an active Simon supporter and I just could not honestly give Walker much of a chance of beating Simon."

Over in the eastern part of the state, Joe T. Connelly, the Democratic chairman of Coles County, was a long-standing friend of Simon and he felt he really had no choice but to serve as a Simon campaign leader in his area. A veteran and respected political science professor at Eastern Illinois University in Charleston, Connelly's support of a candidate often triggered a like response from a number of his students.

Michael Goetz, a product of Springfield Griffin High School, was one of those students in the early 1970s. Goetz, who called himself a foot soldier for his mentor, Professor Connelly, was the EIU campus coordinator for Simon in the primary campaign.

Although both believed Simon would win, Connelly observed at the time that "Walker might have been the best face-to-face campaigner I'd seen" and Goetz was beginning to suspect before the election that his side was showing a bit too much confidence, especially in "the underselling of Walker."

Back down at SIU at Carbondale, the president of the student body during the primary contest was 22-year-old senior George J. Camille, a political science major from Riverton.

A Simon man, he was to acknowledge without hesitation years later that "the local Democratic organization, which backed Simon, was just overconfident.

"The Simon backers were not really working hard for him. A lot of the Simon support in the Carbondale area was lackadaisical. Still, I sure thought he was a cinch to win."

On the Saturday before the primary election, a batch of Simon literature was delivered to Camille. The material was not passed out, Camille said, "because there just was no sense of urgency in the Simon campaign."

Indeed, on that particular Saturday, Camille left Carbondale for Florida, anxious to join other students for a break on the sunny beaches of Fort Lauderdale. ❧

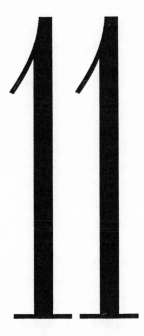

An Upset in the Making

Ten days before voters went to the polls in the 1972 primary election,
Gene Callahan got a disturbing call from his brother Francis, a
farmer back home in Iroquois County and a man with his ear to
the ground.

Francis Callahan, who later would become the Democratic
chairman of Iroquois, told his brother that, based on the things he
was hearing, Paul Simon just might be heading for defeat in the
primary. This was the first time anyone had said that to Gene.

Well, not quite. A few days before, Gene Callahan, Colson
and State Treasurer Alan Dixon, Simon's downstate campaign

manager, had touched base with every Democratic county chairman in Illinois—and only one, just one, Ray Chancey of Jackson County, voiced doubt that the Lieutenant Governor would carry his county.

The rest predicted their counties were in the bag for Simon. A good number said, Callahan recalled, that "we'd carry their county by a margin of 7 to 1 or 8 to 1."

However, that optimism notwithstanding, the outlook for an easy Simon win over Walker was dimming because of certain things that were transpiring.

One broke on March 9 of that primary season when a panel of three federal judges in Chicago issued a ruling that invalidated as unconstitutional a part of Illinois law prohibiting voters from switching political parties within a 23-month period.

The statute was intended to prevent "party raiding," a practice in which members of one party vote in the primary of the other party to nominate a weak candidate. But the federal judges held that the statute blocked constitutionally protected activities by stopping sincere switching as well.

The ruling opened the door for individuals who voted Republican in the 1970 primary to take a Democratic ballot in the 1972 primary. And many apparently did so, the 1972 primary voting pattern would indicate. Furthermore, a lot of those who did so appeared to vote for Walker.

Of course, that is exactly what de Grazia and Bill Goldberg had in mind when de Grazia asked Mary and Andy Leahy, during a breakfast in early 1971 at the Sherman House, to help Goldberg mount a legal challenge to the 23-month rule.

Led by Goldberg, the three went on to file later that year in federal court the lawsuit that challenged the constitutionality of the 23-month stipulation. When the federal panel ruled in favor of the petition early the next year, 12 days before the primary, Walker sensed that it would be a milestone of his campaign.

These were the realities of the situation. Ogilvie was a sure winner in the Republican primary over a nominal opponent, Dr. John H. Mathis, a urologist from Peoria. Thus, many Republicans, now free to ask for a Democratic ballot, felt that they could help Ogilvie more by voting in the primary for the Democratic contender deemed easiest for Ogilvie to whip in the general election in the fall. Dan Walker.

Of course, some of the GOPers crossing over, angry with Ogilvie for his espousal of the state income tax, would not vote for Simon anyway since he, too, had brought up the income tax issue in a way that did not sit well with many taxpayers.

It seemed to matter little that Simon insisted his position on the touchy subject had been perverted by Walker. Even some of Simon's own staffers felt that he needlessly stubbed his toe by unnecessarily broaching the subject.

Halfway through February, with five weeks remaining in the primary campaign, Simon said that a revised tax structure was needed in Illinois and that the state had to move toward greater reliance on the state income tax instead of property levies for funding public education, a position of many liberals. Simon also urged that any hike in the income tax should be accompanied by elimination of the states sales tax on food.

Walker pounced on this one quickly, portraying Simon as a rare candidate promising a tax increase if elected.

Smelling blood, de Grazia ordered that his candidate's immediate campaign schedule be scrapped so that Walker could barnstorm Illinois to demonstrate with multi-colored charts the nightmarish pocketbook hits that would result from Walker's interpretation of Simon's income tax stand.

In short, Walker maintained that the income tax rates for individuals and corporations would have to be tripled to satisfy educational funding and other state revenue requisites under Simon's tax reform idea.

For himself, Walker said that in place of an income tax hike his first obligation would be "the cutting of waste and payrollers from state government to permit a program of tax relief." That program, he elaborated, would include a sales tax credit against the income tax, immediate abolition of the laughable personal property tax on individuals and tax relief for the elderly.

Walker's hammering on the income tax issue finally did prompt the Lieutenant Governor to reply that throughout his public career he had been "calling them as I see them and I am not going to change now."

Still, at the same time, he insisted that "it's clear that I haven't asked for a bigger tax bite, but only a fairer one. I think the people of Illinois have more common sense than some other candidates give them credit for. Glib speeches about easy cuts in taxes without increases elsewhere are pure political hokum."

Nevertheless, the flap over the state income tax, triggered by Simon himself, forced the Lieutenant Governor to respond to the seizure of the issue by Walker, thus for the first time really smoking Simon out of his protective shell in the primary campaign.

Few of the regular Democratic honchos in Simon's corner were apt to argue with the gleeful assessment of Norton Kay that "Paul made a classically dumb political move on this one."

One group of Illinoisans who did not agree with Kay were the men and women who wrote newspaper editorials, at least most of them.

They found Simon's addressing of tax issues refreshingly candid, and many said they were repelled by what they saw as demagogic distortion by Walker of Simon's referral to the Illinois income tax. More than that, many of the editorial writers had come to regard the Walker candidacy as an overservice of press agentry with too little substance.

And they said so in one editorial after another, up and down

Illinois, endorsing Simon over Walker. Save for a handful of newspapers, mainly in the Chicago suburbs, Simon swept the endorsement competition.

He got the nod for the Democratic nomination for governor from each of the four big dailies in Chicago—the Tribune, the Sun-Times, the Daily News and Chicago Today. The four also backed Neil Hartigan for the party nomination for lieutenant governor over Walker running mate Neal Eckert.

Downstate, Kay thought he had a good shot at editorial page support from the Lindsay-Schaub chain, which then included papers in Carbondale, Decatur, Edwardsville, East St. Louis and Champaign-Urbana, as well as a chance for the endorsement of the St. Louis Post-Dispatch. Simon got all of them, along with the backing of virtually every other downstate paper making an endorsement in the contest.

Unlike some of the others, the Post-Dispatch was gracious to Walker as well as Simon in recommending the nomination of Simon, long a favorite of the biggest St. Louis daily.

Labeling both men "liberals in the Adlai Stevenson tradition" and also "men of principle and courage," the Post-Dispatch said that "Illinois Democrats are blessed this year with two candidates for Governor, either of whom could be chosen in good conscience by a voter seeking to do what is best for his state." Simon got the endorsement, though, because of his proven track record in public office, the editorial concluded.

Other parts of the endorsement game were predictable. Like the Illinois AFL-CIO going for Simon. And Walker corralling the Independent Voters of Illinois and numerous other groups of like-minded persons, such as the Independent Precinct Organization in Chicago lakefront wards.

Less predictable, but perhaps more bothersome for Simon than Walker, were certain other aspects of the primary.

For one thing, the primary election would be the first in the state in which persons under 21 years old could vote. Much uncertainty surrounded the role to be played by the roughly 200,000 Illinoisans in the 18 to 20-year-old category who had registered to vote under an expanded enfranchisement granted by constitutional and statutory changes.

Should they vote in large numbers, many observers felt that the political climate in university communities and certain other localities could be changed almost overnight. If so, candidates like Walker fighting regular party organizations might get a boost.

Walker also stood to gain more than Simon from the part of the primary dealing with the fight for the Democratic presidential nomination in 1972.

To the surprise of no one, the Illinois primary had turned into a pivotal contest in the race for the nomination to oppose the re-election bid of President Richard Nixon in the fall election.

In the presidential preference portion of the primary, on the Democratic side, Senator Edmund S. Muskie of Maine was facing former Senator Eugene J. McCarthy of Minnesota. Although the result of that competition was not binding on anybody, McCarthy in particular needed a strong showing to get his candidacy off the ground. Consequently, he had made a strong pitch to college campuses, emphasizing that his rebellious positions in recent years coincided with the views of many younger Americans.

Illinois primary voters also were to elect the bulk of the state's delegates and alternate delegates to both the Democratic and Republican national conventions.

Again, interest was focusing on the Democratic side where slates of Muskie-pledged delegate candidates were opposed mainly by slates committed to Senator George S. McGovern of South Dakota. The Muskie-McGovern fight over delegates extended throughout the state except for the city of Chicago, where Democratic primary voters were expected to elect uncommitted delegates loyal to Daley's machine.

McGovern's candidacy was a challenge of heart and soul to Democratic Party domination by old-line political bosses, meaning that most of his Illinois backers, including persons running downstate for election as McGovern delegates, were opposed to Daley. As McCarthy looked to the college population for support, the McGovern-pledged delegate candidate slates were heavy in many places with individuals tied to universities.

It also was easy to see that numerous McGovern backers were in Walker's corner against Simon—since Muskie had the support, openly or behind the scene, of regular party leaders in many parts of Illinois.

The upshot was that the McGovern and McCarthy candidacies were two more magnets drawing Democratic dissidents and other non-party regulars to the polls on primary day. Sure as all get out, that spelled more trouble for Simon because he was the Daley person in the gubernatorial picture.

For years afterward, many Illinois Democrats looked back on the primary election of March 21, 1972 as gut wrenching. Whether to vote for Simon or Walker was a tough one. Some wrestled with the choice up to the last minute.

Searching of consciences went a lot deeper than usual. The votes of many families were split between Walker and Simon. This happened everywhere.

In prairie author Carl Sandburg's town, Galesburg, Mark and Gladys Lawrence were a respected couple living in a two-story white frame house at 840 Greenleaf Street, a setting that epitomized Norman Rockwell's middle America.

The Lawrences, who had moved to Galesburg from Chicago in the mid 1940s, were very much a part of the Knox College scene at the time of the 1972 primary; he ran the circulation operation at the college library and she was secretary to the president of the small private school.

Both were lifelong Democrats who had watched with fascination the progression of the Walker-Simon contest. As they sat and discussed the race in the book-laden rooms of their trim residence, Gladys Lawrence decided to vote for Walker because she shared his antipathy toward the Chicago machine. If the pair had stayed in Chicago, she almost surely would have been a backer of the independent Democratic movement.

Mark Lawrence gave his vote to Simon, though, because he believed that Simon had proven long ago that he was his own man. No way did Lawrence view Simon as a Daley puppet. Like the writer of the Post-Dispatch endorsement editorial, Lawrence thought Simon clearly had earned the nomination by virtue of his long career in public office.

Gladys Lawrence and her husband were two of the 5,572,478 registered voters in the state at the time. Donald Ed, a veteran elections official in the office of the Illinois secretary of state, estimated that as many as 2,000,000 of them might cast ballots in the primary, a larger than normal turnout.

Besides the governor and lieutenant governor candidates, primary voters also were selecting nominees for other state offices, the United States Senate and House, the General Assembly and county offices. And, of course, there was the presidential stuff.

But the main event remained Simon against Walker. It had captured the imagination of the public and provided Illinois Democrats with their first real statewide primary fight since the Kerner-Lohman-Mitchell race in 1960 for the nomination for governor.

While few, very few apart from the Walker camp thought he could pull it off, the myriad political world of Illinois was coalescing in the final hours before the votes were counted to tip its hat to Walker for a valiant effort against seemingly insurmountable odds. In defeat, Walker was going to at least win some respect. Almost everybody was willing to give him that.

Simon certainly was ready to do so. He well may have been thinking about what he would say to Walker as he flew with his family on the evening of primary day to Chicago, where the Lieutenant Governor anticipated sharing good news with his supporters before the night was over. On the plane with the Simons were Alan Dixon and his wife Joan.

By the time the aircraft approached Midway airport, the polls had been closed for several hours and early returns were coming in.

Upon landing at Midway, the Simon party was met by Gene Callahan, who was not wearing a happy face. Getting Simon and Dixon aside, Callahan told them that the results reported so far were not too favorable.

Later that night, at a hotel in downtown Chicago where Simon and Jeanne and their two children were sequestered with the Dixons, the atmosphere got downright gloomy. ❧

12

Walker Wins—
A Political Fairy Tale

The day after the Illinois primary was one of those sun and fun times on the beaches at Fort Lauderdale that so attracted the college kids from the colder places up north. George Camille and thousands of other young guys in swim trunks were soaking up the rays, their minds on the endless parade up and down the sand of sparsely-clad female bodies.

Camille's concentration was jolted, though, when a friend from Illinois walked up and told him that Paul Simon had lost the primary.

Unable to hide his disbelief, Camille told the fellow he was crazy. Camille then scurried from the beach "to try and find a Chicago paper." He did manage to get his hands "on at least one big city paper...and there it was, Walker had won."

"I still really couldn't believe it," Camille recalled. "I just felt so very sorry for Simon."

About the same time, Alton Telegraph reporter Dennis McMurray was on his honeymoon in Gatlinburg, Tenn., when his eye caught a wire story in the local paper that said Walker had defeated Simon. McMurray also found it hard to believe.

Seven months before, McMurray had covered the stretch of Walker's walk that took him to the Edwardsville campus of Southern Illinois University.

Walker was "such a long shot," remembered McMurray, that the Telegraph considered not even covering his walk through the paper's circulation area. However, Elmer Broz, then city editor of the Telegraph, decided after all to cover Walker because of the "gimmick aspect" of the walk, and McMurray got the assignment.

The lackadaisical reception of Walker at the Edwardsville campus, in the words of McMurray, "left little to excite me about him.

"So, when I read about him beating Simon, I could only figure that a lot of people were sending a very strong message."

That they did. The message was that a majority of the Democratic voters in the primary refused, at least in the gubernatorial contest, to accept the dictates of the party bosses—an espousal of a rebellious attitude awash across America at the time but not previously visible among most Illinois Democrats or, for that matter, the state's card-carrying Republicans.

The denial of the old order in the Walker-Simon race provided one of the most unlikely upsets in Illinois political history, a victory by Daniel Walker that simply was spectacular. A political fairy tale come true, so anomalous as to be unbelievable in even the most farfetched political fiction.

Dan Walker's grandest moment was at hand. The victory over Richard Ogilvie to follow in the fall election would not reverberate through the Illinois political scene like the shock waves emanating from the defeat of Paul Simon.

To pull it off, Walker rolled up surprisingly wide margins over Simon in many downstate counties and scored more heavily than expected in the mainly Republican suburbs of Chicago.

In the end, Walker received 735,193 votes to 694,900 for Simon, leaving Walker with a plurality of 40,293 over the Lieutenant Governor.

When the Republican vote in the primary was added to the Democratic total, it showed that slightly more than 2,000,000 Illinoisans or about 36 percent of the registered voters went to the polls March 21, 1972—making the prediction of Don Ed right on target.

In the race largely responsible for the unusually big primary turnout, Simon carried Cook County and Walker the rest of the state. But Simon didn't win Cook by all that much, while Walker did astonishingly well in parts of downstate.

Walker carried 52 of the so-called 101 downstate counties with a total of 299,709 votes. In the 49 won by Simon, he got 238,459, or 61,250 fewer than Walker, the Chicago corporate lawyer who was an unknown south of Chicago when he announced for governor.

Aside from Sangamon, Madison and St. Clair, Walker handily carried most of the larger populated or big ticket counties apart from Cook. Counties like Peoria, Winnebago (which includes Rockford), Rock Island and Macon (the home of Decatur).

The Walker crowd's assiduous courting of the university communities obviously paid off. He captured just about every downstate county housing a major state university—Champaign, home of the main campus of the University of Illinois (by a wide margin); Jackson (SIU-Carbondale), Coles (Eastern), DeKalb

(Northern), McDonough (Western) and McLean (Illinois State). Madison, with SIU-Edwardsville, was the only one in this gang Walker did not get.

Walker also did pretty well in deep southern Illinois, carrying a sizable number of counties there that, a bit ironically, later would be represented in the United States House by Simon.

Where Walker really walloped Simon, though, was in the densely populated counties around Cook. DuPage was the biggie. In that one, it was Walker 30,820, Simon only 10,890—a 19,930-vote bulge for Walker that in itself almost erased the plurality of 20,957 votes by which Simon won Cook.

In Walker's home county of Lake, the tally was 18,397 for Walker to 7,185 for the Lieutenant Governor, a lopsided difference of 11,212. In Kane, Walker beat Simon nearly 2 to 1; Walker also was a runaway winner in Will. In the other Cook-collaring county with a significant Democratic vote in the primary, McHenry, Walker prevailed 4,264 to 2,538.

Walker's showing in these counties sealed Simon's defeat, especially since Simon hardly came out of Chicago with the victory margin expected for the candidate with the backing of the Daley machine. Simon carried the city of Chicago by 85,311 votes, receiving 371,078 to 285,767 for Walker.

As for the rest of Cook, the suburban townships and a handful of suburbs under the jurisdiction of the Chicago Election Commission, Walker walked away from Simon, 149,717 to 85,363. When this 64,354-vote margin for Walker was subtracted from Simon's plurality in Chicago of 85,311, Simon was left with only the surprisingly small plurality of 20,957 in Cook.

Needless to say, Simon needed a bigger victory in Cook, just as he could have done better in his own part of the state, the populous Madison-St. Clair county area.

Simon did carry Madison in an impressive manner, 20,088 to 12,604, but some had looked for a still wider spread. Simon barely won St. Clair, 16,951 to 15,548—a county in which Simon was a household name and, just as noteworthy, a county with a strong Democratic machine that always followed Daley's lead on state-wide office endorsements. The result in St. Clair left the experts scratching their heads.

Interestingly, one of the few bright spots for Simon was Sangamon County, the seat of state government, where Simon clobbered Walker, 13,291 to 7,739. Walker's attacks on the ruling political establishment, Democratic and Republican, apparently did not sit well around Springfield, a mighty reservoir of state employees and entrenched bureaucrats. Overemphasis could not be placed on the poor treatment of Simon by the big counties collaring Cook. Again, rapidly-growing DuPage was probably the best example. In the fall election, Ogilvie swamped Walker in DuPage by getting more than 62 percent of the vote. In the primary, though, slightly more Democratic votes were cast than Republican, and Walker pocketed an amazing 75 percent of those Democratic ballots.

The most logical reason for this in DuPage—and also in Lake and Will to a great extent—was the federal court ruling permitting the crossovers.

In some normally GOP downstate counties as well as in the largely Republican suburbs of Cook, unprecedented numbers of persons asked for Democratic ballots. The results indicated that Walker was the principal beneficiary, leading to the conclusion that the Walker team made a very strategically successful move in going after the court ruling.

Yet, some in the Walker camp, or at least Green for one, believed that many of those increased numbers of Democratic votes in unlikely places like DuPage actually came from closet Democrats who maybe were going to the polls in a primary for the first time in response to the unusual issues and appeal of the Walker-Simon race. Regular Democratic leaders in the Chicago suburbs just did not know that those votes were there, Green felt.

At the stroke of midnight ending primary day, it was Green, whom Walker like to call his political guru, who advised Walker that he could claim victory by a narrow margin.

"Dave and Vic had consulted our poll watchers in key precincts," related Walker. "Dave then had retired to the bathroom, the only quiet place in our (Chicago) hotel suite, to study figures and think. He emerged after about 30 minutes to say that he thought we'd won."

Green was right, of course, and it left Walker and his cohorts in a quandary. A very nice one, but still a quandary. This crew, in spite of everything, really was not prepared for victory.

At least not for the immediate avalanche of attention to be showered on Walker by the press and others. For one thing, the victor in the Simon-Walker race was expected to hold a press conference the morning after the primary, or to be visible in other time-honored ways, like standing on a busy Chicago street corner the day after the primary to thank passersby for their support.

But, Walker would be asked, probably even pressed, about his future relationship with Daley and other party regulars, at whom he had been throwing darts for so many months. How could Walker now make peace with the Chicago mayor and his followers and still maintain the independent stance that sparked his primary win?

Walker and his brain trust had to think about that. They really hadn't thought that far ahead. There had to have been some doubt that they even would reach this juncture. Now that they had, care had to be taken not to say anything stupid.

Other things needed pondering, too. Neil Hartigan had wiped out Neal Eckert in their bout for the party's nomination for lieutenant governor, 802,449 to 425,021. This left Walker with a fall election running mate loyal to Daley, another complication.

So, Walker did something very unlike himself.

"I came up with a courageous, strategical plan. Cop out! Leave town early and issue a written statement that I was exhausted, had decided to leave on an immediate vacation, and would meet with the press upon my return. All true, by the way."

Off to Florida it was for Walker and his top advisors. Down to Florida to buy time to seek a way to handle the "independent v. regular dilemma."

In the meantime, during the afternoon following the primary, a stunned Illinois political world received a concession statement from Paul Simon in which he congratulated Walker, reiterated that he would support Walker in the general election and stressed that Walker "must now show that he has the ability to unite the party," a challenge in Simon's opinion that would not be easy.

To his backers, Simon expressed regret for "the inadequacies of my campaign, inadequacies which others may see more clearly than I do."

But to those theorizing that Simon probably lost votes for saying the state might have to rely more heavily on its income tax, Simon said he had no regrets "telling people the truth." He added, in what may have been a parting shot at Walker, that he hoped to "never become so eager for any prize that I corrupt the truth, as vile a corruption as any other."

As for Daley, despite one of the most humiliating elections in his career, the mayor professed in public the day after the primary that the Democratic antagonists in the primary would kiss and make up for the fall campaign.

"You win them and lose them," said Daley. "When you win them, you win with humility, and when you lose them, you lose with courage. I've always said a primary fight was a family fight, and when the family fight is over we join as a family again."

Nevertheless, it appeared difficult in the aftermath of the primary to see the party moving in unity toward the November election with Walker at the helm.

Numerous regular Democratic stalwarts were convinced that Walker had assailed them unfairly in order to attain the top spot on the ticket. Should they now bust a gut for him, realizing that they still might not know where they stood with this triumphant maverick even if he won in the fall?

And, speaking of the general election, some observers read good tidings for Ogilvie in the outcome of the Simon-Walker fight.

Quite likely, the Democratic disarray would strengthen the re-election chance of Governor Ogilvie, long regarded as an underdog in the fall election.

Could it be, with this curious state of flux resulting from the Democratic side of the primary, that all previous bets on the fall election now were off? ❧

13
Horse Race with Ogilvie

The astonishing conclusion of the Walker-Simon race made it a tough political act to follow. Many thought Dan Walker's contest with Richard Ogilvie for the governorship would not match up, even though it was the featured bout of the 1972 political season in Illinois.

But it turned out to be a real horse race.

Just as he was against Simon, Walker was the aggressor, at least in the early stages. By now, though, his wolverine tactics were quite familiar to voters. Also, dark horse Walker no longer was an underdog.

At the opening gun of his race with Ogilvie, Walker was the predicted winner. Dan Walker, whose surprise launching of his political candidacy in 1970 was considered political folly, now found himself not even a year and a half later favored to uproot the sitting Governor of Illinois.

Of course, Ogilvie had not helped himself any too much in the matter.

Illinois had 11,251,000 people within its borders then, and darn few of them had a warm impression of their governor. Short and stocky—once even called "dumpy" by a Wall Street Journal reporter, an adjective Ogilvie resented—the pipe-smoking Governor presided over his kingdom like a colorless technocrat, reorganizing, shuffling around or enlarging everything in sight.

He may not have oozed magical charm, but he wrought wholesale revisions in Illinois government that radically altered its face and structure, enabling it to respond much more fully to the concerns in those days over crime, environmental degradation and other issues.

He had vowed to "manage this state as it has never been managed before," and the political scientists and governmental purists gave him high marks for doing just that. To find a better governor of Illinois, in the literal sense, they felt one had to go back a long way to Frank Lowden or perhaps even to John Peter Altgeld.

Of course, Ogilvie had the purse to match. The new state income tax gave him more dollars to spend on programs than were available to most governors before or those since.

One thing was obvious to all. The magnitude of the revamping and higher price tag of state government under Ogilvie made his Democratic predecessors look like pikers.

If it is true as generally assumed that Republicans represent the status quo, Ogilvie was not a very good example. Ogilvie was a leader and a willing spender of state funds and, unlike some of the state's other chief executives, he tried to maneuver the labyrinth of officialdom under him to the cutting edge of what was happening. He gambled that this would pay off with Illinoisans and bring him national attention and respect. Ogilvie in reality was a fellow who liked to take the bull by the horns.

The problem was that he just didn't come across with all of this to a broad enough audience. He seemed to be trapped by his gubernatorial cocoon. The factory worker in Joliet or the miner from Harrisburg never realized that they had this governor so highly regarded in the political science community. They did not get to know him, and he did not appear to go much out of his way to communicate with them.

Never described as charismatic, Ogilvie seemed to have a disdain for dramatics. In a nifty effort at reverse psychology, Ogilvie tried to bolster his standing in the race with Walker by suggesting to voters that personal magnetism was not everything. His campaign poster plugging that theme even became a collector's item.

But in the even then rapidly developing world of image-dominated politics, Ogilvie's shortcomings on this subject could not be overcome. Not when up against the flamboyancy of Walker. Not when the only development that many voters identified with Ogilvie was his successful call for passage of the state income levy.

Ogilvie's fate in his re-election bid might have been doomed from the moment of the first of his scheduled debates with Walker.

The Democrat came out swinging hard from the opening bell of their encounter at a meeting of the United Press International newspaper editors of Illinois at Springfield's Holiday Inn East.

As Ogilvie was leaving the Statehouse to head for the debate, a reporter asked him if he was ready for the direct encounter with Walker.

"Do I look scared?" the Governor replied. Then he held out his hand, palm down.

"Do you see my hand shaking?"

It was not.

Within an hour, though, Walker was lambasting Ogilvie on the same governmental ethics issues Walker had raised against his fellow Democrat Simon.

For instance, Walker pressed the Governor to join him in criticism of well-known Illinois political figures involved in the scandals, revealed during Ogilvie's governorship, growing out of questionable racing stock deals. As did Simon, Ogilvie demurred, seeking instead to sidestep Walker and shift the debate into other areas.

Ogilvie also had a hard time countering the criticisms of Walker on basic bread-and-butter issues of state government, leaving Ogilvie's supporters disgruntled and alarmed at their man's seeming inability to defend himself.

Reporters and other observers, many of whom had been quite delighted over the expectation that Ogilvie would duke it out with Walker, were flabbergasted at Ogilvie acting like he was caught off guard.

The word going around for weeks was that Ogilvie was not about to make the mistake of Simon in not confronting Walker head-on, but the Ogilvie of that opening debate was sleepwalking, giving the impression he was unaware the man facing him did not play by the old rules, not aware that his challenger had no qualms about bringing out skeletons in the closet, anybody's.

Ogilvie's restrained composure had to give way to a more fighting image if he was to have a chance against Walker.

Trying to win re-election on his record was not good enough against Walker. Recitations by Ogilvie of his endless programs could put an audience to sleep. Ogilvie had to get off his gubernatorial high horse, escape from his office, ditch his squadron of security cops and rub shoulders with the real folks.

Ogilvie's opponent, who didn't have to worry about governing the state, still was spending the bulk of his time campaigning on the main streets and byways of Illinois, never missing a chance to say that the state chief executive had to be more visible.

For Walker, the script of his general election campaign deviated little from the shape and tone of what the electorate had seen from him before the primary. More than anything else, he still was banking his chance for victory on what he termed the bedrock of support built by his intensive face-to-face campaigning since the announcement of his candidacy.

National pundits had taken to calling the race the country's most interesting contest for governor, particularly because of Walker's perceived evolvement in the eyes of some into the nation's most exciting new populist. Washington-based columnists already were speculating that a Walker victory would trigger immediate national notice, especially in view of the likely Democratic defeat in the 1972 battle for the White House.

Walker did not see himself as a political populist in the historical context of that term. He did not advocate greater government intervention in business, industry and commerce. But, he did consider himself a populist in so far as his going to the people directly with his candidacy was concerned, and he was not about to quibble over any ink he was receiving from the national writers.

Walker had to concentrate anyway on protecting his reported lead over Ogilvie because it was a very vulnerable one. And that race for the White House was one reason.

If Senator George McGovern, the Democratic candidate for president, fared as poorly in Illinois as many were predicting, Walker might be facing another handicap as threatening as his lack of funds.

This was the reason that Walker sought to sidestep McGovern

and his campaign whenever possible, while Ogilvie seldom hesitated to remind voters of the bid for re-election by President Nixon.

Although saying when asked that he backed the liberal McGovern, Walker was quick to say he recognized that "it apparently is the choice of some to vote for Nixon and Walker."

Consequently, few eyebrows were raised at the estrangement in some areas of the McGovern team from the still largely independent campaign organization of Walker. Many in the Walker camp, although cautious about saying so publicly, were reluctant to integrate their perceived front-running drive with the struggling McGovern effort because they felt Walker had little to gain.

Walker had not even stopped a summer tour of the state by jeep to join most other Illinois Democratic candidates at the party's national nominating convention in Miami Beach, seeing no political profit in going down there. Besides avoiding the convention uproar over the seating of the Illinois delegation, Walker also avoided interruption of the seemingly unending momentum of his personalized campaign.

Too, Walker had not gone overboard, to put it loosely, in seeking rapprochement with the Illinois party regulars after the primary. A number of them made overtures to Walker after his elimination of Simon, but his refusal to commit himself to possible jobs or appointments down the line left them hanging.

Shortly after the primary, Walker made the move that he had decided upon to show his continuing independence from the Daley machine. He asked his running mate, Neil Hartigan, and two other Democrats on the state ticket to resign from their party posts as Chicago ward committeemen. The others were Congressman Roman Pucinski, the Democratic nominee for the United States Senate seat held by Republican Charles Percy, and State Senator Thomas G. Lyons, the candidate for attorney general.

Naturally, none of the three complied with Walker's request, but Walker got the play and impact out of the ploy that he wanted.

Looking back, Walker remembered no more awkward moments following the primary than his campaign appearances at party ward meetings in Chicago.

"At many of these meetings," said Walker, "I would face row after row of often grim-faced precinct captains, hundreds of whom had worked hard to defeat me in the primary. Fortunately, there were always lots of local candidates around that they were closer to than me anyway, so I could give my little speech and leave."

Although appearing from time to time with other members of his party's state ticket, Walker mostly campaigned alone in the contest with Ogilvie, a carrying out of what he called his "individualistic style."

As much as Walker could determine, he got the full support of Mayor Daley against Ogilvie. But nobody expected much trust to develop between the city's established regulars and the many political newcomers in the vanguard of the Walker movement.

Walker strategists did feel reasonably confident that the machine captains in Chicago would deliver, in that they had to go for straight ticket voting in order to protect the Cook County Democratic candidates, the top priority. Elsewhere, the regular Democratic organization was much weaker, necessitating a still crucial role for Walker's personal troops.

No mistake about it, that Walker volunteer force, molded by Cleverdon and now thought to number some 10,000, still constituted the backbone of the Walker campaign.

Walker knew where his bread was buttered. When he came to LaSalle County, he always stopped at the Marder residence, which irritated the regular Democratic chairman of the county more than a little.

The primary victory was like a heady first taste of wine for the neophyte army of Walker. It was political euphoria for most, leaving them wondering why they had not dabbled in politics earlier if accomplishing the seemingly impossible was really this doable. If this collection of ragtag and rah-rah types could oust Paul Simon, the measure of the bland Richard Ogilvie surely could be taken. And they certainly could accomplish this without kowtowing to the Democratic regulars.

Walker's warmest memory of his venture into politics was the spirit in 1972 of his campaign team, from the top people in the West Adams Street headquarters in Chicago to the volunteers operating out of kitchens in the state's farthest reaches.

"They never seemed to doubt that we could win," Walker would say later. "As for me, I didn't even let myself think about winning or losing until near the end. How else could one maintain one's sanity and drive?

"But, it really was like a crusade, and that enthusiasm at every level seemed to carry right on through."

Money still remained another subject. After his primary victory, Walker believed that dough would flow in. It did not.

Finding it "almost as hard to raise money after the primary as before," Walker acknowledged emerging from the Ogilvie race "substantially in debt again." To the tune of $500,000 or more, depending on who was tabulating and which bills were counted as campaign costs.

Walker spent more than $2,000,000 in the race with Ogilvie, a good portion of which predictably went for television ads. Ogilvie's outlay was much higher, as much as three times as much. Of course, in years to follow, the candidates in Illinois gubernatorial contests would spend between them three times the amount put out by Ogilvie and Walker combined.

Little about fund-raising made Walker feel good. The few positive notes, such as a surprising $50,000 contribution from

Daley's Cook County organization, were overwhelmed in the campaign's sea of red ink.

"The worst part of the whole campaign from beginning to end was money," lamented Walker. "Never having enough money to pay bills. Dealing with the people who wanted to get paid, but could not get paid. It really drove us into the ground mentally, the whole fund-raising part. We never had enough money, never.

"One of my closest advisors maintained it was because the 'gimme' crowd knew I wouldn't give jobs or contracts because people gave money. A critic might say it was because I gave off a holier-than-thou impression to those on the political fund-raising circuit."

Whatever, Walker would find himself perplexed at the later number of grand jury investigations into his fund-raising.

"Apparently, it never occurred to them that if I had been willing to take what amounts to bribes, I would never have had the fund-raising problems and debts that I did."

The shortage of dollars for the run against Ogilvie showed quite visibly in the hand-to-mouth existence of many of the campaign's field organizers.

Down south, Steve McCurdy toiled day and night for the Walker campaign. He did not expect to receive a cent, and he didn't. McCurdy was serving a public affairs internship at the time through respected SIU political science professor David Kenney, a program that permitted McCurdy to work full-time for Walker. McCurdy later wrote an academic paper on his experiences.

McCurdy struck up a close friendship in the months preceding the general election with another energetic Walker operative in southern Illinois, David Vaught from over Carmi way. And McCurdy also got to know the hard driving Patrick Quinn, by then the campaign director for southwestern Illinois.

McCurdy assumed that "David and people like Quinn were supposed to get paid," but he added that "I doubted it because there just did not seem to be any money. David and Quinn and others like them just ate their expenses.

"The real Walker campaign was a lot of young guys and gals running around with a buck or two in their pocket."

Quinn was an interesting case, if only because of the unusually strong impression he made on those he encountered and because of his frenetic activism in Illinois public life in the decades to follow.

The living room of the Kolker home in East St. Louis provided free sleeping quarters much of the time for Quinn, the holder of an economics degree from Georgetown University, where he made Phi Beta Kappa, was sports editor and a columnist for the school paper, The Hoya, and attended every anti-Vietnam War protest he could.

Thinking back, Sue Kolker recalled that "Quinn seemed to be everywhere at once, soothing the Walker workers to keep them going and yet trying to play games with the regulars by telling them the Walker effort was no longer completely independent. So serious and still humorous about it all, I never saw a politician work harder. He only slept a few hours each night."

By the end of the campaign's summer, though, many Ogilvie partisans also were not spending much time in bed, having finally awaken to the sobering realization that their hold on Illinois government was in serious jeopardy.

At last, certain individuals had penetrated the Governor's palace guard to get across the message that the selling of Ogilvie's bid for re-election required a repackaged candidate, a less wooden, more humane figure.

With that, they wagered, the situation could be salvaged. After all, Ogilvie had ample campaign funds, at least in comparison to the reputed paucity of Walker dollars, and Ogilvie had a veteran political organization as well as other superior resources, all fertilized by the advantages of incumbency. The only thing still needed was a revamped Ogilvie. Almost overnight, he appeared.

The new Richard Buell Ogilvie stood out in a campaign swing through rural western Illinois right after the beginning of September, the traditional start of the final crucial stage of an Illinois political campaign.

His stop in the Pike County seat of Pittsfield, pig-raising country, said it all. There, lifting a page from Walker's book, Ogilvie spent a fascinating hour in Lindsay's tavern, a popular blue-collar bar right off the town square that was filled with Democrats hoisting a few beers to mark the end of the work day.

Entering unannounced, the Governor plunked down $16 to buy the house a round of drinks, then shot the bull with guys leaning on the bar. No question, the boys at Lindsay's had not been toasted by a governor for quite a spell, and few had thought that Ogilvie would be the one to break the ice.

Only two plainclothes state policemen were accompanying the Governor on this tour—and they remained outside the tavern. Campaign aid Jim Harry, a former high school football star in Pittsfield, did saunter into Lindsay's with Ogilvie, but Harry didn't look like a cop.

The crowning moment at Lindsay's came when Ogilvie challenged some of the watering hole's regulars at the shuffleboard game at the rear. Ogilvie, who was president of the Board of Cook County Commissioners when elected governor, won every single game, much to the disbelief of the overall-clad onlookers. This was truly amazing for a guy cooped up so long in the governor's office.

Chuckling minutes later outside the tavern, Ogilvie predicted that this was only the beginning in his effort "to show people that I am not a stuffed shirt. It is unavoidable that, when you're governor, you get an aloof reputation. You just can't talk to everybody if you're going to be a good governor. But, I can have fun too, and match Walker stride for stride at this game."

Left: Dan Walker (far left) and his brother Lewis with their maternal grandmother Lynch in San Diego in the mid 1930s.

Above: Midshipman Dan Walker at the Naval Academy.

Below: On the first day of his walk through the state in 1971, Walker and sons Charles and Dan, Jr., (in hat) ponder the long road ahead. (Photo courtesy of Dan Walker)

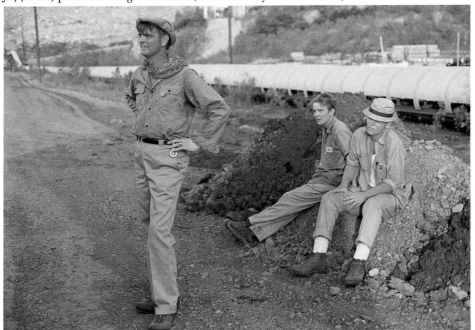

Above left: Not long after the start of the walk, Walker found it necessary to attend to blistery feet. (Photo by Taylor Pensoneau)

Above right: Walker taking a break during his trek through Illinois, a rare moment. (Illinois State Historical Library)

Left: Outside of Trenton, Walker stopped during the walk to dictate his observations into a recorder, thereby compiling some of the information for his later walk journal. (Photo by Taylor Pensoneau)

Facing page:
Above right: Campaigning for governor took Walker to many out-of-the-way places. (Photo courtesy of Dan Walker)

Below right: Walker taking the gubernatorial oath of office from Illinois Supreme Court Justice Walter Schaefer at an outdoor ceremony on January 8, 1973 in front of the Capitol in Springfield.
(Picture copyright State Journal-Register)

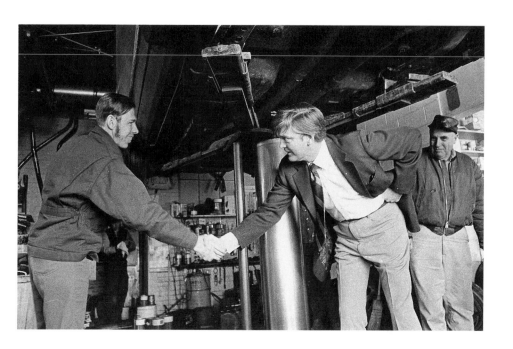

Left: Roberta Dowse Walker, the first lady of Illinois.

Facing page:
Top: The first family of Illinois in the early 1970s, Governor and Mrs. Walker with their four daughters and three sons. Standing from left to right: Charles, Margaret, Julie, Dan, Jr., Mrs. Roberta Dowse Walker, Will (in front of his father), Governor Walker, Kathleen and Roberta Sue. (Illinois State Historical Library)

Below left: The Governor on stage at one of his frequent accountability sessions with the public. (Photo courtesy of Dan Walker)

Below right: Walker found many things to smile about as governor. (Illinois State Historical Library)

Below: Governor Walker (seated behind his desk) meeting in his Statehouse office with members of his brain trust. They were, from left to right, David Green, William Goldberg, Victor de Grazia and Norton Kay. (Photo courtesy of Dan Walker)

Left: Walker often was pictured in a more serious frame of mind, though. (Illinois State Historical Library)

Facing Page:
Top right: Signing legislation passed by the General Assembly in 1975 that greatly revised the Illinois workmen's compensation program, a major victory for organized labor. Standing, left to right, are: Democratic Rep. Thomas J. Hanahan, McHenry; Democratic Sen. Robert W. McCarthy, Decatur; Democratic Rep. E. J. (Zeke) Giorgi, Rockford; and Democratic Rep. John (Jack) Hill, Aurora. Seated, left to right, are: Harl Ray of the State AFL-CIO, Governor Walker and Donald A. Johnson, director of the Illinois Dept. of Labor. (Illinois State Historical Library)

Below right: A familiar sight, Governor Walker conversing with folks in small towns. (Illinois State Historical Library)

Below: Governor Walker presiding at the Democratic Governors Conference in April 1974 in Chicago. Seated next to Walker was another rising star in the party, Governor Jimmy Carter of Georgia. (Photo courtesy of Dan Walker)

Above: After leaving the governorship, Walker and his second wife, also named Roberta, frequently found themselves in the company of celebrities. One such occasion was a reception for England's Prince Charles in the Los Angeles area. Standing, left to right: Walker, Roberta Nelson-Walker, Richard Burton and Elizabeth Taylor. (Photo courtesy of Dan Walker)

Left: Dan Walker in Del Mar, California, a few days before his seventieth birthday in 1992. (Photo by Elizabeth March)

To Sun-Times reporter Charles Wheeler, a familiar face in the Statehouse, the heavy play given the personality aspect of the Walker-Ogilvie race was ridiculous. Even worse, he felt, it had gotten things turned around.

A widely accepted image of the combatants that had Ogilvie cold and distant and Walker more down-to-earth was upside down, as Wheeler and plenty of others saw it.

"Walker always struck a lot of us as uptight, with little personality," opined Wheeler, "while Ogilvie actually was charming in person...really quite personable."

Not many Illinoisans knew that Ogilvie's often impassive face bore a wound from shrapnel that tore through his left cheek when a German shell exploded near a tank that Ogilvie was maneuvering in the Alsace region of France late in World War II. It made smiling physically difficult for Ogilvie, who spent six months in an Army hospital as a result of the incident.

If Ogilvie's governorship had included more visits to the Lindsay's taverns of Illinois, it might have been saved. As it was, that campaign swing through western Illinois, which should have been friendly terrain for the Governor, underscored how out of touch he was with the grass roots.

In many places, people were seeing Ogilvie for the first time since his successful 1968 race for governor against Democrat Samuel Shapiro. A lot of times, in stops at Jacksonville, Beardstown, Mount Sterling, Macomb, even Quincy, he was not recognized (his weight had dropped to 180 pounds from 235 a year and a half earlier).

Could it be that Ogilvie—a Yale man, a lawyer, a onetime federal prosecutor who took on Chicago crime boss Tony Accardo and other syndicate leaders before getting elected sheriff of Cook County—was going to blow it all because he failed to shake enough hands?

Surely not, uneasy GOP stalwarts wanted to believe. Certainly, they told themselves, common sense was going to prevail in this contest.

Ogilvie himself was trying to put it in proper perspective in the closing weeks by telling crowds that "this is a race between our good record and his good looks, and I think most people are beginning to see this as a clear choice."

The Ogilvie record. Editorial writers loved it, and they dwelled on it mightily as paper after paper, including the Chicago majors, endorsed the Governor for re-election. If the press could have decided the election, including most working reporters covering the Ogilvie-Walker race, Ogilvie would have won in a landslide. Ogilvie did not know how high he stood with the media until Walker entered the picture.

In urging the retention of Ogilvie in office, the Sun-Times editorialized that "Ogilvie has brought about great changes for the better in Illinois.

"He has brought the state government from near-bankruptcy to a point where it has doubled state aid to schools; rebuilt highways that were deathtraps; modernized the penal system, crime-fighting agencies and mental hospitals, and written the toughest anti-pollution laws in the nation."

True enough, little of the machinery of Illinois government had escaped the imprint of Ogilvie.

He did revamp state administration of correctional facilities, did enlarge the crime fighting apparatus and did move many elderly persons from crowded state hospitals to nursing and other local care homes.

He improved the state's fiscal accountability through the introduction of annual budgeting—or so it seemed at the time—and through the creation of the Bureau of the Budget within the executive office of the Governor.

While Illinois chief executive, he successfully pushed through the General assembly a program to upgrade the state machinery for fighting air and water pollution, including the establishment of the Illinois Pollution Control Board and the state's Environmental Protection Agency.

A year before the election, Ogilvie obtained legislative approval for a $900,000,000 bond issue for mass transportation, much of which was to go toward construction of a supplemental freeway system.

A lot of what Ogilvie did was coordinated with programs in Washington, meaning that a bigger part of the growing state fiscal load was being shouldered by federal funds. But not nearly enough to preclude the need for more dollars from Illinois taxpayers, if the Ogilvie brand of governmental management was to be executed and paid for.

Ogilvie formally proposed the imposition of the state income tax, which he wanted to initiate with a whopping rate of 4 percent on both individuals and corporations, on the April Fools' Day of his first year in office, 1969. By getting it out of the way early, he wagered, voters might have forgotten about it by the time he stood for re-election three years later. On this one, though, he only was fooling himself.

Feelings of betrayal were everywhere because many in the electorate were quick to say that Ogilvie apparently had tricked them into believing during his 1968 campaign that he would not impose an income tax. Also, Ogilvie's desire for a flat rate of 4 percent stunned the Illinois political world, much of which had looked for him to call for an initial rate of no more than 1 percent (the levy finally adopted was 2.5 percent for individuals and 4 percent on corporations).

Ever the realist, Ogilvie held no illusion that his popularity on entering office would remain nearly as high after his push for the income tax.

Brian B. Whalen remembered the course of things all too well. Whalen was one of the whiz kids in the Ogilvie entourage, a bright faced Chicagoan who came to Springfield with Ogilvie at the ripe old age of 29 to serve as Ogilvie's executive assistant or, as everybody recognized, deputy governor.

When Ogilvie "made the decision to go for the income tax," Whalen related, "there never was any doubt he would go from a popular official to an unpopular one.

"And, indeed, he did."

On the day the income tax finally was approved by the Legislature, the Governor took Whalen to lunch at the Illini Country Club in Springfield and told his youthful assistant that "I (Ogilvie) am now the most unpopular person in Illinois. It will be a tough road on this, but we'll do our best."

Besides Whalen, there were plenty of others in the Ogilvie cadre of whiz kids, a hallmark of his administration, who stood out then and afterward.

Individuals like his budget director, John W. McCarter, Jr., a former White House Fellow, and McCarter's top assistant, George A. Ranney, Jr., who later was a coal industry executive. Ogilvie's legislative counsel, William S. Hanley, another lawyer out of the University of Chicago. Ogilvie assistants like Thomas J. Corcoran, later a member of Congress from northern Illinois, and Ronald Michaelson, who in years to come would be the director of operations at the Illinois Board of Elections. The list of bright young people when on and on, names like John P. Dailey or John W. Kolbe or James B. Holderman, the executive director of the Illinois Board of Higher Education under Ogilvie and later president of the University of South Carolina. Few of these persons had passed their thirtieth birthday when Ogilvie took office.

Ogilvie certainly stuck to the youthful mold in his choice of his 1972 running mate, then 31-year-old State Representative James D. Nowlan from the rustic Stark County community of Toulon.

The lanky Nowlan was a sharp contrast to Neil Hartigan, the

Democratic candidate for lieutenant governor.

Unlike Chicago product Hartigan, with his ties to Mayor Daley and his urbanites, Nowlan, a moderate Republican, had all the earmarks of small town America. Weekly newspaper editor, Sunday school teacher, Freemason, a slow and deliberate talker, an authority on rural problems.

The selection of Nowlan seemingly was intended to try to offset the perception that Ogilvie had fallen down on the courting of rural downstate Illinois, which normally would go Republican.

Of course, the Nowlan-Hartigan contest was not a normal one. Under the new Illinois Constitution of 1970, each party's candidates for governor and lieutenant governor were running as an official team for the first time.

This meant that a person no longer could vote for the gubernatorial candidate of one party and the nominee for lieutenant governor of another party. The framers of the constitution wanted to avoid what they considered the awkward situation that came out of the 1968 election when Republican Ogilvie was elected governor and Democrat Simon lieutenant governor.

As the campaign neared an end, Ogilvie sought to blunt the import of the income tax issue by stressing that part of the levy's proceeds was going to local governments. Too, the Governor had backed, with partial success, revisions in other taxes. They included virtual elimination of the despised personal property levy on many individuals and approval of homestead exemptions on older persons' real property tax assessments.

For his part, Walker told audiences that he would freeze all state taxes for four years, a promise that analysts felt could be met because of the great influx of revenue into the State Treasury from the income levy.

Program-wise, Walker proposed centralization of state responsibility for nursing home administration in one agency and state help for the creation of full-time public health departments in counties then not having them.

The former president of the Chicago Crime Commission pledged to set up crime victim assistance offices, concentrate the efforts of the Illinois Bureau of Investigation on organized crime and seek tougher penalties for the illegal sale of guns and for crimes committed with guns.

Walker also reiterated everywhere that he would work for passage of legislation that would limit political campaign expenditures and require complete disclosure of state campaign contributions.

In pounding away on those proposals, Walker more than lightly suggested that Ogilvie was two-faced on the ethics issues, arguing that the Governor, for example, was continuing to drag his heels on full revelation of campaign money sources—something believed by many to be long overdue in Illinois politics.

To those who paid attention to Walker's campaign stands in the race against Ogilvie, a mixed image emerged, a picture certainly not portraying Walker as a traditional liberal looking to big government for the solution to all of society's ills.

Besides opposing tax hikes, Walker was against "forced" busing to achieve school integration, unconditional amnesty for draft evaders, construction of public housing in big city suburbs and the legalization of pot.

In retrospect, Walker was not a high profile candidate on mainly black-related issues, even though he did back integration, equal educational opportunities, open housing and the repeal of "stop and frisk" legislation on a ground that it magnified already poor police-community relations in black neighborhoods.

Nevertheless, by playing down or turning away in part from the typically unabashed support by Democratic liberals for all causes tied to minorities, Walker was attempting to retain his primary-proven appeal to middle-of-the-roaders and even conservatives angry with Ogilvie and the rest of the Illinois establishment, always the gut target of Walker's campaign.

Walker may have entered the contest with Ogilvie a solid favorite, but by the end of October, a week before the election, many saw the race as too close to call.

Mounting a strong stretch drive, Ogilvie found himself in the final days confiding to friends for the first time that he was confident of victory.

Ironically, the extra support that might push Ogilvie over the hump was thought to be surfacing in Democratic Chicago. Canvasses were showing that Ogilvie was running far ahead of his 1968 campaign pace in both Chicago and its Cook County suburbs. Walker was depicted as holding only a slight edge there, hardly an encouraging sign for him since most Democratic candidates trying to win state wide needed big pluralities in Cook.

Ogilvie could take little credit for his standing in Chicago. Assuming the polls were accurate, Walker was suffering from the hostility toward his candidacy harbored by many Chicago Democrats. Would they not even relent on election day?

On the other hand, voter surveys in normally Republican downstate were giving Ogilvie only a slim lead over Walker. This was certainly true in areas where the challenger was better recognized than Ogilvie.

Still, in the penultimate stage before Illinoisans went to the polls, Ogilvie partisans and more than a few others suspected that Walker simply had finally run out of steam. Walker detractors contended that the public had tired of what they regarded as his generalities and obsession with peripheral matters. Too, Walker critics held, many of his charges had not held water, or so they liked to think.

Walker's promise to eliminate $500 million in waste or unnecessary spending from the state budget drew flak from every direction, with his antagonists arguing that his specific points for achieving the reduction were often spurious and, when added together, producing savings far below the $500 million level.

For instance, some $100 million of the cuts spelled out by Walker would have come from elimination of alleged administrative waste in elementary and secondary schools, an area in which Ogilvie also saw problems. But, it was pointed out that some of the amount to be saved here was in local school budgets and not coming out of the state's allocation for state aid to education.

Walker also brought into play in his $500 million proposal his pledges to increase collections from state income tax cheaters, to put off the building of numerous contemplated projects like the proposed Lincoln dam and lake in eastern Illinois and to assure that only eligible individuals received public aid assistance.

In a number of state agencies, Walker called for the elimination of what he termed ghost payrollers and the termination of contracts to Ogilvie political supporters. Walker even took on spending for what he viewed as an unauthorized air force maintained at taxpayers' expense by the Illinois Department of Transportation.

Walker also called for serious re-evaluation of the need for everybody in a group of 84 public information officers on the state payroll, an area also regarded as ripe for cutting by other challengers of state spending patterns in subsequent years.

Actually, a number of the areas proposed for cuts by Walker already had been targeted by state audit reports or by stories of investigative journalists. When Walker tried to pursue these matters in his campaign, though, many in the know suddenly fell silent or turned away, refusing to help Walker reap political mileage from the issues.

Even when early in the campaign Walker held what most believed to be a commanding lead over Ogilvie, Walker was cautioning his followers that they would be tested sternly by an Ogilvie blitz near the end of the campaign. Walker feared mainly the Governor's television commercials, which, sure enough, were beamed across Illinois in the closing days of the race in rapid-fire fashion.

To tell the truth, nothing about the final days of the contest, Ogilvie's television offense or anything else, came as a surprise to Walker. The ending was predictable, Walker always thought to himself, almost exactly what he expected. Quite quotidian.

If Walker himself had been writing the stories about the windup of his race, he would have described it as follows.

"Ogilvie felt he was in trouble at the end of the general election campaign and went on the attack. Normally an incumbent governor doesn't attack a challenger because it just gives the challenger another opportunity for more publicity. But Ogilvie apparently felt, based on the polling, that he had to attack.

"I had a tremendous lead after the primary, but that lead dwindled away to where a few weeks before the election Ogilvie had caught up with me, maybe forged ahead. But, if so, his lead was thin.

"Then he started dropping a little back, and he went on the air with commercials attacking my Walker Report.

"In our judgment they weren't very good commercials. They featured Ogilvie himself, just by himself, sitting on a stool. He was not the most charismatic person on television, but there he was, hammering away at Walker for being the author of the infamous Walker Report that talked about police riots.

"Now Vic and others on our staff had guessed that was going to be the assault at the end, if there was an assault, so we had our answering commercials ready.

"Ours focused on my support for the 60-day trial requirement, in which I talked about a proposal to try everyone indicted for a crime within 60 days after indictment. The idea had been tested in a poll and the positive response to it was staggering.

"What we had not realized when we were first talking about the plan was that it cut both ways. Conservatives looked at it and saw it as getting people off the streets and into jail in 60 days. To liberals, however, it meant that innocent people would not be languishing in jail for more than 60 days. So, this turned out to be an extremely popular proposal, and we used it as our television commercial answer to Ogilvie's Walker Report criticism."

Of course, Walker already had shown he could use television advertisements to great advantage in defeating Simon. And, just as in the primary, Walker's ads on the tube in the general election were produced by de Grazia's friend from New York, David Garth.

Thereafter, certain that Walker clearly had bested the Governor in the television commercial showdown at the end, de Grazia ventured forth to all within earshot that "we just put him (Ogilvie) away."

In the wake of the impact of the television commercials, and with the general election right around the corner, the Walker strategists put volunteers on every available phone for a final sampling of voters. Even in Republican areas like the Chicago suburbs, the callers found a surprisingly strong response for Walker, so much so that the telephoners just started grabbing phone books willy-nilly and calling every name listed.

No longer asking persons if they were supporting Walker or Ogilvie, the Walker callers just urged those on the other end of the line to "get out and vote, please get out and vote." In particular, residents of western and southwestern Cook County burbs were flooded with these calls.

Finally. Nov. 7, 1972. Election day. All signs pointed to extensive ticket-splitting by the state's 6,215,331 registered voters. This was a requisite for Dan Walker, since Richard Nixon surely was going to blow away George McGovern in the presidential balloting in Illinois and Republican Charles Percy loomed as a hands-down favorite in the U.S. Senate race.

The GOP also appeared quite likely to retain the attorney

general's office, where incumbent William J. Scott, a nationwide attention getter as a result of his suits against polluters, was favored heavily to whip the scrappy Thomas Lyons.

Considering the outlook for Nixon, Percy and Scott, the Republicans seemed to stand a chance for a landslide in Illinois, just like the Democrats had done in 1964 when former President Lyndon B. Johnson swept the state and carried many other Illinois Democrats into office.

But the Ogilvie race clouded the GOP picture. The only thing most analysts felt safe in predicting was that the gubernatorial contest would be decided by fewer than 100,000 votes.

They were right.

Dan Walker defeated Richard Buell Ogilvie for the governorship by 77,494 votes—hardly a minor accomplishment in that President Nixon, Senator Percy and Attorney General Scott all triumphed over their Democratic opponents in the state by lopsided margins.

Walker and running mate Neil Hartigan carried Cook and 54 other counties, leaving the Ogilvie-Nowlan ticket with 47 counties in its pocket.

The final tally gave Walker and Hartigan 2,371,303 votes, or 50.7 percent of the vote for governor, to 2,293,809 for Ogilvie and Nowlan. It was one of the closer races for Illinois governor in the Twentieth Century, but this took nothing away from the impressiveness of Walker's victory.

Walker might have carried Cook County by more than the 99,411-vote plurality he received there, 1,178,446 to 1,079,035.

But, no way could be found to minimize his substantial feat in holding Ogilvie to a 21,917-vote lead in the rest of the state, 1,214,774 to 1,192,857, a poor downstate showing for a Republican governor.

Not that Ogilvie did not carry, and in most cases handily, DuPage, Kane, McHenry, Will, Sangamon, Champaign, McLean and Walker's home county of Lake, all places where the 49-year-old Ogilvie should have done well. Walker may have clobbered Simon in DuPage in the primary, but Ogilvie ran away with the Republican stronghold in the general election, 142,805 to 87,056, giving the Governor more than 62 percent of the DuPage vote.

On the other hand, Walker ran strongly in the key Democratic counties downstate where he had to do so, like Madison, St. Clair and Rock Island (garnering more or close to 60 percent of the vote in each).

And he either beat Ogilvie or cut into his anticipated victory margin in numerous other counties which in an earlier era would have been solid GOP terrain. For instance, Walker's capture of populous Winnebago County in traditionally Republican northern Illinois by 52,566 votes to 40,922 had to really hurt the Ogilvie effort.

To nobody's surprise, Walker lost only a handful of counties south of Springfield, and most of them were little ones.

As if the defeat of Ogilvie was not enough to spoil the election for Illinois Republicans, Democrat Michael Howlett, the state auditor of public accounts, captured the office of secretary of state. That was significant because the nearly 4,200 patronage jobs under the secretary of state made it the most important political base in state government besides the governorship.

However, the story of the election was Walker. Without question, no better story had come out of Illinois politics in decades.

In one political season, like a no-name Clint Eastwood character in one of those spaghetti westerns, Walker had emerged from nowhere, guns blazing, to shoot down three of the biggest, if not the best known, figures in Illinois politics.

First Richard J. Daley and Paul Simon. Then Richard B. Ogilvie, whose loss of the governorship was followed by a financially rewarding career as a lawyer in Chicago. He died in 1988 at the age of 65.

To pull off what he did in 1972, the iconoclastic Walker had to overcome unrelenting opposition at every corner from power groups. He did it through assiduous courtship of the rank and file of Illinois, by never straying far in his two-year gubernatorial campaign from the streets, from hand-shaking and discussion with anyone he met.

When Walker appeared before his jubilant supporters in Chicago on the night of the election, he proclaimed his victory a major stride for the common man.

His triumph, he declared, "belongs to the people...they believed Illinois could be made better."

Walker entered the gubernatorial race as an independent Democrat, and he made it clear to the election night cheers of his followers that he still considered himself every bit an independent Democrat, not beholden to anybody or anything.

Seldom could an individual have been riding higher or sitting prettier in the political spectrum of Illinois. Illinois, his adopted home, the citizens of which now had elected him to the state's most exalted position.

A far cry indeed from that sweltering day during the walk in Old Shawneetown, only 16 months before, when he stood dejectedly in pain, his feet caked in blood and his arrival ignored by the press, questioning to himself the sanity of what he was doing.

To those who were speculating late in 1972 about the future of American politics, the election of Daniel Walker looked to be one of the most far-reaching occurrences.

And 1972 had its share of interesting developments. The death of J. Edgar Hoover. The shooting and paralyzing of Alabama Governor George Wallace in Maryland. President Nixon's landslide victory in his bid for re-election. Before that, in June of that year, the arrest of five burglars inside Democratic national headquarters in the Watergate complex in Washington, individuals found to have ties to Nixon's re-election campaign.

But, the biggest happening, the one to keep an eye on, many persons suspected, well might have been in Illinois where business as usual was tossed out the window in the successful march to the Governor's Mansion by this guy Walker.

The fellow who turned political implausibility into reality, who had shown the underdogs of life that dreams, as far out as they might seem, still came true. ❧

14

The New Governor in Action

As had become his custom, Daniel Walker was whiling away the final
hours of an early winter day in 1992 in the open air of a cafe patio
in the tranquil southern California beach town of Del Mar, gazing
at a spectacular sunset over the placid Pacific.

Home for Walker was an apartment in neighboring Solana
Beach, where there was a balcony from which he also could view
the ocean and, on a clear day, the northern reaches of San Diego
a few miles to the south.

This was the year for Walker to turn 70, and he had found
solace back in this corner of the country where he grew up.

A short hike down the road on a hill in the Encanto community on the eastern outskirts of San Diego still sat the tiny, almost miniature cottage that Walker associated so much with his mother and father's earlier years in San Diego. His dad built it with stone from San Diego's backcountry in the days when his sometime companion was a bottle of Old Grand Dad.

Walker was thinking a lot these days about the old man, like about the time after a drinking bout that the car his dad was driving down a steeply pitched street from the cottage shot off the road and turned over repeatedly before crash landing several hundred feet below. The old man walked away from the wreck.

There was gossip that Dan Walker had a drinking problem when he was governor, but he insisted not. Years later, though, after his difficulties commenced, alcohol did become a problem.

Walker silently turned over these things in his mind on this winter day as he sat, like most around him, sipping wine, clad in a white sweatshirt and blue wash pants.

The weather was mild, a far cry from the cold snap back in the Midwest, back in Illinois where people braced themselves against the bitter winds racing along Michigan Avenue.

But Walker had only warm thoughts on this day of that now distant world of Michigan Avenue and Old Shawneetown and of so many other places once part of his domain.

This was a good day for Walker, one on which he had pushed the nightmarish hell of prison out of his mind, something he was not always able to do in the two and half years since his release. This was a good day because, instead of the specter of freezing Duluth, he was resurrecting in his mind those days 19 years earlier that ushered in his governorship.

Little could rival the exciting satisfaction of the interlude between his election and inauguration.

For a while at least Walker had the best of everything. The suspense, the awful uncertainty were over. It seemed clear now that it all would be worth it. The exuberance of Walker and his people was something to behold.

Walker set about filling these weeks preceding the inauguration, as he put it, "with dramatic and vital activities, such as putting together a cabinet, getting started on the next annual budget, setting up a staff and talking with persons about new programs. Heady stuff.

"Even though you are not yet empowered as the state's chief executive, people look to the governor-elect as their new leader, and they sometimes circumvent the lame duck at the Mansion. This is especially true when the two are members of the opposing parties. A new leader means new enthusiasm and hope for the party that has just recaptured the Mansion, as we did by beating Ogilvie."

Public life in Illinois offers few more cleansing experiences, at least to downstaters, than a change in the governorship. Even many cynics have been known to suspend their pessimism, if only briefly, to give the new chap the benefit of the doubt.

On Walker in particular, one could have an open mind. Nobody had any real inkling anyway of what was to come. He certainly did not seem obligated to the old order like so many before him. Any impartiality toward Walker would not last long, though, especially from those long accustomed to being in the saddle.

The late Kenneth Watson, then a veteran columnist for the old Illinois State Journal in Springfield, profiled happenings under what he loved to call the Statehouse dome.

As he traipsed the halls of the dome-dominated Capitol, the massive building designed in the form of a Latin cross and with a classical facade that is the base of Illinois government, Watson found most of those who worked or hung out there shaking in their boots at the thought of the arrival of Walker. Understandably so.

Even before taking office, Walker would go a long way toward fashioning an administration that appeared as disrespectful of the establishment as did his campaign. Many of those chosen by Walker for key government posts were individuals, like himself, who had spent years knocking without success on the doors to political power.

Few persons familiar with Illinois politics could remain neutral about many of Walker's selections, personages like Abner Mikva, Anthony Scariano, Mary Lee Leahy, Donald Page Moore, William Rutherford. In one of the better understatements of the political season, Norton Kay described the selections of his boss as "persons who were not cleared with anybody in Chicago or elsewhere."

Take Tony Scariano. Walker provided a glaring preview of coming attractions only a month after the election with his bombshell announcement that liberal Democrat Scariano, a peppery outgoing state representative from Park Forest, was his choice for chairman of the Illinois Racing Board.

Scariano, of all people, was to be given a green light to try to clean up what Walker labeled the stink of racetrack politics. Scariano, who repeatedly tried without success to pass bills aimed at reform of the state's racing industry. Scariano, who told an interviewer in 1971 that the racing industry was the most evil in the state and that he would "just as soon introduce a bill abolishing it, but I know this wouldn't pass." Bejesus, whined the horse crowd, anybody but Scariano.

By the arrival of inaugural day, Jan. 8, 1973, it was evident that the accent in the emerging Walker team seemed to be on liberals and Democratic mavericks, with a mix of eastern imports and Walker associates from his days in business. Only a few appointees were from the ranks of regular Illinois Democrats.

Walker's picks, besides providing a foundation for the governmental shake-up promised by Walker, also could give a boost to his intended restructuring of the state Democratic Party.

At last, a chance to uproot the party, so long awaited by Walker and his political chums, was at their fingertips. Their goal of an Illinois Democratic Party more in tune with their idea of participatory democracy—a dream nourished by Walker and the others since the early 1950s—actually could be realized.

To the idealists, the politically enlightened movement of the late Governor Adlai Stevenson, stalled in Illinois for two decades, now was heading for resurrection. Finally, Walker and other once-young disciples of Stevenson were in a position to carry the torch lit by Stevenson. No wonder the reformers felt they seldom had more reason for optimism about the likelihood of an improved governmental climate in the state.

They thought Walker's unusual outdoor inaugural ceremony was certainly a nice starting point. The Walkerites themselves viewed it as being in line with the intensive grass roots nature of his long march to the governorship.

The public ceremony on the front steps of the Statehouse, in front of the statue of Abraham Lincoln facing Second Street, was the first inaugural in the memory of observers that did not take place before a joint session of the General Assembly.

Most everybody wore coats for protection against the subfreezing temperature in the 20s, but not Walker, who showed up in a dark blue suit with a white pin-striped shirt and light blue tie. The man of the hour, flanked near the podium by his wife Roberta and old political acquaintance Angelo Geocaris, didn't flinch at the cold.

The others present, dignitaries and commoners alike, surely did. They shifted from one foot to the other to keep warm as the University of Illinois marching band played the national anthem and the state's poet laureate, Gwendolyn Brooks, read a poem called "Aurora" which she composed for the occasion.

The most memorable part of her work was when she said, "It

is the giant hour. Nothing less than gianthood will do."

After administration of the oath of office to Walker by Justice Schaefer, during which Walker raised his right hand and placed his other hand on the Walker family's maroon-colored Bible, the thirty-sixth Governor of Illinois delivered his inaugural address to the crowd, which by then spilled onto the grounds of the Illinois Supreme Court building east of the Capitol.

Nobody expected Walker to pull any punches, and he didn't.

From his resolve "to sweep the arrogance of bureaucracy from the halls of power" to his pledge to "fight for a government that exists to serve people, rather than cater to the special interests."

In words reminiscent of his hard-hitting campaign, Walker warned, "To those who have grown rich on the public dollar, to those who have won secret grants and contracts, to those in government who put themselves first and the taxpayers second—to you I bring my first message from the people of Illinois: the free ride is over.

"And in the weeks ahead I shall be using the Governor's power of executive order to make this abundantly clear."

The new Governor told the assemblage that his campaign walk throughout the state left him convinced he was taking office in a time of lost faith in the state's government.

During his "voyage," he said, "I listened and spoke to those of you in small communities, on farms and in great cities. I spoke to those of you who work—with your hands and with your minds—in overalls, blue-collars, hard hats, coats and ties...and to some of you who did not work at all because there was no work.

"For all of your differences, what you had to say about government was disturbingly similar. You simply did not believe government was worth your trust.

"This was no partisan view. It was shared by Democrats and Republicans about Democrats and Republicans. It was aimed at no one administration or official. It was instead a pervasive cynicism.

"The people of Illinois—like the people across much of America—simply do not believe that our institutions, including government, can do what they say they will do; they do not believe government understands how they live, what they need, what they want for their families."

The discontent, emphasized Walker, "reaches from Brookport to Galena, from East St. Louis to Zion, from Warsaw to Watseka, from Cairo to Chicago.

"It poses, I believe, the most serious dilemma we face."

Then, getting to the heart of his political creed on this clear wintry day, Walker reiterated a conviction that "here in Illinois and around the nation, the central belief of the founding fathers is sound; the people are the best judge of what they want and need."

Unfortunately, he added, "too many in government do not believe in this American credo; they believe that only experts, politicians, bureaucrats or those with wealth or power can tell people what to do.

"I do not share that belief.

"Let government step back, let people step forward."

Those last words were favorites of his. They were spelled out under the heading "Governor Dan" on a large wooden plaque on a wall of his California apartment, one of the few visible mementos of his governorship.

Walker concluded his inaugural address with a promise well received by many of his listeners but, as Walker would find out, difficult to keep.

"To every one of you, I make this pledge. This government is yours. You created it. You pay for it. And it is time you began getting your money's worth."

Few applauded Walker's forcefully-delivered speech more vigorously than the 100 or so individuals in the crowd who had provided shelter and food to Walker during his 1971 walk through the state. The night before the inauguration, Walker and Roberta took them to dinner at the St. Nicholas Hotel in Springfield, a sign to some observers that Walker had not yet forgotten who had buttered his bread.

In the days before and after his inauguration, Walker was making it clear that he was a man acutely aware of his friends and of those he felt were not. Despite that, few anticipated that he would try to revamp the Democratic Party with such vengeance.

While most county chairmen and other wheelhorses long at the center of the party's makeup were relegated to the bench, Walker was stocking his administration through the power of appointment with persons largely unknown in the Statehouse and other places of governmental power.

It mattered not so much that they were Democrats, Republicans or independents but that they would be loyal to Walker.

Any mystery about what was happening dissolved within the first five or six weeks of Walker's governorship.

The closed and monolithic nature of the party under Richard Daley was seriously under fire. Walker actually seemed to be taking significant strides toward restricting Daley's absolute control of party affairs to the borders of Cook County. To the traditionalists, the time to push the alarm button was approaching rapidly.

Tom Owens, the former Paul Simon man who still was Democratic chairman of Sangamon County, complained that he had not as yet been consulted on one single job by Walker's office and that, furthermore, he did not know of "any veteran Democratic regulars in Sangamon who have got jobs through the Governor's office."

Normally for Owens, who voiced his discontent in an open letter to Walker, the election of a Democratic governor would have opened a door to many jobs for members of his county organization. Jobs—the lifeblood of any successful political operation.

In the general election campaign, many party regulars came through for Walker in spite of his reliance on his own recruits. After the election, the regulars did not expect to be excluded from the fruits of victory.

"I didn't sit on my hands in the campaign," said Leo Obernuefemann, the Democratic chairman of St. Clair County, "and we carried my county handsomely for Walker."

So, Obernuefemann added, "I do expect to get some jobs in his administration filled out of the (regular) organization here. I think we've got to realize some positions under a Democratic administration to keep the party functioning."

But, to the new Governor, guys like Owens and Obernuefemann were just exponents of an old patronage system that Walker despised on grounds that it "can and does breed painters who don't paint, assistants who don't assist and highway workers who lean on their shovels."

In the early days, the Walker version of patronage in government was almost too good for the reformers and altruists to believe.

Unlike his predecessors, Walker had no patronage chief in his office. Outside of high-level appointments, Walker was permitting the filling of many positions by the department directors under whom the employees would actually serve, which was anything but routine.

To underscore his insistence that hiring be done by the government and not by the Democratic Party, Walker was requiring that county chairmen and ward and township committeemen resign their party posts before receiving positions in his administration.

Even more far-reaching was the executive order on patronage that Walker issued a month after taking office. The directive prohibited a state employee from asking another employee to perform political tasks. Also, no employee could be asked or required to make a political contribution.

Although the impact of these Walker policies on the quality of governmental performance remained to be seen, the effect on the Democratic Party rapidly became obvious judging by its quick split into Walker Democrats, Daley Democrats and other factions.

By the end of his first year in office, Walker's attempts to disassociate himself from old-time gubernatorial patronage politics would be mired in quicksand, providing fodder for his unrelenting critics and leaving some of his defenders unsure or confused about what was going on.

Trying to circumvent the regular Democratic and other established channels on patronage, the Walker team would find out, was no cakewalk.

State jobs and who gets them. The lineup feeding at the public trough. To many political professionals, nothing takes precedence to the retention or placement of themselves and their friends and their relatives on the public payroll. It is an obsession, the measure by which the success of a governor's regime is gauged. The quality of programs, the efficacy of services delivered to taxpayers, the image and moral tone of an administration. Those are left to be debated by the League of Women Voters of Illinois. To those who know how matters really work, first things come first. And nothing comes before jobs.

Walker wasted little time trying to affect the touchy state job picture. On his third day in office, he issued an executive order, his first, which required departments and agencies to cut back their number of employees to the levels of the previous Nov. 1. This was intended to lop off some 500 Republican payrollers put on by the Ogilvie administration during its final two months in office, a common practice for a lame duck governor.

Walker also froze the number of overall state employees at the figure employed on Nov. 1, 1972, stipulating in his executive order that "the average staffing level for the period Jan. 1, 1973, through June 30, 1973, shall not exceed the staffing level on Nov. 1, 1972."

That step, plus agency spending restraints dictated by Walker immediately upon assuming office, easily would save taxpayers $10,000,000 during Walker's first six months in office, estimated Hal Hovey, Walker's newly named director of the Bureau of the Budget.

In the order, Walker said that he was "determined to bring state spending under control.

"Over the long run, this will require a careful review of state operations to insure that all employees are actively engaged in delivery of services to people.

"For example, I am convinced that some departments are overstaffed at high paid middle-management levels while there are service levels which are understaffed. These are the kinds of priorities which we must reverse."

So far so good. The real grabbers of attention in those early days, though, were the picks of Walker for many of the posts in his administration. Scariano was only one of a number that got tongues wagging.

Chicago Democrat Abner Mikva, who was a leading liberal spokesman in the United States House of Representatives before his defeat for re-election in 1972, was tabbed to head a state ethics board to be established by Walker after taking office.

The panel was to oversee a disclosure of personal finances that Walker planned to require of major state officials through one of his upcoming executive orders. That would be one way to detect conflicts of interest, Walker felt, thus discouraging corruption.

Remembering that Mary Leahy had spearheaded a drive to incorporate the environmental article in the new Illinois Constitution of 1970, Walker asked the longtime liberal foe of the

Chicago Democratic machine to direct the Environmental Protection Agency, the operation responsible for finding and prosecuting polluters.

Bill Rutherford, a Peoria Republican who for a while was state conservation director under Ogilvie, was asked to serve as Walker's chairman of the advisory council to the Department of Conservation. Since leaving the Ogilvie administration, Rutherford had criticized state personnel practices so much that people in both parties considered him a menace to the system.

Walker picked Donald Page Moore, a Chicagoan and former Department of Justice attorney, to chair the Illinois Law Enforcement Commission. Moore, another liberal, independent Democrat, unsuccessfully had sought his party's nomination in 1972 for state's attorney of Cook County.

Walker asked a former fellow executive at Montgomery Ward, Jack Foster, a personnel expert, to conduct a nationwide search for certain key appointees. One result was 33-year-old Wayne Kerstetter, a onetime methods analyst for the Chicago Police Department who went on to become assistant first deputy police commissioner of New York City.

The Governor asked Kerstetter to be superintendent of the Illinois Bureau of Investigation—the state's "Little FBI."

Another recruit found back East was Jerome G. Miller, who garnered lots of attention for his drive to reform the juvenile corrections system in Massachusetts before coming to Illinois at the urging of Walker to run the Department of Children and Family Services.

Walker liked Miller's record in Massachusetts, where he had moved to close juvenile jails and substitute in their place halfway houses, foster homes, extended parole and probation programs and private psychiatric care.

The Executive Committee in the Illinois Senate, which would recommend to the full body confirmation or rejection of Walker's appointments, was gearing up for a close scrutiny of Miller, as it was for the controversial Mrs. Leahy and certain others, most notably Anthony Dean and David Fogel.

It was bad enough for Walker that the GOP had regained control of the Senate in the 1972 election. Even worse, the Executive Committee was dominated by crusty Republican old liners who naturally did not cotton much to Walker.

Walker campaign worker Dean, named by the Governor to head the Department of Conservation, looked to be facing stiff questioning from the panel because of his conscientious objector background, the same issue that had surfaced when he worked in the 1970 Senate campaign of Adlai Stevenson III.

However, the Executive Committee was sharpening the knives much more for Fogel, the choice of Walker to run the Illinois prison system.

Hard-line penologists in Illinois abhorred the arrival of Fogel, whose innovative efforts to make prisons more humane as the commissioner of correctional institutions in Minnesota were derided by law enforcement officers and penal traditionalists for allegedly making a mockery of the system.

By bringing Fogel to Illinois, Walker thought he was under-lining clearly his commitment to penal reform, to a continuation of the shake-up in Illinois prisons started by Fogel's predecessor, Peter B. Bensinger.

Likewise, with Jerome Miller, Walker got him to come to Illinois from Massachusetts with a promise of gubernatorial support "for exciting and innovative changes in state government."

For Fogel and Miller, rocky days lay ahead in Illinois. But, the selection of them by Walker illustrated far more clearly than did words his intention to cast aside the status quo and plunge ahead without delay to revamp state institutions as radically as he had altered state politics.

Walker would find, though, that getting the General Assembly and the entrenched bureaucracy to go along with his ideas for change was not as easy as convincing voters of the validity of his way of thinking.

In the Legislature, Republicans only held a one-seat edge in each chamber. However, the challenge he faced there was compounded greatly by the difficulty he was sure to encounter from a number of Democratic lawmakers out of the regular party organization, mainly Chicagoans, who viewed his election with mixed feelings.

The Walker gang also could be its own worst enemy, as was the case with one particularly ugly development that tempered the euphoria at the start of the Walker era. The Walker people had nobody to blame but themselves for this one.

Later on, Walker himself, de Grazia and the other insiders wished they never had heard of wealthy Chicago businessman Anthony G. Angelos. Wished they hadn't accepted a $50,000 political contribution from Angelos, even though the money was needed desperately. Wished they had not nominated him to the sensitive regulatory post of state insurance director.

Wished it hadn't come out a few days before the swearing in of Walker that Angelos, whom Walker aids at first described as a prominent financier and philanthropist, had a long association with flophouses and slum properties and alleged financial dealings with Chicago hoodlums. Bringing this fellow into the picture was not a smart move for a new Governor seeking to instill a higher sense of ethics on the government scene. Walker did not need this one.

Another snag in the Walker strategy for a smooth transition into office occurred on Dec. 13 after Walker's election victory. That day, de Grazia suffered a heart attack after accompanying Walker to a luncheon in Chicago of the Third House, an organization of Statehouse lobbyists.

Rushed stricken to the old Woodlawn hospital on Chicago's south side, Victor de Grazia, the Walker intimate always in the middle of everything, suddenly was out of action. After leaving the hospital, de Grazia continued his recuperation at his Kenwood neighborhood home, where he was able to resume helping to put together the Walker governing team.

The totally unexpected illness of de Grazia left Walker brooding, saddened that this should happen to his friend and partner in political dreaming through the years at the exact time the two of them should be relishing fully their moment of triumph.

Walker knew people were not wrong when they said that de Grazia seemed to be almost like a brother to him, even though the two men came from different worlds.

A true son of Chicago, de Grazia was born in 1929 in the Little Italy enclave on the near north side and grew up in the collection of blocks called Lake View not far from Wrigley Field. He was the youngest of the four boys in his family. Two of his brothers would become political scientists and the other a law professor. The oldest brother, Sebastian, would win a Pulitzer Prize for a biography of Machiavelli, the name Victor often was called by most of his detractors and some of his admirers.

Although Victor de Grazia had knocked around at several colleges, Lake Forest and the University of Chicago included, he did not have a college degree. His skills in political theory and conduct were honed on the streets.

All Walker knew was that de Grazia was a "remarkable man," an individual who "understood my way of thinking so much that I felt comfortable in delegating to him decisional areas that I never would have delegated to others." Walker could not fathom the hostility aimed at de Grazia by so many persons.

Dan and de Grazia always had regarded themselves as a team in every sense of the word. That did not change in Springfield, although each recognized that the other had a domain. Vic's was politics; Dan had government.

Walker knew that Vic's involvement in governmental operations was considerably less than most observers believed. When politics and governing sometimes overlapped, Walker had the main say on the government side while Vic's voice prevailed on political considerations.

de Grazia himself, after what had seemed an eternity on the outside looking in, would savor the attention to be showered on him as the top lieutenant and alter ego of Governor Dan Walker. He would be called many things and would be a frequent target of epithets, one of the milder being administration hatchet man.

Most of it rolled off de Grazia's back, except when a Chicago columnist called him the Mussolini of Springfield. Vic didn't like that, nor did Italian-American groups in Chicago. They wanted to protest publicly, but de Grazia said no.

One of the numerous individuals not a member of de Grazia's fan club was Roberta Walker, the new first lady of Illinois. She was convinced that de Grazia exercised too much influence over her husband, power that she did not believe to be always in Dan's interest.

She had more on her mind than Victor, though, as she and her husband entered the Governor's Mansion. Although Mrs. Walker had had little contact with Dorothy Ogilvie, the wife of the departing Governor, Roberta was the recipient of much helpful advice from Gertrude Shapiro, the wife of the last Democrat to serve as state chief executive.

"Go any route with the Mansion you want," Mrs. Shapiro told Roberta Walker. "You can pick and choose what will happen. It is up to you."

Mrs. Walker had not wanted her husband to run for governor, but had known that he "would do it anyway because it was his dream and he did what he wanted to do." However, she had worked hard to help him get elected and his victory had left her thrilled. She was very excited and even a bit overwhelmed by the move into the Mansion.

She loved her family's white brick, colonial style home on Norman Lane in Deerfield, a two-story residence with six bedrooms that was built expressly for Dan and Roberta Walker. They would have to continue to maintain it since it also was the home of her elderly father since his retirement.

Roberta's first year in the Mansion was difficult, much of it spent trying to juggle time between responsibilities in Deerfield and her suddenly expanded public life. She still was an active mother, too, with the two youngest of the seven Walker children, Margaret Ann, 13, and William Marshall (Will), 10, joining their parents in the Mansion.

First and foremost, Roberta Walker would do her best to make the Mansion a home, to inject a personal touch into the private living quarters for the gubernatorial family on the third floor. The state-owned furniture left by the Ogilvies was fine, Roberta thought, but she would bring down from Deerfield one of Dan's favorite chairs and her own sofa. Outside, for the kids, an aboveground pool was purchased by the Walkers and a tire swing was strung up for Will. Margaret soon got a vegetable garden started in a corner of the Mansion yard.

Mrs. Walker, a former elementary school teacher more on the shy side than outgoing, resolved to live in the Mansion with dignity. Living there, she well understood, was a privilege.

Never privy to the thinking of her husband's inner circle, Roberta also knew that it was difficult to get her husband, Vic and the others to listen when she felt she had a premonition about coming events. There was for her in the scheme of things, Roberta realized, an intended place in which she was "to know only what Dan wanted me to know."

Irrespective of that, she was confident that her upbringing in Kenosha as the daughter and only child of a local businessman-politician had prepared her for the role she now faced. She believed that Illinoisans expected and appreciated refinement in their first ladies. Maybe even a bit of a blue blood.

Still, she wished her husband would talk more to her, confide in her, even seek her advice. On matters big and little.

A devout Catholic, Roberta Walker could have told her Protestant husband what to say when he decided to pay a courtesy visit after his election to the Catholic prelate of Chicago, the late John Cardinal Cody.

On the way to the Cardinal's residence, it dawned on Walker that he was not sure of the correct way to address such a major figure in the Catholic Church. Walker finally decided on "your excellency."

So, moments later, as the two were being introduced, Walker said, "I am delighted to meet you, your Excellency."

In reply, Cardinal Cody avoided direct correction of Walker's choice of title. Instead, he held Walker's hand, looked at him with twinkling eyes, and said, "Governor, you are excellent. I am eminent." ❧

Rough Sledding
with the Legislature

Right off the bat, Walker's governorship had a style all its own, a brand darn tough to figure.

He professed he did not want to be a one-man show, a point he really emphasized in delivering his initial State of the State Message to the General Assembly, the occasion of his first appearance before a joint session of the two august bodies.

To make government work, to "deliver the best services at the least possible cost to the people of Illinois," Walker stated, the Governor-led executive branch and the law-making Legislature had "to be partners.

"To do that, and do it well, we cannot have one-man rule. We cannot have war between branches of government."

As they say, famous last words.

Dealing with the General Assembly, Walker was to find, would be the most hair pulling part of his governorship, next to his frustration with the news media.

Getting things straight with the lawmakers was not as simple as that first night of poker at the Mansion, when Walker laid down the law for the card games that would be played regularly during his time in office at either the Mansion or the private retreat he set up on a small lake by Taylorville.

That first poker night at the Mansion after Walker took office. A good story.

Into the Lincoln Study strides the new Governor of Illinois— a big pistol, an old-fashioned six-gun out of the wild West, sticking up out of his waistband. To the astonishment of those present, Walker pulls out the pistol and puts it in the center of the card table.

"Gentlemen," proclaims the new foreman of Illinois government, "we play by my rules. Five-card draw and five-card stud. Table stakes. No wild card games."

That was that. No questions. The man with the gun was the boss. The games would be silent, because Walker wasn't talkative when he held a poker hand. He was a serious player, and a good one. A real pokerface.

Table stakes betting meant that the amount of money on the table was the limit on the dollars that could be wagered. It could get expensive, though, if you lost big at one of these gatherings in the Mansion. One's wallet could be $400 to $500 lighter.

But handling the Legislature just was not as easy for Walker. To many of those seated in the ornate chambers of the House and Senate on the third floor of the Capitol, one floor above the Governor's office, the guy sitting on the second floor was a wild card.

However, Walker's luck up to this stage in getting his way, as the legislators saw it, was about to run out. No way did these guys and gals, Democrats or Republicans, play by Walker's rules. No sir. He wasn't going to get the draw on them.

For Walker, the new Seventy-eighth General Assembly was a buzz saw full of mean hombres who, after fighting among themselves, were spoiling for a go at the new Governor.

It did not take long. Less than three months after taking office, Walker was in hot water with the Legislature, with powerful lawmakers from his own party as well as with Republicans.

In that short time, Walker failed to prevent an embarrassing legislative override of his veto on a bill providing emergency aid to mass transit systems. Nor could he save the nomination of David Fogel, his choice for director of Illinois prisons.

Furthermore, legislative leaders from both parties were warning that this was only the beginning for Walker if he did not enter into more of what they called "political give-and-take" on issues.

If the election of Walker had been a blow to the state's political normality, then the doings in the early days of the new General Assembly drove another nail into the coffin of traditional Illinois politics.

Voters in the 1972 election had left the Legislature in GOP hands, but not by much. Republicans held only an 89 to 88 edge in the House and also only a one-seat advantage, 30 to 29, in the Senate.

In the House, in contrast to the cut-and-dried proceedings in the past, eight roll calls were required before the incumbent speaker, Republican W. Robert Blair of Park Forest, won re-election to the post that quite literally has the power of life and death over bills.

Blair's trouble stemmed from heated opposition on his side of the aisle from Representative Henry J. Hyde, a Park Ridge lawyer and outspoken conservative who commanded loyalty from some 30 of his House Republican colleagues. The Hyde backers were so adamant in their refusal to follow Blair that they planned to caucus separately and hire their own staff.

However, Democratic exploitation of the GOP split was no sure thing because at least 15 Democrats were identified with a liberal bloc that had become increasingly independent in its commitment to reform of House operations. Most important politically, the bloc opposed the old-line leadership loyal to Mayor Daley that had dominated House Democrats for years.

Then, as if having to deal with a chaotic House was not bad enough, Walker's legislative outlook was clouded further by the return to leadership in the Senate of Republican Bourbons.

There, the new president presiding over the chamber was Senator William C. Harris, a conservative Republican from Pontiac and a veteran and often flamboyant legislative wheelhorse.

Harris had to defeat stiff competition from within his own party, mild-mannered Senator Terrel Clarke of Western Springs, to capture his spot, but his victory seemed to ensure one more go-around in the upper chamber for the long dominant Republican Old Guard.

No more exclusive political club could be found in Illinois than the Senate. And its ruling elders for many years were GOP Bourbons, some with political careers dating back to the Depression.

To be fair, when legislative shenanigans in the 1960s plunged the image of the General Assembly to a low point, the Old Guard was dragged reluctantly to the rescue. Its aggressive leader in those days, the combative W. Russell Arrington of Evanston, forcefully whipped the Senate into a model of operating efficiency, one intended to show that the Legislature still could play a full role in government.

The Bourbons' control of the Senate also meant that in most

years few programs made it through the General Assembly without being tailored to the traditionally conservative brand of Illinois Republicanism embodied by the Old Guard.

Naturally, no interests were better served than those protected by the Old Guard—insurance firms and other big businesses, financial institutions, public education, agriculture and strict interpretation of the Illinois Constitution.

However, age, the stepped-up pace in the General Assembly and an increase in Democratic-held seats in the Senate had taken a toll on the Old Guard.

Arrington himself, ailing much of the previous two years from the effects of a paralyzing stroke, had left the scene. Also, a number of other Bourbons had not sought re-election in 1972.

Nevertheless, enough still were on hand in 1973 to elect one of their own, Bill Harris, to the Senate's top spot. It would be the last hurrah for the Bourbons, a final two-year period in power in which they could try to do their best to make life miserable for the maverick Democratic Governor Walker, a last chance to feel their oats. They made the most of it.

Walker's torment by the Legislature during his first years in office convinced him early on that he had to address the situation in the 1974 election, a year that he himself did not have to run.

The 1974 election, an event of midterm for Walker, would present him with an ideal opportunity to translate his appeal to voters into assistance to Democratic legislative candidates sympathetic to the Walker movement for a new political Illinois. The campaign skills of Dan Walker were going to be applied in a number of General Assembly districts in 1974, no doubt of that. He was determined to produce some other new winners on the political scene.

In the meantime, what to do about the damnable Legislature in Walker's first two years in office?

The relationship with the Senate and House was de Grazia's

baby, partly because none of the Walker insiders held any illusions
that this would be an easy job. Walker gave his trusted lieutenant
virtually free rein in this matter. Later, Walker thought that
perhaps he himself should have been more visible and active with
the Legislature.

But, Walker entered office with a firm belief that his administration and the General Assembly were distinctly separate
branches of government, each with its own sphere of sovereignty.
This was one area where Walker intended, at least in the beginning, to respect tradition.

Walker had it in mind to "stay away from the legislators, to not
invade their arena unless invited. I only saw legislators when Vic
said I had to. Otherwise, I stayed away from them. I did not want
to knock down any of the barriers between their world and mine."

To head its legislative liaison team under de Grazia, the
Walker administration recruited Douglas Nelson Kane. Approached on the job by de Grazia before Walker took office, the
33-year-old Kane was an interesting choice.

Born in China where his parents were missionaries. A former
reporter for the Louisville Courier-Journal. Very bright. Quite
liberal. A key Democratic staffer in the House extremely close to
his boss, Representative Clyde Choate of Anna, the House
Democratic leader. Kane had worked for Simon against Walker
in the 1972 primary and he had sat out the general election
campaign afterward.

Although he became part of the Walker team, Kane never
denied his loyalty to Choate, a wily politician whom Walker found
absolutely fascinating but never trusted. Eventually, Kane's closeness to Choate put Kane on what he felt certain was a Nixon-like
enemies' list maintained by the Walker people. But that tran-
spired well after the one year Kane spent fronting for the Walker
administration with the Legislature. It was a year in which Kane
tried his best to do a good job, but always felt he had one hand tied

behind his back.

Kane got to hire his own man to work with the Senate, Michael Duncan, an attorney who went back with Kane to the days when they both were Illinois legislative interns. The House was to be handled by David Caravello, a pick of de Grazia.

Having no previous legislative experience, Caravello was typical of many in the Walker administration who came to their government roles enthusiastic but green.

A onetime seminarian who later taught Latin at a Catholic high school in Chicago, Caravello was one of the group that joined the Walker gubernatorial drive after working in Adlai Stevenson's 1970 Senate campaign. During Walker's walk through the state, Caravello was an advance person, a man on the move as he helped line up the route, found homes in which Walker could spend nights and performed other assorted tasks. A lot of hustle was required of Caravello, a chunky individual who himself was not that crazy about walking. But hustle he did, throughout his years with Walker, and afterward as a successful producer for CBS News in Chicago and Washington.

In the early days of Walker's governorship, the downright hostility of many House members to Caravello prompted an expression of sympathy one day from a veteran Democrat in the chamber, James Holloway of Sparta.

"That poor guy (Caravello) may have the toughest go here because he just can't get any respect trying to represent Walker's interests on bills," remarked Holloway. "It's too bad he doesn't get a little more courtesy now and then because he's really not a bad fellow."

Holloway, a southern Illinoisan with a brother, Robert, in the Walker administration, was among a handful of independent Democrats in the House who tried to give Walker a fair shake as often as they could. They usually were outnumbered greatly, though, by Republicans and the more numerous Democrats under the thumb of Daley.

Sometime cohorts of Holloway in the House's independent Democratic bloc in those days included Glencoe attorney Harold Katz, Highland Park lawyer Daniel Pierce, North Chicago's John Matijevich, Chicago attorney Robert Mann, Tobias Barry of Ladd, Bensenville's William Redmond, Naperville history teacher J. Glenn Schneider, young Michael McClain of Quincy, Taylorville attorney Rolland Tipsword, Eugenia Chapman of Arlington Heights, Chicagoan James M. Houlihan, a newly-elected Walkerite, and black Chicago lawyer Harold Washington, who a decade later would be elected mayor of his city.

On certain issues, Kane did forge coalitions of some Republicans and Democrats not beholden to Daley, but keeping them together was impossible. Most of the time, Kane knew he "just had too few cards to play." Compounding the problem, in Kane's view, was the attitude of the Governor's office itself.

After joining Walker, Kane recommended an administration approach to the General Assembly based on "an informed give-and-take" between the two branches that would lead to "a community of shared values" between the two. Translated, this meant Kane wanted to include the legislative leadership when possible in the Governor's decision-making on issues. Kane favored talking things out ahead of time, seeing where disputes could be avoided.

However, he recalled later, "the Governor's office did not buy this approach, because it basically viewed the General Assembly as an obstacle or a body to be manipulated and not as an equal partner in running state government."

This reflected, Kane averred, "Vic's desire to treat the General Assembly the same way Daley did the Chicago City Council. The Governor would make the decision and then the General Assembly was expected to fall in line."

"Of course, the Governor found out this just didn't work."

That was Kane's conclusion. Walker and others on his team

looked at it differently.

Said the Governor, "We would have been delighted to engage in a meaningful dialogue, but none was possible. Not when the leadership of both parties in at least the House was determined to cut our throats."

Over time, Walker did engage in a discourse of sorts with the General Assembly, including regular breakfast meetings at the Mansion with the Democratic leaders and sporadic appearances at Democratic caucuses.

However, he was particularly distrustful of Chicagoan Cecil Partee, the Democratic minority leader in the Senate, especially on issues of concern to Daley.

Senator Philip Rock of Chicago, an assistant minority leader and another Daley person, was to Walker "a political gentleman who would level with me on how he was going to vote." Unlike Partee, Walker contended, "Phil did not engage in back alley groin kicking."

On Partee, Walker would relate a case in point.

"I could never forget when he told me at breakfast more than one morning that there was nothing troublesome coming up in the Senate that day. But, as soon as the Senate convened he proceeded to lead Democratic senators from Chicago on votes to deny confirmation to some of my key cabinet nominees."

Walker had kinder words for Representative Gerald W. Shea of Chicago suburb Riverside, an assistant minority leader in the lower chamber and Daley's floor leader in the body. Shea was one of those rare legislators who actually read bills and grasped their details, and Walker respected that.

Although Shea was a "shark" to Walker when he worked against the Governor's bills, Walker found Shea "a tenacious ally when he was on our side." In comparison to Partee, added Walker, "when Jerry was with you, he was with you all the way."

Observers of Walker noticed that he seemed to have little

tolerance for fence straddlers. One either was with the man and his cause or was not. Forget the middle ground bit. However, Walker watchers noted, it was especially tricky trying to apply that yardstick to legislators, a number of whom were notorious middle-of-the-roaders.

In his own mind, Walker tried to take a cosmic view of the legislative scene. Of his problems with the lawmakers. Of the light in which the General Assembly and its role was cast, or miscast, by the press and others.

Any realistic appraisal, the Governor believed, would conclude that conflict between the executive and legislative branches was not avoidable in view of the different ways the two entities approached issues. Because of the sharp distinctions between the power base of each branch.

"This conflict happens in every state to one degree or another," said Walker, "but the situation was aggravated in my case because I was to some degree a total outsider, not just a newcomer, and because I was perceived almost as an enemy by the Daley forces as soon as it was apparent that I was not going to always go along with Daley on state matters related to Cook County."

Walker believed that the Chicago mayor had openly run state government during the governorship of Democrat Otto Kerner in the 1960s, years in which Daley worked in cahoots with certain key downstate Democratic legislators and state officials, like the late Paul Powell. Daley also had fared well with Ogilvie, Walker insisted, leaving downstate politically dispirited, irrespective of the occupant of the governor's chair.

The time for an end to Chicago domination of the legislative process was overdue, Walker felt, and at last the right person, namely himself, had reached a position to make that happen.

"In the Legislature, as well as in other areas of politics, I wanted to tip the balance more toward downstate than it had been. The Chicago machine just had too much control."

Yet, Walker would argue, "I could never get across to the media the governmental importance of that division of power between the Democratic Governor and the Democratic mayor of Chicago. They kept seeing it as a personal political battle rather than as a contest over Chicago domination of state government.

"It was a vital, fundamental thing, but my standing up to Daley was reported as pure confrontational politics on my part—often with no mention of the proper governmental overtones involved in regard to substantive policies affecting everybody in the state.

"It was easy with the Legislature, as elsewhere, to just call me a confrontationist.

"But, just as it takes two to confront, it takes two to accommodate. And if somebody isn't willing to accommodate on a reasonable basis, then you can't accommodate with them or you cannot accommodate them. Daley was not known as an accommodator on anything.

"So, when I was beset by superior forces with no intention of accommodating because they could get their way without any fuss, then I had to go public in order to fight them because my only power base was the public. This was the only way I could fight Daley because he had the legislative horses to win any clash from which the opinion and input of the public could be excluded."

Nothing was more of an institution in Illinois than the General Assembly, more ingrained in the state governmental fabric that Walker had lambasted as evil in running for his office.

After arriving in Springfield, a place largely unknown to a lot of Walker people, many of them quickly became wide-eyed at the legislative arena, amazed by its culture and the frenetic subcultures that it bred.

Like the innocents of a Mark Twain novel, the Walkerites surely found it wild and wicked and more than a little crazy.

There was all that seemingly incongruous activity both inside and outside the chambers, as harried legislators dashed pell-mell from the muddle of the chamber floors to the crush outside the chamber doors of lobbyists, protest groups and bewildered tourists wishing they had not wandered to the Capitol's third floor.

Not unlike a stock exchange, the third floor balcony between the House and Senate under the magnificent dome of the Statehouse often was a cacophonous melange of racetrack owners, public aid recipients, railroad barons, civil rights activists, highstrung persons for and against abortion and so on. All trying to forge their deals, or block an individual standing three feet away from making his. The great meeting place, where everyone's interests converged, like no other spot in the state.

Often, when things got hot, well dressed lobbyists would jostle for coveted space along the storied brass rail riding the parapet that circled the balcony of the third floor. That rail, with its elaborate lampposts, the cynosure of so much Illinois legislative lore, and fiction.

Fiction, yes, because most of the boisterous engagements along the shiny rail were superfluous, little more than good theater for those wanting, needing to be seen.

The deliberations that counted usually proceeded away from the crowd in the quiet offices of the legislative leaders behind the two chambers. Inconspicuous back rooms, the deal-making parlors so anathema to Walker.

Governor or not, Walker had a hard nut to crack in the General Assembly.

This became evident early in 1973 with the showdown over Walker's veto of the bill on emergency state aid to the Chicago Transit Authority and other mass transit systems.

Walker asked in his requested revision of the bill that state aid dollars to the CTA be matched by Chicago and Cook County. He refused to go along with the measure's provision of $2 in state funds for each local dollar, saying it was not acceptable state fiscal policy even though shutdowns were being threatened by cash-starved transit operations in the state's urban areas.

So, Daley and other big city leaders concluded they had no choice but to seek the three-fifths vote needed in each house to overturn Walker's veto.

The mass transit package had been hammered out by legislative leaders of both parties after weeks of intense negotiations that almost had paralyzed the General Assembly. During that time, even some Democratic legislators said they had received no guidance on the matter from Walker.

Consequently, many persons viewed Walker's veto as an attack on Daley, whose constituency would be the main beneficiary of the transit aid bill. Of course, the action by Walker would not hurt his already strong standing downstate, where Chicago's problems seldom generated sympathy.

But Walker lost this encounter in the Legislature, where his veto was overridden for a number of reasons. Obviously, Chicago Democrats were not about to support the Governor against the interests of their city and its mayor.

Interestingly, Democrats from other parts of the state also were persuaded to stick with Daley. The fact that the case for Daley was relayed to many downstate Democrats from urban areas by former Mayor Alvin Fields of East St. Louis, an old ally of Daley, illustrated that Walker very much remained up against a still potent old boy network in his own party.

Republicans normally would have jumped at a chance for combat with Daley, but many voted to override Walker because of what they denounced as his demonstrated disrespect for the Legislature.

The veto override fight certainly had more than its quota of spin-offs and subplots. Take the imbroglio over Robert G. Gibson, then the secretary-treasurer of the Illinois AFL-CIO.

Gibson had been nominated by Walker for chairman of the state's Capital Development Board, which oversaw the funding and construction of state buildings. The selection of Gibson, a former Granite City steelworker, was a significant concession by Walker to labor, the state leadership of which had been lukewarm to Walker's election because of its close affiliation with Daley.

However, word got out that Gibson had gone onto the floor of the House to ask members to overturn the Governor's transit veto, saying that immediate state aid to mass transit operations would benefit thousands of union members. Viewing this as an act of total disloyalty, Walker withdrew Gibson's nomination.

After being dumped, Gibson said he was told in a telephone conversation with de Grazia:

"This is war, and you are in the enemy camp. We should have known when the chips were down you would line up with Daley."

A number of legislators contended that they had been offered either jobs or pork barrel projects for their districts in return for a vote to uphold the veto. Walker retorted that such things were not mentioned in calls to lawmakers. Caravello was more graphic, calling the charge baloney.

Later on during his term, after umpteen wrangles with the Legislature, Walker would acknowledge that he "saw nothing wrong with the judicious and careful use of patronage in dealing with the General Assembly. You cannot govern without it. Obviously, it can be overdone. But I don't think we overdid it."

To the end, Walker maintained that he and his crew stood their ground against the more distasteful entreaties from legislators, those "wanting to protect the jobs of their mistresses in the executive branch, the few open to bribes, the few whose word could never be trusted."

In Walker's words, "a job for an uncle, a son, a contributor or a mistress was coin of the realm in Springfield—and always will be. Even some legislators who worked against me did not hesitate to ask Vic for jobs. Sometimes, even a Republican legislator would sneak into my office and ask for a favor.

"Of course, the fact that few of these individuals had given me a vote was, they felt, to be discounted. Their rationalization, naturally, was that as currents shift the legislator who is against you today may be for you tomorrow."

By the time of the conclusion of the first six-month session of the Seventy-eighth Legislature in early July of 1973, the reading on the new Governor was not much clearer than at the beginning of the year. He remained a puzzle.

Nobody would say that the General Assembly had danced to any tune of Walker. Nor had the Governor danced to anybody else's tune. After that, impressions varied from table to table.

Walker really submitted few proposals to the Republican-led bodies. Attempts to inject himself into legislative deliberations were sporadic at best. When he did, he was snubbed more often than not.

Most of those in the business of defining such weighty matters found Walker's first dance with the General Assembly a pretty clumsy waltz. His reluctance to even try to take charge, so unlike his predecessor, left a leadership vacuum that in turn provided an opportunity for the legislators to seize the initiative on governmental policies. But, not surprisingly, this resulted in an unusually disjointed session in which no faction in either of the almost evenly divided houses was able to assert its will clearly.

For his part, Walker sought to remind those who would listen that, unlike some in the governor's seat before him, he did not see new legislation as the principal answer to many of the state's problems. And, too, he realized that the more legislation he pushed, the more rebuffs he would face from the essentially hostile General Assembly.

All of this was not to say, though, that nothing came of the session.

Measures were passed to set up constitutionally required state boards to supervise elections and elementary and secondary education.

There were developments like the approval of a bill delaying for at least several years—and probably longer—state enforcement of regulations aimed at limiting emissions of sulfur dioxide from the burning of Illinois coal. Since the emissions were considered a major cause of air pollution by environmentalists, they would await anxiously Walker's reaction to this measure, which was sought by the coal industry.

Also, persons on both sides in the age-old debate over the death penalty got their juices flowing over a measure sent to Walker that would require a mandatory death penalty for persons convicted of certain kinds of murder, such as the killing of public officials, on-duty police officers and prison guards.

The bill, sponsored by Henry Hyde, was an outgrowth of a campaign to reinstate capital punishment in Illinois. It was drawn in an effort to circumvent constitutional hurdles raised by the United States Supreme Court decision a year earlier against capital punishment. Liberal opponents of the death penalty strongly opposed the bill.

A lot of other issues were addressed.

Walker had voiced support in his State of the State Message for greater legal safeguards for the rights of reporters, calling them "an indispensable fourth branch of government."

Even though "all of us in public life have our moments of displeasure with the media," said Walker, "I find alarming the recent court-imposed limits on the rights of reporters." As a result, he called for legislation "protecting them and their news sources."

Subsequently, much fanfare accompanied the numerous measures submitted during the session that were intended to protect reporters who refused to disclose sources. But the so-called newspersons' shield bills, like many other proposals, would not make it through the GOP-controlled Senate.

Approval of proposed legislation establishing a state lottery and freezing property taxes throughout Illinois was put off.

Legislation that would have created a statewide uniform, professional probation system through the administrative office of the Illinois courts, an objective backed by Walker, was killed by the Senate Judiciary Committee. Other attempts at criminal justice system reforms also went down the drain during the session, mostly because of political jealousies.

In spite of the widespread clamor for campaign funding reform, one of the hottest issues in the 1972 election campaign, the Senate refused to pass a House-approved bill requiring detailed public disclosure of contributions and expenditures in connection with races for state offices, the General Assembly and the judiciary.

Before the end of the following year, though, Walker would be a big winner on this subject. In October of 1974 the state's first campaign finance disclosure statute, finally passed by the General Assembly, went into effect with Walker's signature on it. On this issue, Walker was not to be denied.

A bill to allow 19-year-olds to drink beer and wine starting Oct. 1 of that year was passed by the legislators and signed by Walker before the lawmakers went home.

The General Assembly also approved creation of a new state agency, the Department on Aging, to handle programs and problems related to older individuals. There was a quirk here, though.

Such a plan normally would come from the Governor. But this one was drafted by the new Lieutenant Governor, Neil Hartigan, and sponsored by Blair and Clyde Choate.

Walker did ask Hartigan to work on the problems of senior citizens, but the Governor was not part of the maneuvering to bring about the new agency. The initiative by Hartigan—even though he was a Daley loyalist predictably having little harmonious contact with Walker—still was near the top of the list of idiosyncrasies in a session of little rhyme or reason.

At least, that's what the analysts deduced after the session. Little rhyme or reason.

Privately, Walker was not about to argue. He also didn't really care. The incoherence of the main 1973 session, Walker advocates believed, would not adversely affect their man's apparently solid standing with much of the electorate, partly because of the ill will toward the Legislature harbored by so many in the state.

However, it went deeper than that with Walker.

Although Walker would do his best in the 1974 election to ensure a friendlier General Assembly, he found himself intrinsically at odds with much of the conventional wisdom on the Legislature and its relationship to the governorship and the people of Illinois. In a number of ways, Walker felt, the importance of the General Assembly was blown out of proportion.

For one thing, Walker decried "this continual preoccupation with the legislature in evaluating an administration.

"Most of the books and papers that are written assessing a presidency or a governor look at the executive's program in the legislature. What did he get through the legislature?

"Perhaps defensively, I was never preoccupied with that. I just think it's too much emphasized in the lore and by scholars and commentators."

While the Illinois General Assembly was to Walker "a good sounding board for new issues," the Governor was convinced that "most people in Illinois, and I think this rings true across the country, are much more affected in their daily lives by the operations of the executive and administrative parts of government than by 90 percent of the bills that go through the General Assembly."

After it was over for him, Walker would look back and conclude that "most of the activity of the General Assembly tying up a governor is devoted to things with relatively little impact on the populace at large. The unfortunate part of this is that it can cut into the need to concentrate on management of government, the area where I really tried to spend my time as governor."

In that first State of the State Message, Walker did tell the legislators that "making the day-to-day affairs of state government work better is properly the function of the governor.

"Of the many hats which I may wear, it is the one I expect to put on most often. This is the task I have looked forward to. This is the job I shall enjoy most."

Innovation in government, he had added, "does not only mean creating new programs. It also entails devising new ways to make existing programs more efficient."

To carry this out, Walker had to have good people in important administrative slots, persons he wanted. That was why he was angered most during the session by the almost systematic rejection of a number of his key appointees by the old-line Republican-dominated Senate Executive Committee.

Walker knew the caliber of his administration would rise or fall on the performance of his governing team. He had no choice but to bring many fresh faces into Illinois' corridors of power.

There were winners who would make him proud. But a few bad apples snuck in. And some real characters, too. ❧

16

The Cabinet— Walker's Chorus Line

For a moment or so, Victor de Grazia thought he was dreaming. Sure enough, though, as he awoke from a slumber in Woodlawn hospital, a figure was looming over his bed.

Then, the next thing the groggy de Grazia remembered, the individual was dabbing drops of oil on Vic's forehead from a vial— oil that the dabber said had been blessed by the top religious leader of Greece.

As the uninvited visitor to de Grazia's room wished the patient Godspeed in recovering from his recent heart attack, Vic finally got his eyes open enough to recognize the man. He was the Greek businessman from Chicago whom the Walker people had revealed they intended to name director of the Illinois Department of Insurance.

Anthony Angelos.

Not long afterward, de Grazia would wish that he only had dreamed of Angelos, that the fellow never had crossed the path of de Grazia and Dan Walker.

Later, after all the misery of the Angelos affair had been visited upon the Walker crowd, it fell to de Grazia to end it, or try to. This was not easy for Victor since by then he was taking medicine to help his heart handle tension.

What de Grazia wound up doing was to summon Angelos to Vic's home in Kenwood to inform him that Walker just could not go through with the intended nomination of Angelos. However, the damage was done. Alibi in public as much as they tried, Vic and Dan really were kicking themselves over this one.

Especially since Walker was determined to put together a cabinet that would bring great credit to his governorship and the citizens of Illinois. Second to none.

He wanted experts in their fields to run most agencies, with only a minimum of purely political choices. This meant going out of state in some cases, a decision that earned Walker predictable criticism from the Illinois first gang.

But the nationwide search paid dividends, Walker was convinced, with the recruitment of persons like revenue director Robert Allphin and the courtly and eventually quite popular Langhorne Bond, chosen to serve as secretary of the Department of Transportation.

As might be expected, at least two of the out of staters, David Fogel and Jerry Miller, caused the new Governor headaches. Also, several of the homegrown appointees, such as Mary Lee Leahy, opened a door to recrimination by Walker's political foes.

But, like his appointments or not, political iconoclast Walker tried to stock his cabinet with standouts, some boat rockers like himself. Not like the dull starched shirt, buttoned-down collar types directing so many of the state agencies in the days since Walker. For sure, a large number of those Walker people, the down-home agriculture chief Pud Williams and others, were good copy for the press. Some intentionally, some not.

Although Walker was not exactly an impartial judge, he felt that on the whole he was more than willing to stack up his cabinet against any other in modern Illinois history.

"It was a hard working cabinet, and I spent a lot of time with the members. I believed I should be held responsible for their key decisions and that, in turn, they should be bound by mine. Loyalty up and loyalty down."

As is usual in the course of human affairs, a few old Walker sidekicks were tapped for directorships. Elliot Epstein, Walker's fellow trench fighter in the embryonic days of dissident Democratic politics, headed the Department of Finance.

At the Department of Law Enforcement, which rode herd on the State Police, Walker put Harvey N. Johnson, Jr., in charge. Johnson had been executive director of the Walker-led Chicago Crime Commission and was, along with de Grazia, an assistant director of the study team staff for the Walker Report.

Walker felt comfortable with guys like them, persons who had paid their dues with Walker. Individuals he could trust behind his back, knowing they were sure bets. Walker had to have a certain number of Epsteins and Johnsons around to cushion the administration against the wave makers.

Walker had no intention of being a gubernatorial caretaker, a governmental baby-sitter. Some sectors had to be shaken up— because innovative change was needed and because the electorate expected it from Dan Walker.

Enter David Fogel, and along with him the hurricane that surrounded his nomination to head the Department of Corrections.

The early word on Fogel, when it was revealed he was leaving Minnesota for Illinois, was that he had earned nationwide praise from sociologists and others as a novel originator of penal administration revisions that made prisons more compassionate places. His efforts to liberalize the running of Minnesota's prisons apparently were viewed by Walker as the way to go in Illinois, where penal management changes begun under Ogilvie already had alienated those favoring hard-line operation of the system, including many guards.

Putting it gently, these old-line penologists went bananas over the coming of Fogel.

They threw everything they had into a campaign to discredit the man and his actions in Minnesota, charging that he fathered a permissiveness in that state's prisons resulting in an inmate takeover at the expense of security and penal employees' morale.

Fogel's critics could not believe that once, while Minnesota correctional commissioner, he actually spent several days in the capacity of an inmate at the state's prison at Stillwater or that he opposed capital punishment even when the murder of a prison guard was involved.

Trying to douse the fire in Illinois, Fogel insisted that his programs were necessary to correct "the obvious failures of a fortress-like prison system."

Fogel probably had not encountered anybody in Minnesota, though, like Illinois State Senator John A. Graham, a surly Republican from Barrington who, besides sitting on the Senate Executive Committee, was chairman of the State Commission to Visit and Examine Penal Institutions. His nickname of "Black Jack" reflected his no-nonsense approach to penal management. From the moment the opposition to Fogel rallied behind Graham, Fogel was a dead duck.

In the weeks before the executive panel took up the confirmation of Fogel in early 1973, Graham visited Minnesota and other places to obtain background information aimed at killing the nomination of Fogel. Graham got such an earful on Fogel that, upon returning to Illinois, the senator allowed as how he could "write a book on the things I've accumulated (on Fogel)."

The list seemed endless, even encompassing allegations of left-wing activity by Fogel back in his days in New York and Berkeley, Calif. On the penal side, a lot of the criticism focused on actions by Fogel that either paved the way for premature release of felons or authorized excessive contact between convicts and the outside world.

The verdict of the Executive Committee, sitting in the Capitol's most embellished hearing room, was preordained. All 13 Republicans on the panel, even the few not regarded as conservative, voted to reject Fogel. Eight of the nine Democrats supported him. Since there was no way the full Senate would override the committee, Dan Walker had been slapped in the face.

Through the Executive Committee, the political establishment finally had a clear shot at its tormentor, the new Governor, for one of the first times since he assumed office.

Although rejection by the Senate of even one appointee of Walker would have been a rare happening in Illinois, Fogel was just one of a bunch of Walker nominees for major posts who did not receive Senate confirmation during Walker's first year in office.

Along with Fogel, the best known rejectee was Mary Leahy.

After Walker's election, Mary and husband Andy both were on the transition team laying groundwork for Walker's entry into office. Then, before his inauguration, Walker announced he was naming Mrs. Leahy to run the Environmental Protection Agency.

As for her husband, Walker asked him to serve as liaison between Walker and the multitude of state boards and commissions comprised of gubernatorial appointees and dealing with every subject, big and small, in Illinois. This would not always be an easy job for Andy since Walker demanded balanced representation on the panels for women and minorities, leaving Andrew Leahy often scratching his head at the difficulty in finding, say, a woman who also happened to be black and an engineer. But, unlike his wife, Andy didn't need Senate confirmation for his then $21,996 a year job under Walker.

As it turned out, Mary Lee Leahy would only direct the EPA for a few months. In failing to win Senate confirmation as EPA head, she felt the bitter sting of political revenge in that opposition to her confirmation was spearheaded by Chicago senators bossed by Daley, whom she had antagonized so openly.

The Chicago machine had vowed to remind Mrs. Leahy one day of her legal efforts in the successful move to deny Daley delegates seating at the 1972 Democratic National Convention. That day had arrived sooner than anticipated by the Daleyites, thanks to her nomination for EPA director by the equally despised Dan Walker, and Mrs. Leahy had gotten the message right between the eyes.

Those were anxious days at the EPA, while the nomination of Mrs. Leahy was in limbo. The spirit of employees was down because many felt the agency itself was being dragged through the mud as the controversy over Mary Lee's nomination was being played out.

One day, as all this was going on, the EPA's Springfield headquarters staff was summoned to the parking lot. To the amazement of many, Governor Walker was waiting on the lot to address the hastily-assembled crew, to voice his strong support, not just for Mrs. Leahy, but also for the EPA and its mission. An impromptu pep talk to several hundred state workers by the Governor at an out-of-the-way facility. A new twist.

John (Jack) Moore, chief of the Division of Noise Pollution Control in the EPA at the time, never forgot it.

"It was a very uplifting thing because many of the (EPA) people had never actually even seen a governor," recalled Moore. "It said to us that somebody really was paying attention to us. We were not just some forgotten bureaucratic program off in a corner."

After her rejection, Mary Leahy was given a job by Walker as his liaison to state agencies on environmental affairs. Later on, Walker put her back in his cabinet by naming her director of the Department of Children and Family Services, a post for which the Senate did confirm her.

At DCFS, she was asked by Walker to unravel the chaos linked to his first director of the agency, the import from Massachusetts, Jerome Miller. Miller turned out to be a disappointment to Walker, and the Governor found it necessary to ask him to resign.

As he did in Massachusetts, Miller tried to revamp an Illinois program serving close to 30,000 neglected and dependent children, getting a number of the young persons out of institutionalized settings and into private homes. In seeking to do this, though, Miller had turned the department's management, organization and policies upside down.

"I worked very closely with Director Miller, and I really thought we could pull it off because Jerry had done it in Massachusetts," Walker related afterward.

"However, he just couldn't cope with the much larger department in Illinois undergoing so much massive change. Our department was coming apart at the seams under him. So we failed."

Surprise was evident in some quarters that Miller had not been blocked by the Senate from serving as a director in the first place because of his reputation as a radical administrator back in the East. Also, it seemed clear to many that Walker saw the attention-getting Miller, assuming he had worked out in Illinois, as one of the tickets to national recognition for the Walker administration.

Like Miller, the also controversial Anthony Dean escaped blockage by the Senate and was able to serve as state conservation director.

Leaders of several veterans organizations had pressed the Executive Committee to give Dean a hostile reception, and not just because some persons thought that Dean at 27 years of age was too young for a major cabinet seat in a big state like Illinois.

The veterans also were upset about the conscientious objector status of Dean, a self-styled environmental preservation activist. But Dean prevailed, and proceeded to become a rather adept manager of the Department of Conservation.

Of course, the proposed cabinet member who really caused Walker a black eye was Angelos. The Governor never recovered fully from that embarrassment, which turned into a gold mine for his detractors.

In reality, the nomination of Angelos did not get as far as the Senate's executive panel because it was withdrawn by Walker a little over a week after the Governor took office. Many legislators, editorial writers and leaders of the insurance industry had made a virtual crusade out of their insistence that Walker reconsider the selection of Angelos.

Almost any kind of background check by Walker operatives would have revealed the problems likely to occur in pushing Angelos for a public position.

A few years back, in 1969, President Nixon refused to go along with a recommendation that Angelos be named United States ambassador to Greece after information surfaced indicating Angelos well could be an embarrassment for the country.

A confidential letter that year to Senator Everett Dirksen of Illinois from Robert Walker, then acting executive director of the old Illinois Crime Commission, detailed many situations raising questions about the business and private activities of Angelos, including the charge that he had substantial dealings with Chicago mobsters.

Angelos came into Dan Walker's life shortly before the November 1972 election when he provided $50,000 to the campaign, money sorely needed "to keep the TV commercials going."

Walker knew in accepting the money that Angelos wanted a high profile in any Walker administration.

Every day, Walker later would lament, "elected officials and candidates face an ethical standards quandary, raising funds from people you know are going to want something. It's a tough area. Where do you draw the line?"

To many persons, Walker's nomination of Angelos for Illinois insurance director clearly was inconsistent with Walker's persistent campaign attacks on the traditional political reward practices in both parties. It was great ammunition for those who sought to portray Walker as just another hypocritical politician, no better than the ones he had criticized so sharply.

Another damaging aspect of the Angelos affair was that it dragged on and on. Although Walker aids had not contested initial depiction of the Angelos $50,000 as a contribution, Walker later said the money was a loan, an interest free one repaid in full by the end of March 1973.

This was interesting in that the Illinois Liquor Control Commission, a gubernatorially-appointed panel, had gotten into the act by looking into the possibility that Angelos may have violated state law by contributing to the Walker campaign.

This possibility existed because Angelos was reported to have ties to one or more liquor-dispensing enterprises in the Chicago area, and Illinois liquor license holders were not permitted to make campaign contributions to a party or a candidate in the state.

Although the matter eventually petered out, at least two chairmen of the liquor control body said they were fired by Walker for backing the inquiry into the Angelos contribution, or loan, to Walker.

The first was Donald G. Adams, a Quincy attorney named to the post by Ogilvie. Walker said he canned Adams because the commission had not revoked the licenses of a racetrack concessionaire who had made political contributions.

The other fired chairman was Lawrence E. Johnson, a Democrat and former state's attorney of Champaign County who was named to the liquor regulation job by Walker.

Johnson contended that he was ousted after he rebuffed attempts by persons close to the Governor to limit the Angelos inquiry. Walker's office said Johnson was dismissed because he refused to implement operating efficiencies at the commission.

Ironically, in 1974 Anthony Angelos was denied permission by the state to acquire an insurance and investment company. The person who rejected the Angelos bid was Fred A. Mauck, a relatively unknown individual serving as state insurance director, the position once ticketed for the notorious Angelos.

One cabinet member who did become well known, in part because of his name, was Pud Williams, the director of the Department of Agriculture. A fascinating person, far from bland, Williams would strike up a close friendship with Walker enduring long after their Springfield stay had ended.

Williams was a White County farm boy, one of a group of southern Illinoisans in Walker's cabinet.

Others included Nolan B. Jones, who was living in Cairo when Walker named him director of the Department of Personnel; Russell T. Dawe of Valier, head of the Department of Mines and Minerals; Dean Barringer of Anna, director of the Department of Registration and Education; and Frank Kirk of Carbondale, tabbed to run the Department of Local Government Affairs.

Another cabinet member, Roland W. Burris, who went on to bigger things in the years after Walker, grew up in the south central Illinois railroad town of Centralia. Burris was not as well known in his Centralia High School days as his sports chum and fellow black Bobby Joe Mason, a star basketball player who eventually landed with the Harlem Globetrotters.

But Burris would get his turn in the limelight. Under Walker, attorney Burris served as director of the Department of General Services, the centralized housekeeping agency for state government. This followed a stint as a vice president of Continental Illinois National Bank in Chicago.

Later, in 1978, Democrat Burris was elected to the first of three successive four-year terms as state comptroller. After that, he was elected Illinois attorney general in 1990, thereby establishing himself as another major legacy of the Walker governorship.

The makeup of Walker's cabinet was a true cross section, fully reflective of the great diversity of Illinois.

Every tribe was represented. The medical community included. It had a contingent that embraced individuals like Dr. LeRoy P. Levitt, a Chicago medical school dean who was Walker's director of the Department of Mental Health.

Everybody had somebody in the cabinet, or on one of the boards or commissions, which was the way it should have been. And everyone on board, from the highbrows on down, wanted to spend as much time as possible with the leader, the Governor whose political star appeared so meteoric.

But not many, if any of the persons Walker brought into high places in Illinois government (save for those in the inner circle), were as tight with the boss as Pud Williams—which said quite a bit about Walker and the individuals with whom he felt at ease.

A prominent farm figure and county board member from an out-of-the-way part of the state, the pipe-smoking Williams had a down-to-earth, plainspoken manner that made him appear hokey to city slickers but a rustic philosopher to Capitol reporters starved for characters to cover in the largely sterile atmosphere of state government.

Explaining his outspokenness, which made good copy, Williams opined that "if you don't stand for something, you might as well be a tree." Pud was, assured his wife Dorothy, "no shrinking violet."

Not with the start he had. Robert Junior Williams was supposed to be Robert Pierce Williams, Jr. However, the doctor delivering him was imbibing a little too much at Pud's birth and got the name wrong on the birth certificate. But, Robert J. Williams did inherit the nickname Pud from his farmer father.

No shrinking violet. Hardly an understatement. In the early 1980s, when Williams was unhappy with the daily Carmi Times, he took the bold but impulsive step of founding a rival newspaper, a weekly regional publication called the Southeastern Tribune. Williams was sole owner and publisher of the paper, which came out six or eight times before he abruptly shut it down.

In closing it, he announced that "my purpose was to publish a good paper and show a profit. I succeeded with the first goal but not with the second." Williams lost $75,000 on the venture.

Williams, who was four years younger than Walker, had a 1,400-acre grain and livestock farm in an area named Centerville northwest of the White County seat of Carmi that he and his family continued to operate while he was state agriculture director. After Walker took office, the Williams farm was visited by the Governor, who like to traipse around the Carmi area with Williams, hunting doves and quail.

Actually, Williams never had met or talked to Walker before he was asked by Walker after the election to come to Chicago to discuss with Walker the agriculture directorship. When the two got together, Walker asked him on the spot to take the job.

Williams did, though, have ties to the Walker campaign. Dorothy Williams, who had been Dorothy Given back in her rural Crossville days, picked up on the Walker candidacy when he was walking the state. Also, a young man working on the Williams farm in the summer of 1971 would become a principal organizer of the Walker campaign in southeastern Illinois.

He was David Vaught, a law school student whose late father was a first cousin of Pud's mother. The Vaught family home in Carmi was a beehive of activity for Walker, even to the listing of one phone in the home in the name of the family dog, a black Labrador named Buddy, in a move to get enough residential phones at the house to qualify for a special rate. Buddy Vaught remained listed in the Carmi phone book for a few years afterward.

Another funny thing happened. Love. As the campaign moved along, Williams could not help but notice that Kathleen Marie, the oldest of the Walker daughters, spent an increasing and seemingly inordinate amount of time with David Vaught in his section of the state.

"David and Kathy would visit Dorothy and I, and we were suspecting something was going on between them," Williams said. "But, this was during the campaign, and they denied it." After Walker became Governor, Vaught and Kathleen were married.

Character or not, Williams was a hardheaded boss of the Department of Agriculture, streamlining the operating divisions and striving to protect Illinois farmers from financial losses when grain elevators were going belly up, a national crisis at the time.

He never was at a loss for words. When asked about the health of crops, Williams would say a crop "is in bad shape if I thought it was in bad shape" even though "some of the political image people didn't like me being so blunt."

Blunt to the end.

Pud and Dorothy Williams exercised their prerogative to live in a house provided for the agriculture director and his family at the Illinois State Fairgrounds at Springfield. While there, they presided over numerous luncheons and other functions befitting the first couple of Illinois agriculture.

When they arrived in Springfield, in the words of Williams,

"many people wanted to help me unpack.

"When I left, I had to hire somebody to do the packing." ❧

Life with the Press

Dan Walker really did hate the gridiron dinners put on by the men and women in the Statehouse press corps or, as they were known more formally, the members of the Illinois Legislative Correspondents Association.

Witnesses still insisted years later that Walker, unable to suppress his anger, bit through more than one pipe stem as he watched the elite of Illinois officialdom, mainly himself, ridiculed unmercifully each year in searing songs and skits written and performed by the reporters.

The press crowd gleefully let Walker have it between the eyes at those shindigs. To the scribes, the Governor's personality was erratic, even bordering at times on strange. Most viewed him as a poor sport, with not much of a sense of humor to begin with.

A number of the reporters simply did not like him, and most of those who felt this way made no secret of it. A more perfect target for the gridiron roasters could not be found.

The governorship of Dan Walker was clouded by an abominable relationship with the Capitol press corps and with many of the key editors and editorial writers back in the home offices of the larger newspapers.

The antagonism sorely undermined the public's perception of Walker's stewardship of the office—every bit as much as his storied differences with Mayor Daley and the rest of the state's establishment.

For a man with the political acumen and public track record of Walker, the Governor sometimes seemed to be amazingly inept in dealing with the news media. Or, for that matter, in even grasping the importance for a governor of maintaining credible relations with the press.

In the end, the jumbled tale of Walker and the media was one of miscalculation by a major political figure who stood to have a world to gain by courting the press, a task that should have come naturally for a fellow with the polish and know-how of Walker.

It really did seem that he could have done much more to help himself with the wild bunch in the Statehouse pressroom—an enclave unlike any other part of the Capitol that was experiencing during the Walker years the final chapter of a gloriously robust era.

Certain things, though, got in the way of rational discourse between Walker and the reporters covering him. One was the professed attitude of Walker himself.

Another reason, one more important, was the atmosphere in the pressroom, which was engaging in a period of hardball Statehouse news coverage that had started in the Kerner years and reached a frenzied pitch during Ogilvie's time in office.

For those only happening upon the Illinois governmental scene in the years since Kerner, Ogilvie and Walker, it was understandable that they might have little feeling for the terror and aggravation once inflicted on the high and mighty and the rest of officialdom by the zealous reporters assigned in the 1960s and early 1970s to cover the Statehouse.

In those years, people flocked every day to the first floor newsstand off the Capitol rotunda to grab the morning papers or await the arrival of the old afternoon papers, eager to read the frequent disclosures about the unseemly doings of the elected and appointed officials entrusted by the citizens to run state government.

No office or person on the public payroll seemed safe back then from those reporters hell-bent on snooping into every cranny. No file drawer or voucher on state expenditures was off-limits to their prying eyes.

The Statehouse pressroom in Walker's day was just a darn good story in itself, every bit as absorbing as the unconventional chronicle of Walker himself.

For a man with the stubborn pride of Walker, he would voice almost a touch of repentance when he sought afterward to dissect his much too painful dealings with the press. In hindsight, Walker felt that he would have gone at it differently with the fourth estate, especially the press gang in the Capitol, if political life had given him one more shot.

"In all fairness, I must admit that although I had great problems with the Springfield press corps, I brought a lot of it on myself. I don't blame it totally on them. I did not work to establish good press relations.

"I said that there should be an adversarial role between the press and the Illinois chief executive, and I will always believe that should be the case. That's the way America has always worked.

The two factions were not meant to be buddy-buddy.

"However, I probably carried that thinking too far. By adversarial, I didn't mean confrontational or fighting. I just felt the two should distance themselves from each other. There should be mutual respect, but the reporters had to be critical of me to do their jobs."

Frequently stung by negative stories, leading figures in the Walker administration predictably found themselves blaming Norton Kay, to his face and behind his back, for doing a poor job as press secretary. Making a scapegoat of Kay was an easy out, though, and failed to take into account that Kay's often standoffish manner with the press was in deference to the tone set by Walker and de Grazia, an individual with whom Kay did not like to quibble.

Even though Walker would express regret that he "could not get Norton Kay to work with the press in a relaxed way," he added that "it really was not Norty's fault.

"It was my responsibility to set the conditions of our press relationship, and we didn't realize the errancy of our approach. I should have tempered my position of remoteness somewhat because it naturally was picked up by my staff."

In what some would call a major understatement, Walker concluded that "many of our problems could have been overcome if I had been more conscious of the need for good press relations."

Regardless of Walker's admission thereafter, Kay took it on the chin for Walker's troubles with the press. Not just from Walker's own clique, of which Kay was part, but also from a lot of the men and women laboring in the little cubicles that then comprised the press quarters in the northwest corner of the third floor of the Statehouse.

You see, Kay had come out of their ranks. He had been among those slaving over a typewriter night after night in the pressroom to meet the daily copy deadlines of their papers. Kay certainly should have made it clear to Walker and the others what the pressroom was all about back then. He knew.

As political editor of Chicago's American, Kay inevitably was part of the rough-and-ready world of Chicago journalism that, going into the Walker era, still had four major dailies in the city competing in cutthroat fashion.

The efforts by these papers to outdo each other unavoidably spilled over into the Statehouse pressroom in Springfield, where the bureaus of these papers battled without quarter to dig up dirt on the politicians. Like City Hall in Chicago, the Statehouse was a very fertile ground for the muckrakers.

Actually, Kay and a number of the other Chicago reporters who would spend time in the Capitol pressroom cut their journalistic teeth with the City News Bureau of Chicago, a training ground for young reporters that also fed police, fire and other news stories to the papers and television and radio stations in the city.

Back then, the City News Bureau's operations still featured some of the raucous traits of the Chicago-style journalism so immortalized in the play, "The Front Page," by Ben Hecht and Charles MacArthur. More than a few big names in journalism, including nationally-heralded Chicago columnist Mike Royko, passed through the City News Bureau.

Norty Kay, a son of a Chicago printer, was a fixture in the Chicago newspaper world for a reason beyond his own competence. His wife, Virginia Lee Kay, was a popular columnist for the Daily News. Her death in 1969 shattered his world. It took participation in political campaigns, the Stevenson Senate race in 1970 and then Walker's drive for governor, to bring Kay out of it.

But, back to the pressroom in the Capitol down in Springfield, a place where Kay had been one of the busy performers in the late 1960s and which would drive him up the wall when his man Walker was governor.

By the end of the governorship years of Kerner and Shapiro,

it was clear that the pressroom had changed.

An atmosphere of congenial coexistence, in which many veteran reporters seldom went beyond straight news coverage of officeholders, had given way to a nearly hostile belligerence in some bureaus.

Largely responsible for this transformation was an infusion of younger reporters intent on rocking the boat, refusing to play along with the live and let live attitude of the older reportorial hands on the scene. Some in this new wave even refused to accept the liquor and other gifts that officials (but never Walker) heaped on the Statehouse reporters each Christmas.

These new guys, and the pressroom in the Statehouse in those days was essentially a male bastion, were dispatched to Springfield by editors in Chicago and other places who no longer were satisfied with complacent reporting. The new arrivals burst through the pressroom doors with dreams of Pulitzer prizes for investigative reporting literally dancing in their heads.

To the practitioners of the gumshoe reporting craze that swept the Statehouse, Illinois government was comprised of good people and bad people, with few in between. The evil ones had to be flushed out and, if possible, indicted and even jailed. Putting a crooked public figure behind bars was the ultimate honor for those Statehouse reporters more interested in officials' travel expenses than press releases.

These typewriter jockeys felt they had a higher purpose than reporting the news. They were self-anointed guardians of the public trust in government. Some were damn good at it.

The blood of many an Illinois politician ran cold in those days at the thought of being shadowed by Ed Pound or one of the other crack sleuths working out of the pressroom.

Ethical conduct codes, official investigatory bodies, even the electorate could be ignored or usually discounted by wayward officeholders or bureaucrats. But not those snoops in the pressroom.

Old hands, in government as well as in the pressroom itself, didn't know what to make of these reportorial dicks, who showed little respect for anything or anybody on the Springfield scene. They were just troublemakers.

They came in and out at odd hours, huddled with shadowy sources in secret places, ignored many of the routine press conferences and receptions for reporters and did not hesitate to slam even the old payrollers and hangers-on long given a pass because of their closeness to the more senior, less inquisitive reporters. Hell, they even eavesdropped on each other in the cramped, smoky pressroom, where privacy was impossible.

What was the world, or at least Statehouse journalism, coming to?

A few of these Sam Spades went so far as to work with the Better Government Association, a privately-funded exposer of governmental corruption that had branched out to Springfield from its Chicago base in the years before Walker hit the Capital. The BGA was very unpopular with officials—when they were in power.

If he could have gotten away with it, Walker would have put out a contract on J. Terrence Brunner, a former federal crime-fighting attorney who was executive director of the BGA when Walker was governor.

Walker strongly objected to what he considered ridiculous probes of his administration by the BGA, including its collaboration with the St. Louis Post-Dispatch in an investigation of alleged ghosts on state payrolls during Walker's tenure.

A milestone in the period of intensive Statehouse investigative reporting was the Pound-led disclosure by the Alton Telegraph in 1969 of impropriety by two members of the Illinois Supreme Court in the panel's handling of a case involving former state revenue director Theodore Isaacs.

When the two jurists, Chief Justice Solfisburg and Justice Klingbiel, heeded a call to resign, the reporter bloodhounds had their biggest scalps in the Illinois Capital in years and were hungry for more.

The revelation of Secretary of State Paul Powell's $800,000 hidden fund after his death in 1970 sent the pressroom into a tizzy. Although reporters never could pin down the exact sources of Powell's cash, the investigation sparked disclosures of shady dealings in racing stocks and in other matters that ruined or tarnished the careers of a number of Illinois officials.

It went on and on, from discoveries of clever or zany fund-raising schemes by political figures to exposes of scams in seemingly every part of public life. For the investigative reporters, it was a kind of free-for-all time.

An irony of the matter was that, by the middle of the 1970s, journalism schools would be jammed with students wanting to be muckraking reporters. Their idols were Bob Woodward and Carl Bernstein of the Washington Post, whose investigative disclosure pieces helped bring about investigations of the Watergate break-in, inquiries that in turn forced the resignation of President Nixon.

However, Illinois government officials had been a target of the Woodward-Bernstein style of hard-hitting reporting long before the Watergate burglary occurred in June 1972.

At the start of Walker's governorship, the press corps consisted of a daily contingent of about 30 newspaper, radio and television reporters and photographers, a number that would swell for the concluding weeks of a legislative session and for other more newsworthy occasions.

Interesting individuals they were. The pressroom, during the Walker years, was certainly a collection of fascinating personalities. Hard driving. Irreverent—many to the core. Some good writers. Some not so good. A number of people around long enough to know where the skeletons were buried, including more than several persons willing to write what they knew.

But the common denominator was that everybody was a unique individual.

Those pressroom types. Like hardworking Robert Kieckhefer, head of the United Press International bureau, and his feisty UPI sidekick, Tom Laue. Like John Camper, the witty chief of the old Daily News bureau, and his predecessor, the cherubic Henry Hanson, an artist and balloonist who still came to Springfield when Walker was governor to cover the General Assembly. Like finicky Burnell Heinecke, the son of Freeburg who ran the Sun-Times office.

Like the untiring William O'Connell of the Peoria Journal Star, a walking encyclopedia on legislative doings. Like the Tribune's urbane David Gilbert, who would be one of the first to join the gubernatorial campaign of Walker's successor, Jim Thompson. Like hefty Richard Icen, an astute analyst for the Decatur-based Lindsay-Schaub Newspapers. Like the highly respected Bill Miller, who pioneered radio coverage of Illinois government through his news feeds to stations around the state.

By the start of the Walker period, the much-feared Ed Pound, then with the Sun-Times, had departed Springfield for Chicago to torment the Daley machine. But, his old investigative running mate, Taylor Pensoneau, the Post-Dispatch man in the Statehouse, remained on the scene in the Walker years. The other big St. Louis daily, the Globe-Democrat, had Thomas Amberg, a son of the paper's late publisher, covering the Illinois Capitol during much of Walker's term.

Sun-Timesman Charles N. Wheeler III, another pressroom performer in Walker's time, also had strong journalism roots. His dad was a Sun-Times copy editor and his grandfather, Charles N. Wheeler, had been political editor of the Daily News and, before that, an Illinois Statehouse correspondent early in the century.

Unlike most of his pressroom colleagues in the Walker years, Wheeler was not gone from the Statehouse press corps shortly after the departure of Walker. He remained a fixture in the Sun-Times bureau, seeing many public figures come and go. At times the liberal Wheeler changed his opinion about some of those he covered. But not about Walker. It was harsh and it went as follows.

"Dan Walker was probably the phoniest politician I ever met.

"He cynically created a political image for himself apart from reality. Here was a corporation lawyer who dressed up in a bandanna and work shirt to pretend he was something other than what he was.

"Many thought he was a real liberal because of the Walker Report. But he signed the death penalty legislation while he was in office. He was definitely not a liberal."

Wheeler had plenty of company in the pressroom in his reading of Walker. Not that other governors were adored by the press corps.

Otto Kerner was viewed as aristocratically aloof. Samuel Shapiro wasn't in office long enough to show he was gubernatorial material. Dick Ogilvie could have displayed more gubernatorial oomph, but he did become eventually a good fellow in the lexicon of the pressroom, especially after his defeat by Walker.

None of these predecessors of Walker, though, touched off the emotional hostility that so many in the pressroom felt for Walker.

Nobody in the press crowd in the Walker days was a better writer or a more caustic satirist than John Camper, an Ohioan out of Kenyon College who ran the Daily News bureau in Springfield from 1970 to 1975. He was not among the Walker haters, but years later, when associate chancellor for public affairs at the University of Illinois at Chicago, he still expressed amazement at the animus of the media gang toward Walker.

As hard as it was to believe, recalled Camper, "there was unity in the pressroom because of the disdain for Walker.

"At the same moment, it was a fun time in the normally crazy atmosphere of the pressroom because you always came in each day knowing Walker was going to pull some stunt or get into a confrontation that would make news. His inconsistencies, his staging of things...all were great for our business, although we weren't always sure where the benefit to the state of Illinois could be found.

"Of course, there was never any shortage of people coming around to us trying to dump dirt on Walker."

All in all, Camper concluded, "Walker had terrible press relations that made for an impossible job for Norty and Mark Clark. The skepticism about Walker got so strong that both of them and us had trouble at times keeping straight faces in dealing with each other."

Mark Clark was a young Philadelphian reporting out of the Springfield bureau of Chicago Today when Kay tapped him, not long into the Walker administration, to be deputy press secretary.

Upon his "going over" to the other side, Clark was asked by Kay about the pressroom moniker for Walker of "werewolf," an obvious point of interest in the Walker inner sanctum.

Whatever Clark's reply, the truth was that the appellation was coined by Camper because of what the Statehouse scribes perceived to be Walker's frequently fierce glare and periodic changes of positions on issues.

So, how did Walker get into such a pickle with these people on the floor above his office in the Statehouse? These conspicuous know-it-alls who called him werewolf behind his back.

Part of the answer, and quite likely a major part, lay in his stunning 1972 primary victory over Paul Simon.

As Walker himself saw it, "Paul had a good record, and the press in the Capitol liked him and thought he deserved or had earned the Democratic nomination for governor.

"Then, along comes this guy Walker out of nowhere, with no elected experience in government, and he tries to take it away from Simon. The reporters in Springfield made it very clear that I did not have a chance and, further, many did not want me to have a chance. There were always ones out there who never forgave me for beating their man Simon."

In private, Walker would not have gotten an argument on this from a lot of the Statehouse reporters back then. Some would have gone as far publicly as did Camper in acknowledging that "without doubt, Paul Simon was very close to the press corps because he almost was one of us."

Beyond that, the Statehouse press battalion was to a great degree a part of the Illinois establishment that Walker had challenged so strongly in his quest for the governorship. His attacks against the failings of the ruling order necessarily implied, the Statehouse reporters figured, that they had not been doing their job very well either.

Also, in seeking to overcome his underdog status in taking on the establishment, Walker was seen by many in the media as guilty of too many gross exaggerations or misrepresentations of facts. And all the time, his media detractors argued further, Walker was holding himself out as better than the rest of the political world he was accosting. Consequently, Walker was adjudged by the press to have asked to be evaluated by a higher standard, meaning that when he stumbled he was going to be criticized twice as much as the next person. This explained his hard treatment by the press over the Angelos affair right off the bat in his governorship.

One situation in particular sealed Walker's fate with the reporters in the Statehouse.

With the early March 1973 date for Walker's first state budget submission rapidly approaching, reporters understandably were getting antsy since the Governor's office had not scheduled any media briefings ahead of time on the always complicated fiscal plan.

The proposed budget presented each year by the governor is the best blueprint available for what the governor has in mind for Illinois government and the taxpayers. Because reporters liked to do a thorough job in covering it, they welcomed the briefings on the many segments of the fiscal program that Ogilvie and other state chief executives had orchestrated prior to the day of the budget's unveiling to the General Assembly.

The pressroom assumed Walker would follow this pattern. However, reporters were stonewalled by Kay or his secretary, a little Los Angeles gal named Wendy Feldman, when they inquired about briefings or, at least, getting the printed budget material in time to write credible stories.

Not this time. No written background was released to the media until Walker started his formal presentation of his proposed $7,027,485,000 budget for fiscal 1974 to a joint session of the House and Senate.

This virtually ensured that first day stories and broadcasts on the budget, the most important, would convey what Walker wanted to say. It would be his spin, and only his, leaving reporters furious that their initial budgetary stories would be neither balanced nor researched properly.

Kay knew this was not the way the press thought a railroad should be run and that playing it this way would undermine seriously his standing in the pressroom. He was right.

"Doing it like that," he noted accurately, "was the best way to get our version out with the first shot." But, he added, "it was a short-term gain and a long-term loss.

"I knew that would happen, but I took the rap. It contributed to my image as a devil incarnate."

The Statehouse press people also got the short end of another Walker practice, flying around the state, say from Rockford to Moline to Peoria to Carbondale, to announce this program or that development to local reporters waiting at each stop.

The Capitol journalists in Springfield, used to getting all such news first, either were ignored on these occasions or given the word no earlier than the reporters in other parts of the state. It was another way to cut the Statehouse crew down to size.

Of course, Walker also saw this tactic as a logical course for taking his positions on issues directly to regions of downstate Illinois where he was more popular than in Springfield. He went over well on these fly arounds, especially with local newspersons getting a rare opportunity to question a governor.

"I knew some in the (Statehouse) pressroom got their nose out of joint over Walker doing that," observed Ray Serati, the veteran head of the Statehouse bureau of Copley News Service and a man with lasting allegiance to his small town roots in the southern Illinois community of Herrin.

But, added Serati, "why couldn't a reporter in Rock Island or Carbondale ask just as good a question as the people in the Statehouse?"

While another governor with the poor Statehouse press relations of Walker might have ventured into the pressroom to attempt to disarm his critics, Walker did not. He just could not bring himself to do it.

Save for rare exceptions here or there, Walker's style did not include drinking, backslapping, pleading his case or fraternizing with members of the Capitol press covering his administration.

After leaving office, Walker was one of the first to take note of the frequent stops in the pressroom by his successor, visits often entailing friendly chitchat between Governor Thompson and reporters as well as a beer or two. Not many aspects of Thompson's lengthy governorship were cultivated more personally than his rapport with the press, and it paid off in spades.

Oh, Walker did make an effort now and then.

Saturday night poker games for Statehouse reporters and

certain others were not infrequent occurrences in the frame home on Springfield's South Fifth Street of Bob Estill, the Capitol bureau chief for Springfield's State Journal-Register.

One night at these games, not too long before midnight, in sauntered Governor Dan Walker himself, all alone, to join the astonished cardplayers in a few hands. It was not a complete surprise to Estill, who had been alerted by Kay that Walker might do this.

Still, Estill was "astounded that he really came because some of those sitting there that night were not his greatest admirers.

"The Governor walking into the poker game that evening was, for him, the same thing as walking into the lions' den."

Even though Walker had only minimal contact one-on-one with those reporters writing about him, he read a surprisingly large amount of what they wrote. The Governor was a self-described "newspaper person." He did not watch television, not even coverage of himself on the tube's news programs.

As for the print media, Walker left the governorship heavily disappointed, especially over his visits to the editorial boards of the Tribune, Sun-Times and Daily News—which he viewed as uncomfortable exercises in frustration. Walker often felt that the editorial writers and top brass at these sessions just did not like him. He found them neither open-minded nor, to his surprise, erudite about many of the difficult issues he tried to raise.

The Governor long had believed that "one of the reasons why the public does not pay much attention to editorials is that they are so frequently out of touch." His personal experience as Illinois chief executive bolstered that opinion.

In meeting with the editorial boards in Chicago, Walker contended, "I rarely had intelligent questions from the working members of those editorial staffs. They seemed to be incapable of understanding the real heart of state government financing problems, or even trying to comprehend.

"The word 'ivory tower' applied here with great force. They were often just as blind and prejudiced and uninformed as many of the politicians they frequently criticized."

In parts of Illinois away from Chicago, Walker discovered newspapers "more refreshing to deal with" because the reporters were "more honest and straightforward."

To many in Chicago journalism, most of the media elsewhere in Illinois was depicted sardonically as the pygmy press. Thus, any inference of downstate media superiority by Walker, or any other person, would have been met with snickers.

Yet, Walker pushed that notion, swearing that "in many ways, downstate journalists are smarter. They come to the point faster, eschew the angles more frequently and don't try to second-guess you.

"Many Chicago reporters—mainly in the print end—thought they were smarter than anyone in government when they actually knew very little about how state government operates."

Paranoia between the Statehouse press corps and the office of Illinois governor melted more quickly than snow in August with the exit of the Walker administration. Things changed so rapidly that it was hard, less than a year or two after Walker was gone, to fathom the hostility that had existed.

As the United States attorney in Chicago, Jim Thompson worked the press beautifully in furthering his prosecutorial agenda. He didn't miss a beat in continuing this pattern when he moved to the governor's chair.

Thompson no doubt was much more of a believer than Walker in an old adage which held, in the words of John Camper, that "you should not get into fights with people who buy ink by the tank car load."

A lot about the pressroom itself had changed from Walker to Thompson. Before Walker left office, the press crew had moved to new and fancier quarters in the Capitol, accommodations remodeled for the reporters at a cost to taxpayers of $550,000.

The new pressroom did not even sound the same. The Walker years were the last in which the click-clack of typewriters filled the air before the arrival of the monotonous drone of the computerized equipment that replaced typewriters, telecopiers and the last vestiges of Western Union in the writing and transmission of stories.

The lineup in the pressroom was diminishing also, leading to less cutthroat competition in reporting. Chicago Today ceased publication in 1974, while Walker still was around, and the Daily News died several years after Thompson took office. Also in 1974, the two Springfield dailies were merged into one paper, the State Journal-Register, a move that in reality improved significantly journalistic quality in the Capital city.

The big break for Thompson, though, was the departure from the pressroom of most of the investigative big guns who had hounded Walker and, before him, Ogilvie. Compared to the group of tigers Walker and Ogilvie had to contend with in the pressroom, Thompson faced a largely Milquetoast band of reporters.

Take away the old-fashioned digging of widely-read columnist Mike Lawrence, who also ran the Statehouse bureau for the Lee newspapers, and spadework was hard to find. If there was second-guessing of Thompson, it often came only from Illinois Times, a spicy, liberal weekly based in Springfield that began publication in the mid 1970s.

For Walker, the press was a two-edged sword. Without the coverage of his walk and other features of his upstart political venture, Walker would not have been elected governor. But, the antipathy that followed between Walker and at least the bigger Illinois media sorely undercut any appearance of smooth sailing by the Walker administration.

In the years following Walker's departure from Springfield,

new arrivals in the pressroom would be told that their predecessors were instrumental in the bringing down of Governor Daniel Walker. A heady claim, perhaps, even in the world of journalists where reporters are not shy about taking credit for happenings.

One thing was certain, though. The press coverage drove the Walkerites up the wall, creating for them a diversionary problem that undeniably detracted from their march toward greater political success.

To lay the blame for the press albatross on Kay was too easy, but Kay took much of it nonetheless. Kay did not bounce back overnight from the fall of Dan Walker, believing bitterly that one of the greatest and most promising developments in the modern annals of American political leadership was short-circuited prematurely. To have come so far against such stiff odds in such a short time, and then to watch it all slide down the chute. The hurt was deep for Kay.

Only after a long while had passed was Norty Kay able to conjure up all the positives of the Walker movement and start feeling better about his once in a lifetime role in it.

By then, he was a partner in the Haymarket Group, a Chicago-based public affairs firm. And by then he was happily remarried to Sandra Blau, still another University of Chicago product in the Walker vanguard, who had several roles in the administration, including the managership of the governor's office.

Kay could look back on the whole thing then with more equanimity. Well, maybe not all of it. Like Walker, he still despised those gridiron dinners. &

 **Governing Illinois**

As governor of Illinois, Dan Walker plunged right in.

He had worked too hard to capture this plum position to not give it everything he had. No way would Walker be a figurehead. Walker intended to be a hands-on governor, an executive determined to do everything within his reach to ensure that the citizens of his adopted state were getting their money's worth out of Illinois government.

The Illinois Constitution said that the governor "shall have the supreme executive power" in the state, and Walker was dead set on exercising that omnipotent authority right down to the day-to-day affairs of the sprawling bureaucracy he had been elected to head.

More than anything else, Walker wanted to be recognized as a good manager of government.

He sought to show the electorate that he could live up to his campaign theme to bring government closer to the people, to make it more attuned to the real needs and desires of the governed.

Trying to get a handle on the maze of Illinois governing structures was a daunting challenge, a task admittedly beyond the capability and energy of most politicians. But Walker had not the tiniest bit of doubt that it was a ready-made situation for a person like himself, willing to loosen his tie, roll up his sleeves and get on with it.

The Governor was also confident that, along with the favorable attention he surely would be receiving, his political future would take care of itself.

Re-election to his office in 1976 naturally was the next logical step in his political progression.

Still, the disillusioning political chaos in Washington in the early 1970s, culminating in the first resignation ever by a president, looked to make the White House quite vulnerable to an outsider not tainted by the moral turpitude of the leadership in the nation's Capital. In thinking of the presidential election in 1976, Governor Walker of Illinois just might be in the right spot at the perfect moment.

In fact, by the time that the 1976 election was at the nation's doorstep, Walker had received enough positive mention by national pundits to merit inclusion in the speculation about possible contenders for the Democratic nomination for president. Enough notice to cause uncertainty within the Walker inner circle. David Green, never one for convention, wanted to skip another run for governor and enter the New Hampshire primary early in 1976 as an announced candidate for president. But he was outvoted by the others—de Grazia, Goldberg, Kay and Walker himself.

"We bucked Dave on that one," said Walker. "We thought we could win another dramatic Illinois gubernatorial primary victory, and then, if it wasn't too late, enter the presidential race in April. We thought that would be the safer route, but it turned out not to be."

For a while, there was a chance that Walker would not run for anything in 1976. At least, he had decided in the summer of 1975 against going again for governor.

"I was tired of it all.

"Tired of the unending media attacks, tired of the difficulties with Daley and with the Legislature, tired of the developing marital problems, which in politics often come with the territory.

"I was growing tired of my inability to take charge and forge ahead, as of old.

"I told the top staff of my intention to retire. It was Vic who talked me out of it in the late summer or early fall of that year."

The Walker governorship was that of a man who attempted to be all things to all people. Unlike his successor, Walker insisted on involving himself heavily in the nuts and bolts of governmental direction. Yet, unlike his predecessor, Ogilvie, Walker also persisted in trying to maintain contact, personal as well as spiritual, with the parts of Illinois seldom identified with the state power structure. What Walker called the other Illinois, his favorite segment of Illinois.

Striving to remain down to earth, Walker ran the office on high octane. It left him exhausted. Yet, he would have done even more if he could have found the time.

Along with every other responsibility on his overloaded plate, Walker for a time considered appointing himself director of the Illinois Department of Public Aid. That would have been a unique wrinkle. A sitting governor also serving as director of one of his own departments.

There was a postscript to that idea, a sentimental tie. Walker had been secretary and then acting chairman of the old Illinois Public Aid Commission before it was replaced in 1963 by the new department as the agency for administering public assistance programs in the state.

When Walker assumed the reins of Illinois government, the costs and caseloads in the public aid system were soaring out of sight, a dilemma faced by governors before and after Walker. For his part, Walker did not duck the situation.

Shortly after becoming governor, Walker launched an attack to combat cheating in public aid, including elimination of the 7 percent of the recipients that Walker held to be ineligible for benefits. He also went after other kinds of fraud linked to a program requiring $1 of every $5 spent by the state.

Although the get-tough policy could not arrest the steadily increasing cost of welfare, Walker was able to show that the roughly 1,090,000 persons receiving assistance late in his administration—roughly 10 percent of the state's population—exceeded only slightly the figure at the start of his term in office.

Public aid remained a boiling pot of problems, some aggravated by the economic downturn in Illinois while Walker was governor. His first public aid department director, Joel Edelman, resigned in 1974 after a falling out with the Governor's office. To some legislators and federal officials, Walker never could do enough to curtail cheating in the system.

But Walker was able to stamp out many of the brush fires constantly threatening the public aid program (partly because healthy state finances in his first years in office provided him with the necessary dollars). Making it clear from the beginning that he would not let the welfare system engulf his administration, Walker incurred the wrath of some social liberals but endeared himself to numerous middle-class wage earners outraged at the growth of the public assistance rolls.

The public aid agency was one of the largest of the 22 departments or code agencies under Walker that administered major services, programs and regulatory functions of state government. The directors of the departments were named by the Governor, appointments that of course had to be ratified by the Senate.

Aside from the code departments, the Governor's so-called cabinet agencies, the executive branch of Illinois government captained by Walker also included a myriad, a veritable web, of boards, commissions and bureaus either regulating or dealing in some fashion with almost every facet of human endeavor in Illinois.

A number of these entities, like the Environmental Protection Agency and the Illinois Commerce Commission, were bigger and better known than some of the code departments. The bottom line, though, was that Walker was held accountable for the performance of all of them.

Since this was the case, Walker did his level best to put his stamp on each agency, to not let them run themselves without direction or input from the Governor's office.

Walker felt his political persona exemplified change, and he carried that thesis right into his relationship with the agencies. Policy shake-ups, sometimes more, were the order of the day.

The Governor came off as a conservative in what he wanted to do here, as a liberal reformer in the way he proceeded over there. Labeling him was tricky; he was such a farrago. However, no person mistook Walker's intent to revise the workings of Illinois government.

Not through the creation of new bureaucracies, in the style of Ogilvie, but by getting much more out of the existing framework. To Walker, larger government did not mean better government.

In actuality, as Walker staffers would jest, he had little choice but to make a fresh start of things because Walker arrived in the governor's office to find the place stripped of files and records. Not even a piece of paper could be found listing appointees or vacancies on all those boards or commissions, which created an administrative circus.

When Alberta Doud sat down at her desk on the day she went to work as Governor Walker's personal secretary, the attractive brunette from Riverton, just 27 at the time, found nothing in her desk drawers but a bottle of aspirins.

Starting from scratch. That's the way the Walker people looked at everything.

As with the state budget. Here Walker opted for a new approach by instituting zero-base budgeting, a process developed in the business management field a few years earlier by Texas Instruments and other firms in the private sector.

With these practitioners, zero-base budgeting entailed a procedure based on simple logic in which each manager was asked to break down his or her proposed annual budget into small parts dubbed "decision packages." In each of these, the manager stated what he or she intended to accomplish, the cost involved and the benefit to the overall organization. After comparison of these "packages" to the organization's long-term goals, the packages were ranked by top management and sanctioned to the level affordable.

In bringing this idea to Illinois governmental budgeting, Walker said it would work in the following manner.

"Zero-base budgeting requires each state agency head to stack his or her programs with the least important on top and a price tag on each.

"That allows the Governor, with his Bureau of the Budget, to review the programs in line with the comprehensive state objectives and fiscal picture and then prioritize those programs within the dollar realities of the budget. Spending allocations are approved accordingly, meaning we can shift funds from low priority areas."

William Barnhart, a reporter for the Hinsdale-based "Little" Trib when Walker was governor and later associate financial editor of the Chicago Tribune, recalled that "zero-base budgeting was in vogue in the business world in the early 1970s, and Walker pushed it as his version of state fiscal reform."

Barnhart thought, however, that application of the concept appeared to have been abandoned by Walker's budget crew several years into his administration.

Walker insisted, though, that utilization of zero-base budgeting techniques assisted him greatly in bringing the state budget under control and, consequently, ending the spiraling growth of Illinois government. At least for a while.

And, by doing this, Walker emphasized, he was able to avoid calling for tax hikes or new levies while he was chief executive of Illinois.

Being able to pull that off was no minor feat, especially since state spending did increase during the Walker period. Although not by much in the first two years of his term.

In his second proposed state budget, the one covering fiscal year 1975 (which began July 1, 1974), the Governor asked for approval of appropriations totalling $7,886,436,000, only $236,135,000 above the total appropriations for fiscal 1974, the first 12-month period subject to a Walker budget.

Come early 1975, and time for Walker's third budget, the one for fiscal 1976, he called for legislative approval of an operating plan based on a record amount of $10,750,606,000 in appropriations. It seemed like a lot of money at the time, although the figure pales in comparison to the budgets of later governors of Illinois.

(In 1976, Walker's fourth and last year in office, he recommended a budget of $9,908,000,000 to the General Assembly, considerably below the figure the previous year.)

Walker had to go to considerable effort while in office to avoid raising taxes, particularly after the financial cushion from the added revenue from the Ogilvie-approved Illinois income tax had been absorbed by increased state expenditures.

By 1975, a year of economic recession in Illinois, Walker was cutting it close in betting that he could push the Legislature to sign off on that record budget proposal of close to 11 billion dollars without hitting taxpayers for any additional money. He got away with a good deal of it, including the no new taxation part, with the luck of a Mississippi River gambler and adroit fiscal management.

Walker was all over the ballpark during the budget donny-brook in 1975. After being regarded as a fiscal conservative during his first two years in office, he was then tagged a liberal spender when he called for the biggest state budget in history. He did this in 1975 before the impact of the recession hit home in Illinois, triggering drops in sales and income tax revenue.

Thus, shortly before the end of the 1975 legislative session, Walker again became the fiscal conservative as he went on evening television live and statewide to marshal backing for a broad cut in his own proposed budget, admitting his original approach was based on faulty state revenue projections. He conceded that outlays could not be as great as he had planned from the state's General Revenue Fund, which financed state aid to education, public aid and basic state operations.

On the other hand, his message that night still underscored the one point in state fiscal policy on which he would not budge. No tax hikes.

Noting that Illinoisans were facing either a tax hike or reduced government spending, he vowed that the choice was obvious as long as he was governor.

"In time of economic trouble, it is wrong for government to increase taxes," the Governor said. "Millions of Illinois citizens already have tightened their belts—to the point where it hurts."

He added, "People rightfully expect government to live within its means, to meet declining revenues by reducing spending. People don't want a tax increase, and I am opposed to one."

In the end, 1975 was like every other year in Illinois government in which the mighty forces in public life duel over the state budget, leaving the taxpayers out in the trenches in breathless suspense over the perpetually epic battle over state dollars. After much wrangling, a budget is always approved, and 1975 was no exception.

Walker, the liberal-conservative during the budget drama, was at the windup kind of a middle-of-the-roader.

State Comptroller George W. Lindberg, a Republican, and others with a conservative political slant, like the Illinois Chamber of Commerce, chose to depict Walker as a foolhardy spendthrift, recklessly pushing the state toward bankruptcy.

In the minds of Democratic legislative leaders, and by 1975 they were running the show in both chambers, Walker invariably was threatening to shortchange education and the welfare community, which the final budget figures showed to not be true.

Walker just rolled with these punches, knowing that in spite of his real or imagined shortcomings in the tumultuous budget deliberations, he had protected the taxpayers. No tax increases. The thing he had promised to do, and the thing that could count heavily with voters in the 1976 election year, depending of course on what Walker decided to do.

Besides holding the line on taxes in that major session in 1975, Walker took pride in the fact that the General Assembly passed and he signed legislation providing additional tax relief for senior citizens and disabled individuals. That could come in handy later, too.

It was easier keeping a lid on taxes if a governor could squeeze more money out of existing revenue sources. Walker tried to do this, with positive results, through the Department of Revenue and the person the Governor brought in to run the agency, Robert

H. Allphin, who had been tax compliance manager for PPG Industries, Inc., of Pittsburgh.

Heeding an order from Walker to get "more dollars, the maximum amount we can," out of the department's collection of taxes, Allphin went to work immediately, shaking up the department and hightailing it after thousands of individuals and corporations failing to file state income tax returns or remitting only a part of their tax liability.

Although the income levy already had been in effect for nearly four years when Allphin took over, the department never had filed a civil suit seeking a judgment for back taxes as well as penalties or interest—even though 7,000,000 returns were being filed annually.

Allphin was fixed, in this and other areas of state taxation, to give tax cheaters more than a slap on the wrist. By the end of Walker's first year in office, the revenue agency had brought charges against 174 state tax dodgers, resulting in criminal convictions, prison sentences and fines that reaped many additional dollars for the state's coffers.

With the social agencies, the Governor plowed ahead with policies, some pushed already under Ogilvie, that Walker deemed humane advancements in the state's handling of the mentally ill, the disabled and others with serious problems.

At the start of the 1960s, some 50,000 persons were jammed into state mental hospitals, the bulk of them receiving little more than custodial care. By the time Walker left office, the number was down to 12,000 residents in the 28 facilities operated by the Department of Mental Health and Developmental Disabilities (the new name given the mental health agency while Walker was Illinois chief executive).

The transfer of many of these persons from large state hospitals to community-based quarters had proceeded under Ogilvie, and Walker pursued it on a ground that care for these individuals at the local level was a much more compassionate way to go.

In public aid, while the Walker administration continued to try to weed out ineligible persons from the rolls, the monthly allotment for many welfare families considered truly needy was hiked through the use of a simplified flat grant payment system.

Since its inception in 1964, the Department of Children and Family Services had been an administrative bucking bronco for governors, and the list would include both Walker and his successors, Thompson and Jim Edgar.

Too often, critics contended, the very agency established to act as guardian for children neglected or abused by their parents had turned many of the kids into victims of the department itself. Time and again, it was charged, neglect, bungling and laziness colored the agency's handling of child abuse cases. Social workers and others in the department's 3,200-person work force seldom got credit for doing anything right.

Walker had a hot potato on his hands shortly after he took office when it was discovered that, before he was governor, the department had quietly placed about 800 youngsters under its guardianship in out-of-state facilities in Texas, Missouri, Oregon and several other states. Furthermore, the word was that a lot of these wards, regarded as unmanageable in their home state, had been shipped to brutal atmospheres in sometimes unmonitored or unlicensed facilities.

The Walker administration put a rush order on a plan to get most or as many as possible of these children back in Illinois, believing that wards of the state in Illinois should be in homes in Illinois whenever possible.

Retrieval of these youngsters was managed better by Jerome Miller than much of the other business handled by him as Walker's first director of the department. After botching his attempt to radically reorganize the agency, Miller was sent packing by Walker.

This led to the directorship of the children's agency in the latter part of the Walker administration by the highly-trusted Mary Lee Leahy and to the restoration under her watchful eye of a semblance of order in the agency's functioning.

But in the long run, with the increasing breakdown of families and other negative societal trends affecting youngsters, the Department of Children and Family Services continued to face the next thing to a mission impossible.

By originally backing liberal penal reformer David Fogel for director of the Department of Corrections, it was assumed that Walker seconded many of Fogel's proposals for more humanizing of the penitentiary system.

Even after the Senate sidetracked the Fogel appointment, the person who did get the directorship, Allyn R. Sielaff, also seemed to have every intention, with the blessing of Walker, to improve conditions for inmates.

Sielaff intended to have prisoners spend more time outside prison through the development of work release programs and furloughs for inmates. He didn't want to build more prisons, which became a reality later under Governor Thompson. Instead, Sielaff, a lawyer and social worker who had been commissioner of the Pennsylvania corrections bureau, planned to spend money on inmate-related programs and on projects like advanced training academies for guards. He also had ideas about dealing with gangs in prisons, which Sielaff saw as a major headache in the Illinois system.

As of mid-1976, though, when Sielaff was leaving his Illinois post to become administrator of Wisconsin prisons, his leading accomplishment may have been his claim that at one point while he was director nearly every prisoner had his own cell. However, the rapid increase in prison population while Walker was in office, from 6,000 to some 9,000 inmates, had forced the department to increase cell occupancy before Sielaff left Springfield, prompting a warning from the departing director of troubled days ahead.

As for Walker himself, the Governor felt later that he had been mistaken in nominating Fogel for prisons director, believing that Fogel indeed would have been too liberal for the job.

The Governor clearly was coming down on the side of the anti-crime backlash across the country. In 1973, Walker signed into law the bill sent to him by the Legislature that restored the death penalty in the state for certain kinds of murders. He approved it after the General Assembly accepted revisions to the measure requested by Walker in an attempt to remove what he termed objectionable features.

His approval incensed liberals, who noted that Walker had opposed capital punishment in his campaign for governor. Walker replied that he went along with limited imposition of the death penalty because the will of the citizenry seemed to him clearly in favor of it.

(However, in September 1975, the Illinois Supreme Court ruled the reinstated death penalty unconstitutional, upholding a lower judicial ruling that the statute was invalid in its establishment of three-judge circuit court panels to review and pass on death sentences.)

In fairness to Walker, it was an era when even penal reformers and more than a few of the General Assembly's liberals were adding their voices to those insisting that harsher measures were perhaps the only recourse for protecting society in the Illinois criminal justice system.

Through the years, moves to get tough with criminals had been supported in the state mainly by persons from either rural downstate areas or conservative ethnic neighborhoods in Chicago. Halfway through his governorship, Walker also appeared to be squarely on board.

That was when he said he favored the imposition of flat sentences on convicted criminals, elimination of parole and an end to the concept of rehabilitation as a key factor in deciding whether a prisoner should be released.

The Governor was seeking, in his words, to reintroduce "the concept of punishment for committing a crime rather than rehabilitation..."

No, Walker insisted, his approach was not designed to satisfy those who wanted to lock up criminals and throw away the key. He just wanted to replace rehabilitation-based parole with a scheme under which a convict's sentence would be reduced one day for each day he served without a serious infraction of the rules.

Again, this seemed the correct political position in view of the growing feeling against making life any better for criminals. Yet, there could be little doubt that Walker's posture on criminal justice would lead to an increased prison population.

His first year in office, Walker got high marks for handling several tests to his authority at the state's prisons.

At the Menard penitentiary at Chester, an uprising by 38 inmates ended after Illinois State Police released nausea gas into a building the convicts held. A guard hostage was freed. Walker ordered the release of the gas after determining that the conditions for using it were right.

He also orchestrated the successful defusing of a potentially deadly hostage seizure incident at Joliet's Stateville prison, and came away looking tough but conciliatory.

When he took office, he said, "I made a point of preparing for these explosive possibilities. I knew only I could accept responsibility for that kind of prison situation."

What Governor Dan Walker never could have been prepared for, though, was the prison situation in which he found himself 11 years after leaving his office.

In a devastatingly ironic twist, the man who once was lord and master of his state's penal institutions found himself on the other end as an inmate in the federal penitentiary at Duluth. He was locked up there for 18 months, and by the time he walked away from it on June 29, 1989, more than 30 pounds lighter than when he went in, Walker had been through purgatory.

The guards at Duluth knew exactly who Walker was, and who he had been. Now they had him under their thumb, this fellow at one time so high and powerful. He deserved taunting and he got it. Much more so than many of the other white prisoners, a large number of whom were drug dealers or smugglers.

To survive prison, Walker had to grope deep within himself for an inner resolve to not capitulate to "an atmosphere that was very bad for me psychologically."

Walker said he knew that "the prison stay of Otto Kerner had broken him as a man," but that "I was absolutely determined that wouldn't happen to me."

Getting out mentally alive, Walker learned, required "living within myself in a way I never imagined was possible."

Was this the way it was for many of the thousands incarcerated in Illinois when he was governor? Yes, Walker wondered about that. Had the inmates in Illinois reviled him as a despot?

But hadn't Walker always addressed their grievances, even when they were rebellious? Although Walker had won that dramatic hostage showdown at Stateville, he quickly directed changes at the prison, like more guards and better toilet facilities. Improved toilets, a big deal inside those somber walls. He later realized that all too well because at Duluth Walker put in his time on the toilet detail.

It might have been even more humiliating at Duluth, Walker reasoned, if he had lorded it over people as governor. However, he had gone the extra mile to avoid putting on airs or to exercise all of the perquisites available to the head of one of the richer states in the country.

Unlike other governors, Walker did not let his name appear on highway signs welcoming people to Illinois. He forbade the display of his picture in state offices, and refused to permit his name on fishing and hunting licenses. Car telephones, even for Walker cabinet members, were banned.

Walker wanted to lead by example, setting a pattern designed to diminish the remoteness of the governor's office from the populace. He expected the same of his staffers and administrators.

His own office in the Capitol, although secluded, was relatively small and austere. Not by accident, it was the same office Walker used in 1952 when he was an aid to Governor Stevenson.

With Walker using this office, a kind of back corner retreat, the larger and more ostentatious office nearby used by his predecessors was converted into a conference room during the Walker years.

Walker could find solace in his little office, about the only place away from the Mansion he could think things out, not worry about being on display, his every move scrutinized, every word recorded. In the at least several hours each day that Walker tried to spend in his office, he could be free from all but a handful of trusted individuals.

Goldberg, de Grazia, Kay. And Alberta Doud, who surprisingly came to Walker's office not from his campaign but from the Ogilvie administration. The insider, though, who probably saw the Governor more than anybody else was Mary Parrilli, Walker's administrative assistant.

Another brunette pleasing to the eye, Mary Parrilli had been Walker's executive secretary at Montgomery Ward and, before that, a legal secretary for him at the Chicago law firm. Always around, she had assisted him in preparation of the Walker Report.

Not married during her years with Walker, which came to nearly two decades, she became almost a part of Walker's family, handling among other things his financial affairs, including his tax returns. She even kept an eye on the fiscal doings of the Walker youngsters when they left home for college.

Pete Wilkes was another figure in the world of Walker who couldn't be ignored. Wilkes was a young state policeman who headed security for the Governor. Wilkes, who dressed in plain clothes, was with the Governor when he was away from his office, especially on the road, more than any other person.

Assigned to Walker after he won the general election, Wilkes turned out to be more than a tough guy bodyguard for his boss. The two became close friends. Wilkes was the only individual who always knew the whereabouts of Walker, even when the Governor departed from the schedule that dominated, or was supposed to control, his time.

Ogilvie was quite security minded, which might have been expected from a former sheriff of Cook County. However, Walker cut back in this area, often settling for just a car driven by a state trooper out of uniform with no lead or trailing vehicles.

Walker knew he could not ignore security, and was confident that Wilkes ran a tight ship on the matter. But the Governor refused to flaunt the protection thing, believing that "there was little anyone could do anyway to stop an assassin determined to get you."

Although Walker had been told that he needed two troopers with him all the time, he reduced it to one as much as possible.

When walking, he allowed only one trooper to accompany him. In cars, depending on the occasion, there could be two, one acting as the driver. Upon entering, attending or leaving events, no trooper was permitted to walk with him, heeding Walker's wish to "keep at a distance."

Threats to Walker's safety were made, but as he put it, "nothing ever happened." Wilkes never informed Walker of the threats, but did ensure that protective measures were taken. The Walker style could leave Wilkes miserable with worry.

When the Governor wanted a little side trip or other departure from the routine, Wilkes always took charge of the situation personally.

If confidentiality was necessary, Walker noted, "Wilkes would be the only one with me, although there would be one trooper ahead, whom I never saw, making on-the-spot arrangements."

Should a crisis occur while the Governor was on the road, he said that Wilkes "always knew where to find the closest private room with a telephone or medical facilities. If it was a problem requiring state police or National Guard action, I'd simply use Pete to relay the command orders. He could take care of it while I was on the phone with the protagonists in the crisis."

The image portrayed by Walker also did not allow for the limousines associated with most governors and other constitutional officers in Illinois. Walker had the limos sold when he took office and rode instead in ordinary Chevrolets—much to the displeasure of First Lady Roberta.

Walker himself had second thoughts about this later, saying that "foolishly, I thought this would make points for me...like people thinking that here's a governor giving up limousines to ride like a regular citizen.

"But, in retrospect, I don't think many voters give a damn.

"Actually, if anything, it caused some problems."

Other governors hated Walker at their conferences, he felt certain, when they rode in Cadillacs furnished by General Motors and Walker tooled up in a rented Chevy.

Or, at important gatherings in Chicago when Daley and other bigwigs sailed through police lines in luxury cars while Walker was being stopped by cops unable to believe a governor was arriving in a humble Chevy. Those occasions necessitated extra jawboning by Wilkes.

The image game also meant that the speed at which Walker was driven had to be taken into account. After he would fly into Williamson County Airport near Marion, for example, the conspicuous number one license plate was kept on the car to be used by Walker only if the speed laws were going to be obeyed. If the trooper driving Walker had to exceed the speed limit for the Governor to meet a scheduled commitment, then "random plates" were affixed to his car. This little switcheroo was a common practice especially in southern Illinois, where Walker wanted to avoid any sign of appearing uppity.

Walker had fallen in love with southern Illinois, the launching pad for the walk that propelled him to the Governor's Mansion. He was at ease down there, far more so than in the hustle and bustle of Chicago and other places up north where the bulk of the state's population resided.

To the often harried Governor, southern Illinois was a respite from the headaches of public aid roles, abused children, the political rancor of Mayor Daley, the snooty big city newspaper crowd, the animosity of the General Assembly.

Without doubt, the lower region of Illinois, much of it poverty stricken, posed every bit as much of a challenge for state government as the rest of Illinois. Maybe more of one considering that so few people really lived down there.

But Walker seemed to shake off his demons in the hours he managed to spend in southern Illinois, and they added up to a surprisingly large number. Walker couldn't wait to roam those small Bible Belt towns on weekends, strolling into cafes, musty stores, barber shops.

Down there at least they knew this was no run-of-the-mill governor. There was real affection for Walker, in whom people recognized an almost kindred spirit.

You never knew where Walker would pop up in central or southern Illinois. Once, after hunting with Pud Williams, the Governor and his agriculture director walked into a quaint restaurant in Enfield run by a popular woman named Alice. The eatery was even smaller than the White County village. It couldn't have had more than six tables.

After Williams properly introduced Alice to the Governor, she asked Walker to sample her chili. Which he did.

Did Alice wash the spoon used by the Governor? Nope. No way. That spoon was hung on a wall of the tiny restaurant.

Walker wrapped up more than a few of his days in the foot of the state with a late evening steak in a restaurant in Marion operated by Tony Castellano, who had stuck out his neck politically for Walker in the early days of his candidacy. The patronizing of the steak house by Walker put it on the map of significant places in Illinois during the Walker era.

Often, after dining with Tony, the Governor would be provided with a jug of martinis by the restaurateur to imbibe on the plane flight back to Springfield.

Walker had a rule against serving liquor on state planes or in any of his cars.

But he would bend the rules. If it was late and the day's business was over. If nobody else was around. And if he had just ended one of those wonderful days in southern Illinois and was returning to Springfield, and to the tough chores there of being governor of Illinois. ❧

Dealing with the Issues, Big and Small

Walker and his political sidekicks hardly thought small. They went after their state's biggest enchilada in their first run for public office. When Walker got the governorship, it was hard to fault his crew for looking ahead with covetous glances at Washington and the country's premier political prize.

Success in this business required—in addition to ability—gall, incredible self-assurance, pretentiousness, all the luck in the world and faith in more than the zodiac. Walker had all of these and another trait even stronger—an ambition to succeed that was for him an overwhelmingly burning desire.

Few around him could miss it. Certainly not George Kelm, who had much in common with Walker. They had met at Northwestern law school, later were law firm partners in Chicago and both lived in Deerfield where they were active in Democratic politics. To Kelm, who would go on to lead an Illinois coal company, Walker was an especially talented, industrious and productive attorney and, to boot, a very likeable guy. The only problem, Kelm found, was "knowing where Dan might be coming from because the guiding light in his life was his own ambition.

"His aspiration overrode everything else. He told me his ambition was to be president of the United States."

Surely, for Walker, being governor would be a great apprenticeship for the presidency.

He wanted to operate the machinery of Illinois government in the manner of a freewheeling board chairman, tinkering here, prodding there, refusing to fit any one philosophical mode, in no way handcuffed to the historic or recent traditions observed by most Illinois governors elected in a more conventional manner. If anything was predictable about Walker, it seemed to be his unpredictability.

Well, yes and no. Walker could be counted on to do what was expedient, thought many of those attempting to follow the performance of what they saw as a most difficult-to-define individual in the governor's chair. If that made him less than predictable, they surmised, so be it.

Walker didn't go in for labels anyway. Imaging was his thing. It was his political shtick, the root of his appeal. His candidacy was sold as an outgrowth of the general mistrust held by so many of the "little people" against those in power. Walker's handlers were not that concerned if the Governor came across as shallow to those only comfortable with nice, clear-cut political categorizations.

No question, to win the office, Walker desperately needed the support of Illinois' liberal community and other dissatisfied groups to hurdle the state power structure. If it even became fashionable to call him a populist, which it did, then that was okay.

Walker as governor maintained, though, that persons tracking him had to understand that the severe underdog nature of his campaign necessitated certain posturing that did not reveal the whole Walker.

The truth at the time was that Walker actually agreed with President Nixon and others who were critical of the large-scale social welfare programs initiated in the 1960s by Democratic leaders of the Federal Government, believing that billions in tax dollars were wasted in these efforts.

Nor was Walker pandering to big business when he stressed early in his gubernatorial years that "we need to remind ourselves continually that America is great not simply because of our government, but also because of our unique private enterprise system." This was the former Montgomery Ward executive talking, and he had every intention to use his administration as a catalyst for private enterprise initiatives in the state.

He did not want to go down as another anti-business Democrat. But he did in the eyes of some. Thanks almost solely to the tremendous success of organized labor in 1975 in getting the General Assembly to approve a restructuring of the Illinois workmen's compensation program that left business leaders fuming.

Union chieftains argued the changes long were needed to give injured employees a fairer shake. But employer groups complained bitterly that the revisions imposed costs on businesses so exorbitant that commerce would be driven from the state.

Walker sided with labor in going along with the revisions, believing that injured workers and their families were entitled to better service and quicker payment under the program. Critics countered that the legislation as implemented fell far short of its good intentions by subjecting all involved to unreasonable red tape made worse by slipshod administration.

To the business community, 1975 went down as a year of legislative infamy and Walker was branded a decidedly pro-labor governor.

This reading of the situation overlooked Walker's attempts to address concerns of Illinois business in other areas. He also got shortchanged on the labor side in that in spite of labor's leap forward with Walker's help in 1975 most of the Illinois union leadership knifed Walker politically when he sought re-election in 1976.

Next to dealing with labor, what Illinois business leaders found most irritating in the early 1970s was the aggressiveness of the state's enforcement of its antipollution program. Walker agreed that more of a balance had to be struck on this matter, resulting in a noticeable change of heart by the Illinois Environmental Protection Agency.

By the start of Walker's second year in office, Richard H. Briceland, a former federal antipollution official heading the state EPA at Walker's request, served notice of an end to what Briceland called the days of the "big stick approach" to polluters.

In its place, Briceland stressed, his agency was resorting to legal action against contaminators of water and air only after the failure of more conciliatory means to secure compliance with the Illinois antipollution rules.

Until then, the EPA had pursued polluters with little quarter or favoritism shown even to major firms. That angered industrialists, who complained of embarrassment from state officials arbitrarily seeking fines and other penalties before trying more agreeable methods of resolving issues.

Down the road, though, Briceland would find only minimal success with what he termed "the sincere and good faith efforts which I have made in attempting to work constructively (with industrialists)."

Vigorous implementation of the antipollution program by Ogilvie had sparked a backlash of political resentment in many places, of which Walker was very aware. Still, developments showed that Walker was not a pussycat either on environmental law enforcement.

Take the time in 1975 when antagonism between the state and Granite City Steel Co. got so heated that EPA officials took the seemingly unprecedented step, at least in Illinois, of using a search warrant to seize pollution test records from the company. The search warrant was issued after the state agency contended that the steel firm knowingly had released misleading information to the EPA in an effort to create an impression that the company was complying with the state antipollution program. After officers of the firm objected strongly, a Madison County circuit judge ordered the return of the documents to the firm.

The following year, the EPA and Granite City Steel reached an accord on a major program to control emissions believed by state officials to be a major cause of air pollution in southwestern Illinois.

Prior to Ogilvie, the attention given environmental issues by an Illinois chief executive was not that important in measuring gubernatorial performance. For as long as anybody could remember, the Illinois antipollution effort had been kind of a one-man show featuring a feisty old-timer named Clarence W. Klassen. The chief state sanitary engineer and an employee of the state going back to 1925, Klassen had run the state's programs to combat dirty air and water out of his hip pocket.

However, by the time Ogilvie left Springfield, the Illinois antipollution thrust had ballooned into a multi-agency setup nourished by a library of strengthened regulations and a whole new crew of engineers, lawyers and bureaucrats. By not hesitating to use this upgraded weaponry against polluters in a heavy-handed fashion, Ogilvie got high marks from the environmental crowd.

After Ogilvie, the perception of each governor on environmental issues depended on who was doing the beholding.

To ardent environmental advocates, Walker and later Thompson failed to pursue polluters with the fervor of Ogilvie or William Scott, the Illinois attorney general during the Ogilvie, Walker and early Thompson years in office.

Slow but steady reversal of the degradation of Illinois' water and air continued under Walker and then Thompson, but minus the fanfare of Ogilvie's time.

Unlike many environmentalists, leaders of Illinois industries and other major targets of the pollution-fighting program did not view Walker as a foot dragger on enforcement. The Walker flamboyance may not have been as visible on environmental protection as on certain other matters, but Walker stood his ground against moves by business forces to stymie or weaken the program.

Unfortunately for those hoping Walker might be lukewarm on the environmental front, his walk through the state was an eye-opener. He winced at the trash littering the landscape and could not help but smell the fouled water of so many streams. When the walk party reached the bank of the Mississippi at East St. Louis, son Dan was reluctant to stand in the water for a photographer, fearing blisters on his feel would get infected.

As governor, though, Walker still held to the idea that negotiation and compromise had a place in the state's efforts to bring polluters into compliance with control standards. While he wouldn't hold hands with polluters, he said he recognized that pollution abatement requirements could not outstrip or overtax the capabilities of industries and other sources of pollution. There had to be a middle ground.

No air quality issue was more contentious during Walker's governorship than the sulfur dioxide emission controversy, a subject with life-and-death implications for the Illinois coal industry.

This hot potato hit his desk when the coal industry pushed through the Legislature, during Walker's first months in office, the bill that would have prohibited for several years or even longer the enforcement of state rules designed to reduce emissions of the pollutant sulfur dioxide from the combustion of Illinois coal. After that, Walker was lobbied vigorously by those wanting him to sign the legislation and by environmental organizations opposing it.

Walker vetoed the measure, and delighted environmentalists gave him a thumbs-up.

But that hardly put the issue to bed. For the rest of Walker's days in office, and for years thereafter, Illinois officials, coal producers, coal-burning utilities and environmental leaders wrestled with the sulfurous emission question—a complicated kettle of fish that would surface in Congress in the 1980s as the so-called acid rain issue.

Few goals of the Illinois antipollution program were as difficult to attain as sulfur dioxide control. There was just so much involved.

Illinois was a leading coal mining state, and most of the coal mined was high-sulfur. Curtailing the use of this resource would mean mine closings and many thousands of unemployed miners in southern and central Illinois, regions where mining was virtually the lifeblood of the economy.

Governor Walker was quick to realize that, while implementation of the sulfur dioxide control regulations appeared inevitable, steps had to be taken to provide for the continued use of Illinois coal.

Now Walker did not enter office as a big fan of the coal industry. In the early days of his walk in the southern part of the state, he frowned at the scarred acreage from old mining operations abandoned decades earlier. After he became governor, he approved a pioneering state program for the reclamation of some of these eyesores.

However, the Walker era also was colored by a national energy crisis. Mideast oil embargoing and other foreign policy upheavals were forcing big hikes in petroleum and natural gas prices, making it fairly obvious that the United States had to rely even more on its coal for satisfying domestic fuel requirements.

This plight, unsettling as it was, offered in the mind of Walker hope instead of gloom for large regions of downstate because of the great potential in the massive coal seams under much of Illinois.

As a result of this thinking, one of the major initiatives of the Walker administration was launched: Illinois coal development. The commitment of public funds and other resources to elimination of the dirty emissions resulting from the burning of the state's high-sulfur coal.

A centerpiece of this undertaking was Walker's successful call for passage by the General Assembly in 1974 of a program providing for the issuance of $70,000,000 in general obligation bonds to stimulate development of Illinois' coal reserves. It broke with past tradition by putting Illinois tax dollars behind an attempted rescue of the state's shaky coal industry. In ensuing years, the money from the bond proceeds was spent to help underwrite projects at industrial sites and utility plants demonstrating the clean use of Illinois coal.

Walker's offensive on coal had other features too. He staged publicized conferences with national figures to focus attention on the state's coal. He had Illinois bid to become the location for almost every project proposed by federal officials for shoring up the marketability of coal. He personally beseeched executives of coal firms to open new mines in the state. Some did.

The Governor tried everything he could to make Illinois the capital of the coal universe. He made Sid Marder his point man in the quest.

Walker had persuaded Marder to come down to Springfield from Peru by appointing Marder to the Pollution Control Board. Marder was the Governor's eyes and ears on the panel, but Walker had another job in mind for the scrappy little engineer.

Under Walker, an Illinois energy office had been operating to work out fuel allocation problems and other tasks necessitated by the energy crisis. The office had been run by Denis Hayes, the same Denis Hayes given the lion's share of credit for putting together the celebrated Earth Day observances across the nation.

But Hayes was to depart, and Walker asked Marder to step down from the pollution control panel to upgrade the Hayes operation into an energy division in the Department of Business and Economic Development. Although the division was given responsibility for a lot of things in the energy field, including energy conservation programs and the pushing of alternative energy systems, the main game was coal development.

Marder and his staff, Sheridan (Rusty) Glen and the others, had a full-time job in itself just trying to line up projects that the state's coal development bonds could support.

As the state's energy boss, Marder got a candid view of Walker that few state officials, even high ones, ever get of a governor.

Without question, Marder remembered, "I was handling a hot area, important enough in those times that the Governor would call me into his office frequently to ask how the projects were going.

"Believe me, the guy (Walker) was a very tough boss, really demanding. He pushed my operation to the limit. He wanted a coal development program, and the state got one. Or at least the solid beginning of one."

Marder still chuckled years down the line, when he was an environmental consultant to major Illinois businesses, at Walker's "eye for detail."

Once, while Marder was trying to work out an undertaking with General Electric Co., he showed Walker a letter from Marder's office on the subject.

After reading the communication, Walker admonished Marder for a "dangling participle" that Walker found in the document.

"As I left his office," said Marder, "he told me to correct what he called that mistake in the letter.

"A dangling participle. I kid you not. The Governor of 11,000,000 people was worried about my dangling participle."

Walker liked Marder, seeing in him many of the characteristics of the Walker movement. A bantam rooster (albeit one with a New York accent) displaying the pugnacity of a street fighter on his sleeve. Marder liked to duke it out, never thinking twice about stepping on toes.

Plenty of other Walker people also were like that, giving rise to the feeling that the Walker crowd was, well, just too darned abrasive. That's why an individual like Langhorne Bond stood out. Of course, Bond never was regarded as one of the Walker guys.

Contrary to a number of other Walker administration officials, Bond made few serious enemies—even though he had a most challenging assignment, directing the huge Department of Transportation.

Illinois leaped to the top among the states during the Walker years in the receipt of federal money for transportation. When Bond, an attorney with much experience in Washington, was not searching the national capital for dollars, his lieutenants were.

Bond also spent considerable time in Washington lobbying for approval by the United States Department of Transportation of construction of a new airport for the St. Louis area on an Illinois site near the Monroe County seat of Waterloo.

That project did not go forward, but Bond was successful in finally paving the way for the long sought wrapping up of the interstate highway system in the heavily populated Illinois part of the St. Louis area. This was a mighty accomplishment in view of the welter of headaches involved, from the need to save historic sites and preserve precious park acreage to the addressing of minority hiring concerns and the delicate wading through the local government hodgepodge in that congested vicinity.

Bond's personal emissary in solving these complications in what still then was called the East Side was Gary R. Fears, an imaginative hustler from Granite City who became adept at finding shortcuts through red tape. Fears, one of the young campaigners for Walker's gubernatorial bid, was on Bond's payroll. It later turned out that Fears was a leading bankroller of Walker's failed bid for renomination for governor in 1976, loaning the effort more than $26,000, a tidy sum in those days.

The reputation of Bond as a Washington insider convinced Thompson to ask Bond to remain Illinois transportation secretary when Thompson succeeded Walker. However, Bond accepted an appointment in 1977 from President Jimmy Carter to be administrator of the Federal Aviation Administration.

Bond's slot in Illinois was filled by Thompson with another Walker administration person, John D. Kramer, a onetime head of the Highway Action Coalition, which had lobbied in Washington for the use of federal highway trust funds for public transit.

Bond brought Kramer from Washington to a top spot on his staff in 1973. In turn, Kramer became the right arm of Bond in the money-raising game in Washington.

Unlike some individuals in the Walker administration, Bond showed that he knew how to compromise. As a result, he managed to accommodate the competing road construction demands of Democrats and Republicans, Chicagoans as well as downstaters.

He did get bruised, though, when he killed with Walker's blessing most of the proposed supplemental freeway system in the state that had been pushed by the Ogilvie administration, an undertaking with a tremendous price tag.

The Walker administration, or any other for that matter, needed the verve that Bond brought to the scene. A man of irreverent humor, Bond was a conspicuous pursuer of the good life. He was a pilot. He lived in an elegant Italianate mansion in Springfield. He had a Triumph Spitfire in which he zipped around many midwestern racetracks.

Although raised in Virginia, Langhorne was born in Shanghai, where his father directed the China National Aviation Corp. The Bond family left China because of its war with Japan. Later, Bond's father was a vice president of Pan American World Airways.

Prior to joining the Walker team, Bond ran the National Transportation Center, a nonprofit research operation based in Pittsburgh. While there, he developed the "articulated single-deck transit bus," an unusually long vehicle designed to bend in the middle when it turned.

The transportation department was not the only Illinois agency chasing funds in Washington. The health of the state budget, not to mention the welfare of many programs, depended on landing many hundreds of millions of federal dollars each year. Most of the individuals handling this task were not as well known as Langhorne Bond.

Joe Wilkins, for one, patrolled the back hallways of Washington to obtain the maximum federal money available for Illinois public aid and mental health programs eligible for federal matching funds.

Wilkins, a Vietnam War veteran from the small fruit shipping town of Cobden in Union County, had learned the ropes in Washington with the Department of Defense. Sniffing out elusive federal dollars also came naturally for Wilkins because as an Air Force captain in Vietnam he served with the intelligence-gathering Team 95.

It was not unusual for Wilkins to find himself huddling in Washington with a Walker budget director or even Bill Goldberg to "report firsthand on my maneuvering to get our hands on money that would let us balance our budget back home."

Of course, Wilkins was a largely anonymous toiler for the state, as were so many others with responsibilities crucial to the success of an Illinois governor. State mine inspectors. Economic development officers. Nursing home regulators. The list was endless.

One reason that Walker ran well in rural areas in the 1976 Illinois primary was because the Department of Agriculture had maneuvered adroitly to protect farmers against catastrophic losses from grain elevator failures.

Grain elevators did go belly-up in the state when Walker was chief executive, as was happening elsewhere, but Pud Williams insisted to his final day as ag director that his fellow farmers were shielded from resulting financial setbacks in an unprecedented fashion.

The individual given a lot of the credit for handling this ticklish matter for the Walker administration was Sparta farmer Robert W. Holloway, the superintendent of the Division of Agriculture Industrial Regulations in Williams' agency. Democrat Holloway was hired for his patronage position by Williams after Holloway worked for Walker in his gubernatorial campaign. Not one to rest, Holloway continued to work his 400-acre cattle and grain farm in Randolph County on weekends.

In overseeing grain elevator regulation for the state, Holloway recalled, "we worked intensely with local bankers and other key persons in farming communities to combat elevator failures and their disastrous results.

"There were a lot of problems, yes, but no total elevator failures when Dan Walker was governor. We acted to prevent that.

"We moved successfully to deal with crooked grain elevator

operators, acting in this area much better than had been the case previously in state government. Total losses were avoided. Farmers depositing or storing grain in the elevators never had such protection from the state."

During the ag directorship of Williams, his agency even closed the financially-troubled elevator that his family owned near the Wayne County village of Golden Gate.

His family, said Williams, "paid off every farmer involved. Nobody lost a dime. My department treated the Williams Grain Co. like everybody else—even though it was a hard thing to do." (At the time, Williams was not involved in the operation of the elevator because, at the direction of Walker, Williams had put his holdings in Williams Grain into a blind trust to preclude a conflict of interest.)

The ag department, as it turned out, was one of the most visible agencies in state government during Walker's watch. Agriculture could catch the public eye because of the many uncommon matters that came across its path.

Like when the department moved to eradicate a serious outbreak of tuberculosis in herds of beef cattle in Madison and Greene counties, or attempted to advise law enforcement officers and Walker himself on combating an alarming hike in cattle rustling. Yes, cattle rustlers right here in Illinois.

Every day, it seemed, the crew of Dr. Paul Doby, the veterinarian supervising the agency's Division of Meat, Poultry and Livestock Inspection, was hauling in livestock slaughterers or meat processors committing grisly violations of the state's dead animal disposal law and related statutes.

Heck, Williams' boys even were in on a surprise raid by Washington County Sheriff Tom Hale on a cockfight in a sawmill near Coulterville. That made good reading, particularly for the millions of Illinoisans who had little knowledge about cockfighting or rustling in their state.

Unfortunately, the Walker years were ones of deepening economic trouble for Illinois farmers. Across the country, farmers were going out of business at a rate of close to 2,000 each week. The small farm sector especially was in a tailspin.

Higher operating costs for farmers and falling prices for their products were adding up to financial disaster for many, spawning anger and hopelessness throughout the midwestern corn belt. On many Illinois tracts where the farmhouses were not deserted, the occupants were leaving a good part of the land idle or planting noncash crops in an effort to force a jump in the price of farm products.

The picture was not as bleak as the scene in many of those classic black and white photos of rural poverty in the Great Depression taken for the Farm Security Administration, many of them shot in Illinois. But people were seeing the handwriting on the wall.

The farm economy was not an isolated situation. When Walker took office, many other parts of the state's economy were in the early stages of an anemic period. With the winding down of the Vietnam War, industry was plunging into a severe recession and inflation was as rampant as folks could remember.

Illinois traditionally had been a mecca for small towns, but the vitality of many of the places with 5,000 or fewer souls was ebbing quickly. Their storied squares were being vacated, leaving shells of buildings only suitable from then on as sets for movies extolling the vibrancy of what once had been. The fabled myths of small town living were evaporating into just that, mythology, as the jobs and commerce and even health care disappeared.

Rural Illinoisans were feeling more and more estranged from the expanding urban areas of the state. When governor, Walker witnessed an amusing move, only partly tongue-in-cheek, to incorporate 16 counties in rural western Illinois into a separate state named the "Republic of Forgottonia." Its promoters claimed their end of the world was treated like an inferior stepchild in comparison to the rest of Illinois, whether the issue was road construction or anything else affecting the economy.

Really, they had a point. A person could make the rounds in Springfield for years without hearing mention of many of those 16 counties. Warren, Scott, Mercer and Henderson, to name a few. Hardly any of the Capital hotshots knew where Henderson could be found and as for that county's seat, Oquawka, none had even heard of it.

Not that the bigger Illinois cities, those that did have recognizable names, weren't changing either during the Walker era. While the little towns were becoming reserves for the poor and elderly, the larger communities were seeing their core areas decimated.

Whites were fleeing from the old established neighborhoods to outlying areas to avoid the influx to the inner cities of blacks and other minorities. In turn, the downtown retail centers would surrender their vitality to the massive shopping malls that, not too many years beyond the Walker governorship, ringed most Illinois cities of any significant size.

These commercial leviathans, catalysts for more Illinois societal changes than any Illinois governmental policies, homogenized much of the Illinois landscape in remarkably quick fashion. Wal-Mart. Now there was a real force for transformation.

When Walker took office, he inherited an agency with responsibility for promoting mercantilism in the state, the Illinois Department of Business and Economic Development. Kind of a taxpayer-supported chamber of commerce.

It had evolved out of an operation begun in Governor Kerner's days and known then as the state's economic development board. The idea for the program came mainly from a young fellow from Chicago, Victor de Grazia, who ran the economic board's undertakings for a while at the request of Kerner.

By the time Walker arrived, the state's chamber of commerce was just one more bureaucracy. Like every candidate for governor, Walker had pledged to kick the department in the rear to get more visible movement in promotion of the economic climate.

But this was not an easy assignment, especially with the nation mired during the Walker years in what was to be the country's most serious recession in three decades. During Walker's last stage in office, the inflation rate topped 9 percent and unemployment in the United States was more than 8 percent, and Illinois was no stranger to the situation.

This made it tough for Walker and his BED directors, Howard R. Fricke and Joseph P. Pisciotte, to make people believe the agency's almost always routine claims of great success in protecting the Illinois job base.

As often happens, much of the notice accorded a far-flung operation like BED, with offices scattered around the world, focused on just one or two things, such as the coal promotion campaign under Marder or the agency's effort under Walker to lure moviemakers to Illinois.

Funny but true, in the last part of Walker's governorship the name of BED employee Lucy Salenger probably was more recognized in many places than that of her boss, Joe Pisciotte. She was a persuasive West Coast woman with Hollywood connections who laid a lot of the foundation for the numerous movies to be shot, from that point on, in Illinois instead of southern California.

This was typical of the Walker governorship as a whole, where the little things or one-shot deals would be most remembered by all but the political scientists.

For instance, Walker's signing of legislation partly lifting the state's prohibition against the open burning of leaves registered favorably with millions of Illinoisans.

But it was doubtful that even a few of those same millions realized that the Department of Insurance under Walker made

Illinois one of the first states to move to eliminate discrimination against women and singles in the sale and coverage of health and life insurance. Or that the department may have been the first in the nation to use a professional testing firm to prepare and administer the license examinations for brokers and agents—a step designed to further protect the public from unqualified license applicants. Or that the department was requiring affected insurance companies to file written reports on all complaints by policyholders to the department.

Or that, under Walker's leadership, Illinois was in the vanguard of states moving against so-called redlining by firms, the discriminatory practice of withholding home-loan funds or insurance from black neighborhoods on grounds that they were poor economic risks.

For sure, reporters on the Statehouse beat found much more newsworthy the quick cuts by Walker in the state's public relations programs—the slashing of the budget and staff of the governor-controlled Illinois Information Service and the sharp reduction in the number of the individual agencies' public information officers, spokespersons and plain old flacks. Press releases from Walker's office were way down from Ogilvie's time. Of course, Walker had promised to wield an ax in this area as part of his vow to trim governmental fat.

Still, this was a small-fry step in the Governor's game plan for getting a handle on state government. Lopping off some press agents wasn't going to change much of anything, but it looked good and was the kind of nickel-and-dime stuff that people identified with. Which was certainly okay, as far as it went.

What Dan Walker really wanted, though, was recognition as the governor with the managerial skill and brains to compel better service for the populace from the bureaucracy. He hoped to be viewed as a man on top of things. He wished those voters who had put him in the governor's chair could see him doing his homework, outfoxing the rigid bureaucrats, getting them off dead center on this or that issue.

That was the real challenge, the tough thing to pull off. It took considerably more ingenuity than his signing of the bill creating the Illinois State Lottery on December 14, 1973.

Although he had reservations about increasing the scope of gambling in the state, Walker finally had accepted the argument that the lottery was desirable because of the many millions of necessary new dollars it would bring to Illinois' general revenue coffer. He also suspected that by approving the measure he would be producing a major legacy of his governorship. Naturally he was right.

By such things as lotteries are governorships measured. ✦

Out of the Public Eye

Here he was, Governor Dan Walker, not very long after taking office, sitting in the White House at a formal dinner for the nation's governors and their wives. Another milestone in his meteoric political career.

Walker, that rising populist out of Illinois, was seated next to the wife of the President of the United States. Pat Nixon had not said anything yet to Walker, but the Governor was sure she would and he was thinking about what he would say to the spouse of the most powerful political leader in the world.

He knew he'd have to measure his words. Still, he could not

help but feel excited at being this close to her. But how would the ice be broken?

Finally it happened. As Walker bantered lightly with a woman on his left side while eating bits of salad, the woman to his right, Mrs. Nixon, tapped his arm. Turning to the wife of Richard Nixon, Walker smiled as pleasantly as he could and waited for her first words.

And they were: "Governor, you are eating my salad."

Blushing, he knew she had him, knew he had screwed up. He always had been confused about the placement of salad plates. Never had gotten it straight. It was just one of those things.

In formal settings, Walker observed wryly, "things didn't always go as gracefully as I would have wished."

Now and then, the Governor even seemed cursed at these events. Jeez, there were some moments, and often at the most inopportune times.

The dignity of the occasion was so thick you could cut it with a knife when the Governor and Mrs. Walker were hosts for a grandiloquent dinner for the justices of the Illinois Supreme Court and their wives.

White ties and tails in the Mansion's executive dining room. Decorum was being observed so closely that night that old B.I. Beeler, the main butler at the Mansion, had not hidden a drink for the Governor behind a plant as he usually did during gatherings at the Mansion so Walker could work in some sips without having to carry a drink or go to the bar.

The dinner with the justices was going hunky-dory. After the completion of the main course, Walker felt at ease and decided to allow himself the luxury of leaning back in the antique Louis XIV or whatever armchair from which he was presiding over this august occasion.

Disaster. It came with the sound of a god-awful crash shooting through the room, waking up everybody.

As Walker reclined in his chair, its back went out and both the Governor and the chair toppled backward to the floor. Walker ended up on his back, his legs propped straight up by the overturned chair. B.I. Beeler stood over the Governor, aghast with horror. The dessert tray in the butler's hands was shaking.

Looking up, Walker saw only the lanky figure of Beeler, clad as always in black suit and bow tie, the butler's gold teeth glistening. The Governor wondered whether Edith Doty, the housekeeper for the Walkers in their private living area upstairs, had heard the resounding thud of his spill. Also, there still was the matter of the presence in the room of the members of the Illinois Supreme Court.

Visions of what they must be thinking flashed through the mind of Walker, still in a supine position. Not a sound, not a breath could be heard.

Finally, Walker heard a voice, a high-pitched feminine one, saying, "I am glad, thank God, it wasn't me. Can you imagine my feet sticking up like that, my skirt down and all my petticoats showing?"

That brought down the house.

Later, Walker was told that the commentator was the wife of Justice Robert C. Underwood of Normal.

With this kind of luck, no wonder the Walkers did not socialize with the state's other major elected officials. No way could Walker relax with the Hartigans, Mike Howlett, Bill Scott, Mayor Daley. That would be stretching it too far.

"Oh, of course, there were the gala affairs to which those people were invited," said Walker. "And sometimes they came, except for Daley.

"Too, we had parties at the Mansion, maybe one a month, to which different groups of people were invited."

However, few of the functions at the Mansion seemed to be of much real political benefit to Walker, a situation that political guru de Grazia did not like at all.

The Governor also did practically no entertaining in Chicago, which he later felt to have been a mistake since "that would have been a very good way to woo the establishment."

Although both had staffs at their beck and call, neither the Governor nor Mrs. Walker had much control over their lives. Their exalted status created numerous downsides, including a severe limit on what Walker labeled "the important quality time together that every family needs."

Really, what was it like being the Governor of Illinois?

Walker captured the job with few preconceived notions of what to expect. What he did find out, and pretty quickly, was that he was the leading player in an unending drama that had for its stage the entire state of Illinois.

First and foremost, Walker discovered, "you rarely stop because your life is no longer in your own hands.

"You have illusions that you will be able to govern, but to a certain degree that is a fantasy. You live according to a schedule made up by other people. You have to depend on other people, your key assistants, because the job is just too overwhelming. They are supposed to have the pulse of what is going on at all levels and coordinate accordingly. I had to adhere to their prioritizing, or everything would fall into chaos.

"A governor loses many of his friends because you're not allowed to see them. So they eventually feel you're high-hatting them. Their inevitable reaction is that now that he has become a national figure he no longer has time for 'us peons.' And perhaps, to be honest, it is only human that a smidgen of pomposity does subconsciously insinuate itself into your innermost thoughts when you are in a position like governor.

"If you are an honest public servant, you suffer financially. You lose most of your money unless you are super wealthy going into office—which I was not.

"It's tough to get much real exercise and, despite the common conception of daily elegant dining, you eat all the wrong foods.

"You are always on stage and must constantly guard every word you utter for fear it will find its way into print, will be taken out of context or will offend some significant individual or group.

"Most everyday pleasures and relaxation are denied you. Once you are really there, you realize that you truly do belong to the people. No movies, no serious reading, no hobbies. Even thinking becomes a luxury.

"Oddly enough, since virtually everything is done for you, you lose a lot of the everyday sharpness that got you there in the first place. And for a variety of reasons, your sex life suffers.

"Sure, you get to attend all types of formal dinners and 'important' parties, high-powered political gatherings and the like. But you can't stay at any of them for any decent length of time. And for every function you attend, if only briefly, you risk offending 10 other groups that invited you to events the same day.

"I knew, of course, that some are better at this life-style than others. Some enjoy it to the hilt. As for myself, on a scale of one to 10, I considered it a six."

So, did Walker find it unbearable serving as governor? Not at all.

Insisting that he "would not want in the end to present a bleak picture of the job for which I fought so hard," Walker allowed as how "the rapid pace" actually suited his manner. Too, before becoming governor, Walker was not much of a party goer anyway. The social hobnobbing of Dan Walker came after the governorship in a fashion that nobody could have envisioned when he was governor.

Walker did not give a hoot about movies, and the absence of a sustained family home life was not exactly a new twist for Walker, a workaholic most of his life.

His only hobby, tennis, was not a casualty of his governorship.

Many days in Springfield began at a wee hour in Washington Park with a match against Bill Goldberg, who had been a tennis player at Highland Park High School.

Another thing, Walker did manage some time for himself. Most governors do, and Walker was no exception. For a person with so much at his fingertips, though, Walker's private moments largely were spent in modest surroundings.

A gun person, and proud of it, Walker found the hours to make it out to the fields and marshes in pursuit of ducks, quail or doves.

If he loved anything more, it was his little hideout down by Taylorville. This was a place befitting the self-styled commoner in the governor's chair and not the spiffy yacht skipper of later years.

Whispers held that it was a cabin deep in a woods in Christian County, a secret, almost mysterious refuge where big deals were cut. More accurately, the retreat was a double house trailer on a small man-made lake next to bigger Lake Bertinetti by Taylorville, which did happen to be the seat of Christian County.

Walker owned the trailer, which he himself warmly called "the cabin." The Governor paid about $25,000 for the setup out of his own pocket; not a cent of state money went for it. It was on property owned by C. F. Bertinetti, the Democratic chairman of Christian and an unusually close political ally of Walker.

The Governor had the trailer furnished just the way he wanted, its kitchen, dining space, living room, three small bedrooms. The existence of the retreat certainly was not a secret, but few individuals besides the Governor's hunting or cardplayer buddies got invited to it. State business was not conducted there.

Walker often drove to the trailer in the jeep that he owned, the same red, white and blue vehicle he had used during the summer stage of his 1972 campaign against Ogilvie. The Governor would zip around Taylorville in the open jeep, visible to all as he drove alone without security people to a grocery or to fetch catfish bait for the fishing back at the trailer. From time to time, he'd get caught up in the endless train of teen-driven hot rods cruising the square in Taylorville.

To the core, Walker was a shotgun person. Never owned a rifle. Learned to hunt with his dad and was just too attached to his father's old double-barreled L.C. Smith shotgun to give it up.

But he shied away from the hunting spots and lodges frequented by his predecessors and other big shots around well-known areas such as geese-rich Horseshoe Lake at the bottom of the state.

Instead, Walker would seek permission from farmers to hunt in their fields. Or a hunting partner would get the approval.

For Walker, a typical mid-state foray for doves or quail would take him to a farm near Standard City, a speck on the map of Macoupin County. Accompanying the Governor might be Vince Demuzio, whom Walker helped elect to the Illinois Senate in 1974, and quite likely another Carlinville Democrat, then State Representative Ken Boyle. The party also well may have included Jerry Gross, the owner of a Carlinville haberdashery who had become a friend of Walker through Demuzio.

Away from the public eye, Walker could be carefree at his trailer by the little lake. This could mean playing poker far into the night with Bertinetti, Demuzio and Wally Heil, a Taylorville furniture dealer with whom Walker had become quite close. Or skimming across the small lake in the 12-foot sailboat Walker purchased.

On a good tack, the Governor might run for as much as five minutes. Frequently though he ended up in the water or went aground, prompting Bertinetti or Heil to question kiddingly whether Walker truly was a graduate of the Naval Academy.

Walker couldn't wait to duck out when possible to hightail it down to his retreat. More than once in a blue moon, he recounted, "we would lay a pattern of jugs across the lake before we started playing poker. The jugs were milk bottles half filled with water, fitted with three-foot lines and baited with hooks.

"Then, later at night, two or three of us would get in the boat and run the pattern, shining a light on each jug. If it was dancing, we knew we had a fish on the line. Netted, it usually turned out to be a catfish, which I would skin and fry the next day.

"This little game could almost get to be dangerous when we did it after several hours of drinking. Especially if the lake was choppy, and the jug was being pulled across the lake by a big catfish. Governor drowns battling catfish! I didn't want anyone reading that."

One thought on the mind of Walker when he lined up his retreat was a belief that it would give his family needed relief from the public spotlight. But he got an impression right off that Roberta did not like it. The way he saw it, he had to drag her down to the place.

But she did not remember it that way. Her husband was mistaken, she felt, if he had that perception. But then there were other subjects on which the two failed to sufficiently communicate during the hectic, taut years of the governorship of Dan Walker.

A strained marriage in the Illinois Governor's Mansion hardly was a condition limited to the Walkers. State troopers assigned to Mansion security have whispered privately of strange behavior by more than one of the women cast as Illinois first ladies in modern political history.

Mrs. Roberta Walker was not the subject of any of those tales. If anything less than complimentary was said about her, it was that she seemed to be a reluctant first lady of Illinois.

Roberta Marie Dowse certainly did not grow up thinking she would ever find herself in that role.

She was the only child of Richard Dowse, a businessman and Republican politician in the Kenosha area, and Margaret Ann DeLany Dowse, whose family roots were with a Democratic clan in Lake County, Illinois. A grandfather, Patrick Henry DeLany, served in the Illinois House of Representatives.

Friends of Roberta Walker in her later life probably would have been surprised to find out that her mother, Margaret DeLany, had been a suffragette who marched in the streets. Few could see the refined, always proper Roberta Walker picketing for any cause.

In her words, "I grew up in the Depression and was in the tail end of the period before the modern women's movement. Younger women in the movement probably felt I was not enough of an activist, maybe not outspoken enough."

Although brought up in Kenosha, Roberta, who was raised Catholic, went to a Catholic high school, St. Catherine, in the nearby Wisconsin city of Racine. (Her mother was Catholic; her father was not.)

As things so often happen, a high school classmate of Roberta, Don Iselin of Racine, went on to the Naval Academy, where he had a roommate named Dan Walker.

When Iselin came home from the academy to Racine for the Christmas break of 1944, he was accompanied by Walker. Iselin still saw Roberta in those days because his girlfriend and later wife was Jacqueline Myers of Kenosha, the closest friend of Roberta.

To make it short, history should record that Roberta was introduced to Dan Walker when he joined Don Iselin on that yuletide break in 1944 and that, before Don and Dan returned to the academy, Dan and Roberta had gone on their first date (to a Chicago night club).

As she later put it, "things progressed from there." Things like a visit by Roberta to the Naval Academy in the spring of 1945 and the continual correspondence that comprised much of their courtship.

She was so different from many of the women Walker had encountered in his earlier sailor days. To her, Walker's initial "bump on the log" social tendencies became overshadowed by the many positive qualities of this young man from an impoverished background who seemed so obviously intent on making something of himself.

They were married on April 12, 1947, in the rectory of St. Mark's Catholic Church in Kenosha. On March 1 of the following year, Kathleen Marie was born, the first of the seven children.

She was followed by Daniel junior in 1949, Julie Ann in 1950, Roberta Sue (Robbie) in 1952, Charles Richard in 1954, Margaret in 1960 and Will in 1962.

With a family of that size, Roberta Walker, a Wisconsin college graduate, would have little time to pursue her intended profession as an elementary school teacher.

She was tied to the home front in Deerfield because her husband was a man always on the go. His involvement with all those rebellious Democrats, his drive to make his mark with his law firm, the crime commission role, the demands of the Montgomery Ward job. Plus, there always seemed to be an extraordinary undertaking tying him up even more, like the Walker Report.

Roberta and the youngsters attended Mass regularly, but her Protestant husband seldom accompanied them.

It was because of her endless hope that her husband would spend more time with his family that she was not elated at his decision to run for governor. But trying to talk him out of it was futile, she realized, so she did whatever she could to help.

Understanding her husband as well as she did, Roberta knew that he never did anything halfheartedly and those who took his candidacy lightly were sorely underestimating him. Well before the primary election, she was sure in her heart that he was going to win. She could not believe that the vaunted regular Democratic organization was so oblivious to what was happening.

By the same token, Roberta Walker "also knew that we were in trouble in the primary in 1976, but I could not get anybody to listen to me."

She never could accept her exclusion from the little circle of advisers surrounding her husband. After Walker, Thompson left no doubt of the high stock he put in the counsel of his wife, Jayne, and Thompson's successor, Jim Edgar, relied heavily on input from his wife Brenda. But the relationship between the Walkers was not viewed like that.

If she had "known or been told more," Roberta Walker insisted, "I certainly could have helped more."

The Mansion definitely was her territory. She governed it from an office that she set up on the lower level. She and her personal secretary, Geraldine McDermand, party arranger and menu planner Margaret Kolom and Marge Dowling, who kept an eye on the antiques and other furnishings, had their hands full dealing with hundreds of functions at the Mansion.

Walker daughters Kathleen and Julie were married while their father was governor and their wedding receptions were held in the Mansion.

Roberta Walker presided over this world with a stately comportment that her husband could not always match as he fought to contend with the helter-skelter in the Statehouse a few blocks away.

Yet, she sensed an absence of the kind of cooperation between her office and the Governor's crew that "was necessary to permit me to do the kind of job I really wanted to do.

"On some events the Governor's staff wanted things done or served a certain way at the Mansion. I did not always agree, and I'd put my foot down. So, yes, there was friction."

Her understanding, Mrs. Walker recalled, was that "the Mansion was not to be used for political things. No fund-raisers. Nothing like that.

"Because of the way Dan came into office, both Dan and Vic had indicated that we really had to watch using the Mansion for things overly political. I felt that was their game plan and that I was responding to it. I never knew that I may have been viewed as an obstacle to more political use of the Mansion."

Before the end of her husband's years in office, Roberta Walker worked with the Executive Mansion Association and Illinois historian James Hickey in overseeing the completion of the refurnishing of the Mansion, which had undergone renovation while Ogilvie was in office. This entailed trips by Mrs. Walker to New Orleans and other places to procure certain antiques for the restoration.

She also was a frequent traveler around Illinois, often because of her involvement in state and private programs for helping the aged and the handicapped. She led a delegation of Illinois business leaders on a trade mission to Japan and other points in the Far East, and she was at the head of another Illinois business contingent on a trade outing to Brazil.

At all times, the natty little first lady of Illinois vowed to herself to "make a conscious effort not to become isolated from the public" because she "could easily see where this might happen" to a governor's wife.

Of one thing Roberta Walker was very sure.

"After the inauguration of Dan, I felt I lived a lifetime during the next four years."

And, when those four years of Dan Walker's governorship were over, so was the marriage of Roberta and Dan.

Deeply disappointed with his political downfall and departure from the governorship, Walker reached a conclusion that his marriage was just one more factor in the vexation and frustration then gripping his life. In his mind, the marriage had run out of gas. The demands of the governorship had provoked an incompatibility that bred too many spats.

With the end of the Springfield days, Roberta wanted to return to their home in Deerfield, but Walker could not bring himself to go along with a resumption of that earlier part of his life.

Their 30-year marriage ended in divorce in 1977, the first year out of office for Walker. Roberta did not want the divorce, but grew to see at the time that it was a perhaps inevitable outcome of what she perceived as her husband's failure to come to grips with the latest dramatic turn of events in his life.

Years later, in assessing the chapters of his life, Walker would regret the grief inflicted on Roberta by the end of their marriage. Stabs of pain would go through him when he thought of the hurt she experienced upon learning in the years after the divorce that Walker had become involved with another woman while governor.

The Capitol press gang may have called Walker werewolf behind his back, but in the eyes of many of the women he met across the state Walker was not hard to look at.

Some suspected there had been a closer than office relationship with Mary Parrilli, his long-standing secretary and assistant. And, as governor he had learned quickly after taking office that too much conversation with one woman or attention to another at an event anywhere in the state could trigger rumors even before he was out of the town. It mattered not whether he was in southern Illinois or Chicago. He had to watch it with women just like he had to avoid being caught looking bored or inattentive at the head tables at which he found himself night after night.

At one political gathering, Governor Walker met a woman from a small downstate town that he wanted to see again. He got his wish. Several secret meetings between the two ensued, always away from Springfield.

He was much more attracted to another woman whom he was with at social functions while governor. He began seeing her covertly and the relationship turned into a passionate affair.

She was a Chicago socialite, a younger woman believed by Walker to be a very lovely lady. Their frequent times together included discreet lunches and meetings in suites at Michigan Avenue hotels. Walker's security chief, Pete Wilkes, always was aware of the arrangements involved in the matter.

The woman in the affair, which lasted a bit beyond Walker's governorship, was not the woman who became his second wife.

The second Mrs. Walker also was named Roberta. When they first met, Walker still was governor and she was Roberta Nelson, a DuPage countian who represented developmentally disabled individuals on state issues that affected them.

Roberta Nelson, a mother of three, had written a widely-read book on creating community acceptance for the handicapped and was active in the putting together of what would be the Illinois Epilepsy Association. She would become the first executive director of the association and Walker would go on the organization's board after leaving the governor's office.

There was no relationship between the two while Walker was governor or so long as he was married, but after his divorce one thing led to another rather quickly.

On November 24, 1978, Walker was married to Roberta Nelson, who was divorced from her husband, an investment executive. The marriage of Dan and Roberta II took place in an Episcopal church in Elmhurst.

To Walker, marriage to the good-looking, outgoing, dark haired Roberta, 14 years younger than he and an active Republican, offered a new lease on life.

Walker still felt he was politically strong and capable of another run for major office. More than that, though, Walker wanted to enjoy life and prosper, and he was convinced that his attractive new wife complemented a revitalized Dan Walker.

Some said that he wanted people to sit up and take notice of him again, just like they did in the days of his governorship when he really was a mover and shaker. ❧

Still Looking Good

Back in 1974 and early 1975, few Illinoisans would have guessed that Dan Walker would not win another election. Although the road was bumpy, with ambushers lurking at every turn, the Governor seemed by most signs to be forging ahead in his fight to ensure a new political era in his own image.

Folk singer Bob Dylan's hit, "The Times They Are A-Changin," may have been a theme song of the 1960s, but it still held true in the following decade. Social turbulence might have been subsiding, but the system remained up for grabs.

Unable to extricate himself from the Watergate mess, Nixon

became in 1974 the first president to resign. Polls showed unyielding distrust of government across the country, breeding continued strong discontent and political alienation. Not too far into the 1970s, girls were allowed to play in Little League baseball and one big electric power firm started using municipal refuse as a boiler fuel.

In Illinois, where voters signaled their desire for change by electing Walker in the first place, political upheaval was continuing. Walker was making sure of that.

The 1974 election, midway through Walker's term of office, left the Democrats in control of almost everything at the top of state government. Most notably, Democrats gained control of both houses of the General Assembly for the first time since 1937.

Governor Walker had a big hand in this. In both the primary and general elections, he stumped hard for not just Democratic legislative candidates, but particularly for ones that would be loyal to him. He got results, enough so to make the 1974 election a watershed in the Walker political revolution.

He followed this by successfully opposing at the start of 1975 the ascendancy to the House speakership by Clyde Choate, the veteran Democratic leader in the body. To Walker, Choate was the kind of manipulator who gave politics a poor reputation.

It truly was a period in Walker's governorship of political prosperity. A lot of things were happening.

Illinois Republican Chairman Don (Doc) Adams even found himself having to worry about the impact of a country-western record on Walker commissioned and promoted late in 1974 by the Illinois Democratic Fund, a money-raising operation of the Governor.

"A Winner Walkin' Home: The Ballad of Dan Walker" was written and recorded by Stan Hitchcock of Nashville and was being sold by Walkerites for a couple of bucks. The record also was being used at fund-raising concerts for the Governor.

The song called Walker "a man who means just what he says" and extolled other virtues of this man whose "body's tired but not his soul." While skittish Republicans searched their ranks for a songwriter, the Illinois political world wondered what Walker would do next.

While the wondering was going on, the United States Supreme Court handed Walker good news late in 1974 by upholding his executive order requiring certain state employees to disclose their financial holdings—a part of Walker's effort to impose tougher ethical standards for state employees so as to ensure greater honesty in government. His order had made Illinois a leader on this matter. Some in the state bureaucracy had argued that the disclosure order violated their right to privacy.

(However, Walker was not successful in getting the judiciary to agree that he could require companies seeking or holding state contracts to disclose their political contributions.)

The final months of 1974 also were a time when Walker finally seemed to be making headway on political fund-raising, a never ending headache.

At center stage on this was the Illinois Democratic Fund. Set up by the Walker team in 1973, it became the arm for raising capital for the Governor's ongoing political activities.

Before the IDF, no fund-raising operation of consequence existed statewide for Democrats. Without one, Walker knew he would have little success in grabbing at least part of the state Democratic financial clout away from Daley's Cook County organization, a money source Walker obviously could not rely on.

Downstate Democrats did not dispute the need for the IDF, but they found it hard to swallow the Walkerites' argument that the IDF was designed more to assist the party's candidates than the Governor's political career.

Of course, the IDF was not to be confused with the less noticeable All-Illinois Democratic Committee, which was still trying at the end of 1974 to eliminate the sizable deficit remaining from Walker's campaign for governor.

For one thing, David Cleverdon, the former organization director for Walker's gubernatorial campaign who was directing the IDF, stressed that the names of many of its donors had been disclosed. This was not true for the United Republican Fund, the nearest thing to the IDF in the Illinois GOP.

It also was not true for the All-Illinois Democratic Committee, which had not been open about the money raised to erase the deficit or about still unpaid bills from Walker's 1972 campaign effort—much to the consternation of the Chicago media and others second-guessing Walker.

But the Walker crowd preferred concentrating on the more positive IDF because it signified the future and things to remember like the day of Oct. 7, 1974. IDF Governor's Day. Walker showed on that occasion that he could raise dollars with the best of them after all.

A limited number of Illinoisans were invited by the IDF to participate in the day's activities—to the tune of a $1,000 donation by each. Enough persons accepted the offer, Cleverdon said, to net the IDF close to $100,000.

For a start, the contributors had an afternoon of golf and tennis at Springfield's Oakcrest Country Club with Stan Musial, Lee Majors and other sports and television celebrities.

Then, the day ended with a seven-course dinner at the Governor's Mansion, an affair at which the food was prepared under the eye of Jovan, the proprietor of one of Chicago's finest restaurants. This was obviously one occasion on which the Mansion clearly was used for political purposes.

To those hanging around the edge of the Governor's Day events, Walker appeared far along in moving from a party outlander to the leader of a new political establishment. There was a great distance from the political have-nots of his 1972 campaign to the luminaries with whom he rubbed shoulders that day.

The IDF had concentrated up to that point on getting small contributions from persons who had not donated previously to either party.

Or, in the words that day of Cleverdon, it was true "we really haven't gone after the fat cats in the past. We have aimed at, and gotten, the little donors, the ordinary folks."

But, as for those willing to fork over $1,000 on Governor's Day, Cleverdon found them "also to be plain folks, but ones who have done well in life...persons now willing to pay that much money to be high rollers or just to be with famous people."

Nevertheless, most of the money collected on Governor's Day was used to finance the television commercials and other activities of Walker in support of certain Democrats running in 1974 for the General Assembly.

For a while, Walker approached the 1974 election season with a hands-off policy in respect to almost all of the legislative primary races in the Democratic Party. Well into the primary campaign, he had done little more on the surface than express support for the re-election of two Chicago Democratic legislators not supported by the Daley machine, independent Senator Dawn Clark Netsch and Representative James Houlihan, a longtime political ally of the Governor.

A few weeks before the primary, though, Walker abandoned any pretense of being above the fray by throwing himself into numerous contests in support, most often, of underdog candidates opposed by regular Democratic organizations or running in Republican areas. Not many persons were surprised by Walker's involvement. Polls available to his office indicated that few legislative contenders would suffer from his backing.

Walker was the first to realize that nobody stood to gain more from a Democratic Legislature than himself. A claim by the Governor to have helped or even been instrumental in bringing the General Assembly under the wing of his party could not hurt his national image.

To be honest, many observers believed that Illinois Democrats could not help but score legislative gains in 1974 because of unease with the GOP over the Watergate political climate and the downfall of Nixon. Too, Illinois Republicans only held a one-vote margin in each branch of the General Assembly going into 1974.

Still, Walker and his lieutenants injected themselves into that year's electoral picture with a vigor seldom exhibited by a modern era Illinois governor not on the ballot himself.

Accentuating the push, de Grazia took a two-month leave of absence from his governmental post before the general election to coordinate Walker's campaign activities, a period in which Vic's salary and expenses were picked up by the IDF.

de Grazia also waged a successful campaign to oppose approval in the 1974 election of a proposed Illinois constitutional amendment that would have virtually stripped Walker of his amendatory veto power.

That controversial authority, granted to Illinois governors by the 1970 Illinois Constitution, permitted the chief executives to make substantial changes in bills passed by the Legislature, enough so that critics argued that the amendatory veto power usurped the power of the General Assembly.

(Legislators can vote to accept a governor's recommendations on a bill, paving the way for it to become law, or they can seek to override an amendatory veto or they can do nothing, in effect killing the bill.)

The Walker team did not go undefeated in General Assembly contests where the Governor himself or his operatives were active in 1974.

Walker's people could not give Joseph Pisciotte enough of a boost to unseat incumbent Republican Senator Stanley Weaver of Urbana in eastern Illinois. This was the same Joe Pisciotte who was executive director of the Illinois Constitutional Convention of 1970 and later Walker's economic development director.

In a contest much closer to home, the Walker forces could not bring about the election to the Illinois House of Walker son-in-law David Vaught of Marion. Obviously, that was an eye-catcher, the headline contest of the primary campaign downstate.

Those were still the days when each General Assembly district sent three House members to Springfield. Each party would nominate two candidates in the primary, and voters would elect three of those four to the lower chamber in the general election.

In 1974, the Fifty-ninth Legislative District covered 10 counties and parts of two others in the southernmost part of Illinois. The Democratic primary field for the two nominations for the House included House minority leader Choate and another incumbent, Benton lawyer Richard Hart, as well as Vaught.

The 26-year-old Vaught, then working for the administration of his father-in-law as a tourism official, viewed Hart as the most vulnerable and attacked him as being bought and sold by the coal industry, to which Hart was in fact quite close. Nevertheless, Vaught's candidacy really ticked off Choate, to put it mildly.

As it turned out, Democratic primary voters in the Fifty-ninth District selected Choate and Hart over Vaught, thought by many to be too much in a hurry to capitalize on the position of his father-in-law. Walker did not ask Vaught to run, had reservations about it all along, but in the end plugged hard for Vaught. When the primary was over, it was hard to tell who was more hot under the collar at the other, Walker or Choate.

Stung as he was by Vaught's defeat, Walker still came out of that election year smelling like a rose. The Governor's pain was eased by results in many other parts of the state.

Like in the election to the House of Harold D. Byers, a Highland book salesman who was a Walker campaign chairman in Madison County in 1972 and anything but a favorite of the regular Democratic organization in Madison.

And in the Forty-ninth Legislative District in central Illinois, where Walkerites never hid their enthusiasm in both the primary and fall election for the Senate candidacy of Carlinville's Vince Demuzio, a former executive director of the Illinois Valley Economic Development Corp., who was just 32 at the time.

Demuzio, whose coal miner father had come to this country from Italy in 1928, won a spirited Democratic primary contest with Mayor Russell Masinelli of Staunton and went on to oust Republican incumbent A. C. (Junie) Bartulis of Benld in the general election.

Demuzio's district was one of a number in which Walker campaigned in 1974 by touring in his trademark red, white and blue jeep. Delighted at getting back out on the campaign trail, Walker seemed to be everywhere at once, especially in the weeks before the fall election.

The Governor and his jeep might be in Carlinville or Gillespie one minute, but word reaching the Statehouse an hour or two later would have him in Kankakee or Fairfield or Pekin.

Returning to the side roads and blue highways, the Governor, garbed at times in jeans and work shirts, was calling attention to candidates who at first may have been given little chance of victory.

A case in point was Jerome J. Joyce, a portly Kankakee County farmer from Essex seeking to wrest away a Senate seat from the heavily favored Edward McBroom, a Kankakee businessman and stalwart of the GOP bloc in the General Assembly's upper body.

Only a few did not at first share the view of Rick Davis, a reporter for the Kankakee Daily Journal, who "surely thought McBroom had a lock on the seat." But, observed Davis, "Walker really succeeded in drawing eyes to the Joyce candidacy, so much so that a whole lot of people in that area really believed that a Joyce victory was Walker's top objective in the election." Joyce won.

Another Walker success story in 1974 was the election to the Illinois House from south central Illinois of Democrat William L. O'Daniel, a Wayne City grain farmer.

In view of his own background, the Governor just naturally liked O'Daniel. He was a son of a tenant farmer in Kentucky who brought his family to southern Illinois in the Depression and bought a farm near Golden Gate. During World War II, young Bill was an Army paratrooper who was wounded in action in the Philippines. Coming out of the war a hero but penniless, O'Daniel started his own farming operation on a shoestring in Wayne County. By the time he sold out in the mid 1970s, O'Daniel had built his undertaking into a nearly 4,000-acre farm that was one of the largest grain producers in the region.

Walker also was O'Daniel's kind of guy. To O'Daniel, Walker was "the type of person we needed in government, a man in touch with the real people but also with a business background. He was my style of Democrat.

"Dan was an inspiration for me to run. I was fresh off the farm, green as could be politically. He was of tremendous help to me in 1974. Without Dan, I might not have been politically successful."

Walker was the speaker at O'Daniel's first fund-raiser, which packed the gym at Fairfield High School. The two men also made the rounds in O'Daniel's sprawling district in the Governor's jeep.

Republican legislative candidates tried to combat the invasion of their backyards by Walker with charges that his governorship was stumbling because of his state budget cuts and allegedly unfulfilled promises. Some of the GOPers were depicting their races as informal plebiscites on the popularity of the Governor. They were gambling his appeal had waned. They guessed wrong— at least in many downstate districts.

"In 1974," said Richard N. Luft of Pekin, "Dan Walker was still very popular in my district. So, when you can get a popular sitting governor to come into your district and campaign all over for you in an open jeep, like I did, it's quite beneficial to say the least."

Luft, who had been the elected auditor of Tazewell County, lost a race for the Illinois Senate in 1972. He then was legislative liaison for the state transportation department during Walker's first two years in office before running for and winning a seat in the Illinois House in 1974.

The investment of time and effort by Walker in the 1974 election would assure the leaving of his fingerprints on Illinois government for decades after his own departure from the scene.

The most immediately evident outcome of the 1974 balloting, though, was the Democratic sweep. Besides the party's capture of both branches of the Legislature, Adlai Stevenson III easily won re-election to his United States Senate seat and Illinois Treasurer Alan Dixon retained his office in a cakewalk.

The Republicans also lost their hold on a majority of the state's 24 seats in the United States House, with Democrats emerging from the election with a 13 to 11 edge in the congressional delegation.

The political career of Paul Simon was resurrected with his election to the United States House from southern Illinois. Ten years later, Simon would win election to the United States Senate and in 1988 this man once politically vanquished by Walker would launch a serious bid for the Democratic nomination for president.

Democrats' rare control of the General Assembly and governorship at the same time would last only two years because of the party's loss of the governor's office in the 1976 election. But, with the exception of one two-year period, the House remained a Democratic bastion for decades. And Republicans would not regain a majority in the Senate until 1993.

Few results of the 1974 election were more personally satisfying to Walker than the stunning failure of his bitter Republican nemesis, House Speaker W. Robert Blair, to win re-election to a seat in the lower chamber.

Blair, a Walker tormentor at every turn, had his eye on the Republican gubernatorial nomination in 1976 and had shown he could raise both the funds and issues to be taken seriously. He also had assembled a very politically astute staff, it was later recalled, that included at the top rung an executive assistant from Charleston, a dapper young man named Jim Edgar.

Walker may have been out of sight after 1976, but he could not be forgotten. Not with individuals like Demuzio, Luft, O'Daniel and Jerry Joyce figuring so heavily in Illinois legislative happenings in ensuing years. Demuzio was even Illinois Democratic chairman from 1986 to 1990, a post hardly ever held by a Democrat outside the Chicago area.

Plenty of others with Walker ties made it to the General Assembly in the years after Walker. Jim Rea, Alfred Ronan and Michael Curran, to name a few.

Rea, the man from Christopher, ran a branch of the governor's office in southern Illinois while Walker was governor and then, in a career as a House member and state senator beginning in 1979, was a wheelhorse for legislation affecting the lower part of the state.

Chicagoan Ronan was an agency official in the Walker administration before serving for more than a decade in the Illinois House where he was an influential wheeler-dealer and chairman of the transportation committee.

Mike Curran. An interesting story, like so many coming out of the Walker movement.

Grows up in Quincy, the oldest of 13 kids of Duke Curran, who was widely known from his football playing days at the University of Iowa. Young Mike himself gets a degree in creative writing from the University of Illinois. Joins a brother, Mark Curran, as one of a tiny number working in Adams County in 1972 for the election of Walker. Like Walker, Mike said he believed that "machine politics needed checking." When Walker is governor, Mike works for a while for the state transportation agency. When Walker seeks re-election in 1976, Mike is a salaried worker for the campaign with responsibility for Springfield, Quincy and the Quad Cities. Out of sight after that until he resurfaces politically in 1982 by surprisingly capturing a GOP-held House seat representing Springfield, enabling him to embark on a path in the lower chamber as a champion of the interests of education and state workers.

After the 1974 election, Walker would not again taste political victory—with one exception. He stopped Clyde Choate from becoming speaker of the Illinois House in a confrontation at the start of 1975 that turned the lower chamber into a three-ring circus.

The House speakership is in the mind of many the state's second most powerful post and one and all assumed that Democratic capture of the House in the 1974 election would mean the virtually automatic elevation of Democratic minority leader Choate to the presiding officer's chair when the new Seventy-ninth General Assembly convened in January 1975.

But Walker decided he didn't want Choate to be speaker, contending that Choate was unfit for the position because he was a protege of the late Secretary of State Paul Powell, a Democratic power broker whose almost legendary dealings remained the talk of the Illinois political world long after his death in 1970.

"We were trying to improve the image of Illinois government," Walker would say afterward of his opposition to Choate. "Clyde in the speakership did not fit in with what we were trying to accomplish."

Years later, Choate had a wry comeback.

"So I was bad for the image of government? Well, I didn't go to prison."

Political enmity between Walker and Choate was not always

the case. When Walker entered the governorship, Choate recalled, "I thought he was a hell of a guy with real presidential potential." Prior to their falling out, Choate had warm memories of hours spent with the Governor in hunting blinds around Ware, not far from Choate's town of Anna, and of poker nights at the Governor's Mansion. It was Choate who taught Walker to play two-handed poker on a flight they once shared from Carbondale to Springfield.

Like Walker, Clyde L. Choate was a person of humble origin. Born in West Frankfort, one of 14 children of a farmer-miner. Grew up over in Union County. Just one more poor kid in the Depression.

But Choate already was an established political figure while Walker was a law student at Northwestern.

Choate was elected to the House in 1946 when he was 26 years old, and a hero of World War II. Not long before going to the General Assembly, when Choate was working as an apprentice railroad brakeman in St. Louis, he read in a newspaper that he was to receive the Congressional Medal of Honor for valor in action in France. When President Truman presented the medal to him, Choate recollected, "he said that he would rather have it than be president."

Throughout his 28 years in the House before 1975, Choate built a reputation as a master of legislative maneuvering who had a leading hand in the passage of much of the major legislation of his time concerning public schools, labor, veterans and government reorganization. He joined fellow southern Illinoisan Powell in pushing legislation to trigger the development of Southern Illinois University and many other public improvement projects in the southern section of the state.

Vienna-resident Powell was incredibly adept in bringing home the bacon for southern Illinois, and Choate was right there with him. To do this, they had to scheme unmercifully, employing every wile they could muster, which sometimes meant either playing ball with or conning the more numerous Chicago area legislators. Only through such extraordinary dealings on its behalf could southern Illinois remain competitive in the legislative process. But many righteous folks could not see that.

Unfortunately for Powell, he was remembered mostly for the $800,000 in cash found in his Springfield hotel apartment and Statehouse office after his death.

Although the origin of the money remained a mystery, investigations into the matter brought out many things in Powell's past, including a business relationship with Choate. Clyde was also among the politicians who had joined Powell in sometimes lucrative horse racing investments.

Choate could not, and did not, argue that he and Powell were not friends and political allies. But Choate took umbrage at being called Powell's protege, insisting that he was every bit as much of his own man in public life as Walker.

To that, the Walker camp would counter that it was hard not to notice that Choate frequently sided with Mayor Daley in the legislative encounters between the Governor and the mayor.

Choate was convinced, though, that the quarrel with Walker stemmed from Choate's refusal to back David Vaught over Dick Hart for one of the Democratic nominations for the House in Choate's district in the 1974 primary.

"That had to be it, my refusal to support the Governor's son-in-law," surmised Choate years later when his mind flashed back to a day late in 1974 when he walked into the Statehouse, bought a Chicago Daily News in the rotunda and promptly read that the Governor could not back him for speaker.

"I had just left the Mansion, where I met with Walker on legislative strategy, and he hadn't said a thing to me on the subject of speaker. When I saw that paper, I was hurt, sick and mad as hell."

The marathon dogfight that followed when the House got down to electing its speaker in January 1975 wore out everybody. But it was fun at first, especially for the reporters.

Highlighting the very first day of the 1975 session was not the usual harmony of opening day but a god-awful shoving match in the House between a lobbyist and a legislator, a definite no-no.

Bystanders had to jump between the two just as the lobbyist, a steelworkers' union operative, was winding up to throw a punch at Representative John Matijevich after the legislator had pushed the lobbyist off the House floor. The lobbyist was trying to rally support for Choate for speaker and North Chicago Democrat Matijevich was strongly opposing Choate.

Enough of the other Democrats felt like Matijevich to deny Choate the 89 votes needed to get elected speaker even though the Democrats then controlled the chamber by a 101 to 76 margin. And even though, in the early balloting, Choate had the backing of the sizable Chicago Democratic bloc taking direction from Daley.

Walker would never dominate the House, but he now had enough Democrats following him in his opposition to Choate to prevent the southern Illinoisan from winning. At the same time, no other Democratic aspirant for speaker could get the necessary votes either, setting off a deadlock that endured through ballot after ballot after ballot.

Somewhere along the line, Daley abandoned his support for Choate and ended up, along with Walker, backing the compromise candidacy of diminutive Democrat William A. Redmond of Bensenville, a DuPage County village a stone's throw from Chicago. So, for a few days, Walker and Daley were working toward the same goal.

Ironically, even the backing of Daley and Walker still could not secure victory for Redmond in the speakership contest until seven Republican representatives crossed over to finally give him the needed 89 votes. That occurred on the ninety-third ballot. Nobody could recall anything like it.

The low-key Redmond became known as a conciliatory individual in the three terms in which he was speaker. The same was not said about the real muscle in the Redmond speakership, the shrewd young Irish lawyer from Chicago who was Democratic majority leader under Redmond, one Michael J. Madigan.

When Madigan himself became speaker in 1983, the House entered an era of discipline under ironfisted control from the podium that was unthinkable in the chaos that often gripped the House in the years before Madigan.

Back to 1975, the blocking of Choate's move for speaker was hailed by Walker partisans, particularly ones who saw issues as either all white or all black, as a great victory for the Governor. Intervention in a legislative leadership battle to that degree by a governor certainly was not common. Risks were involved, win or lose.

Life with the Legislature did not get that much easier for Walker. The most obvious explanation was that the House, after the speakership contest, was as balkanized as ever with the Democrats splitting their loyalties between Daley, Walker and, yes, Clyde Choate.

The Governor continued to take his lumps, such as in the General Assembly's rejection in 1975 of his request for approval of an accelerated state construction program of more than $4 billion, an ambitious plan to fight the recession and unemployment by pouring state bond funds into the faltering Illinois construction industry to create as many as 30,000 new jobs.

For members of Walker's legislative liaison team, every day was hazardous duty. When state Senator James Donnewald of Breese lined up Ronald Messina for a job with the Walker administration, the 27-year-old urban affairs specialist fresh out of St. Louis University had little inkling he soon would feel like a war veteran.

Assigned to work the House with David Caravello, New Jerseyite Messina "quickly realized I had to get up every day ready for a fight. With all the Democratic factions, absolutely nothing came easy for us. Long nights. Seven days a week. But, it was the most exhilarating period of my life, professionally."

Never, added Messina, "would I ever experience another time like the 1975 session. The Choate issue was the most exciting thing I ever worked on. And the gains in benefits that year by organized labor were simply unbelievable."

In any kind of normal political milieu, 1975 might have finally been a year in which Walker could have settled down in the governorship, eased away a little from the constant intensity of his public life. But nagging annoyances always were popping up, some of his own making.

With the state's first campaign finance disclosure law at last signed by Walker and in effect, the Governor's Illinois Democratic Fund was filing public reports with the Illinois Board of Elections showing that many of the top contributors to the IDF were individuals with firms doing business with the state.

Many of those bankers, housing developers, contractors, engineers and other donors also had contributed to other governors in previous years when political contributions did not have to be revealed.

Critics of Walker pointed out, though, that he had been quite critical of Ogilvie for accepting donations from state contract holders, in particular road builders.

Also hurting his image in 1975 were the disclosures, mainly by the St. Louis Post-Dispatch, of numerous individuals on the payrolls of various state agencies who actually worked on political or other projects for the Governor's office that had little or nothing to do with the departments paying the individuals.

These persons were dubbed "ghost payrollers" in regard to the agencies compensating them because regular personnel in those agencies never saw the "ghosts." Walker indignantly retorted that the practice was as old as the hills in Illinois government. Making a big deal of it with his administration was grossly unfair, he insisted.

There were plenty of other irritations as 1975 moved along.

For instance, because of the refusal of the General Assembly to approve necessary funding, Walker closed the statewide network or branches of his Governor's Action Office, set up by Walker to be a hallmark of his administration. Staffed with Walker people, these local offices fielded requests for help from persons finding it impossible to penetrate the interminable bureaucracies of the state agencies.

From mid 1974 to March 1975 alone, Walker noted, some 45,000 "cases" were handled by the GAO network.

Most likely, things like the GAO setback would not have happened if Walker had reached any kind of political accord with Daley. However, an amiable relationship with Daley was not in the cards. Never really was. Never really could be.

The Governor, proud and stubborn Dan Walker, could never in any way bring himself to pay the price for peace with the mayor. That cost, Walker was sure, fell nothing short of complete capitulation to the mayor on any issue he deemed important.

And, at any rate, the Governor's strategists still were gambling that Walker's interests were best served by a continuation of the hostility between Walker and the man who was both mayor and Illinois Democratic boss.

By the middle of 1975, the relentless fighting with Daley had gotten on Walker's nerves. It was a primary reason that a tired Walker began to entertain thoughts about just hanging it up and not going for re-election.

Still, be that as it may, the whole Illinois political world knows that Walker did seek to retain his office in 1976. Furthermore, when he formally announced on Oct. 1, 1975, his intention to do this, Daley was the target of as many Walker broadsides as ever.

By all signs, a rerun of the tone of Walker's 1972 campaign was in the making—at least if Walker had his way.

Standing at a press conference in Chicago, the Governor declared in announcing his candidacy for re-election that, although he had not "satisfied the politicians," he would always "fight for what is right for the people regardless of where the chips may fall."

The Governor openly challenged Daley to back a candidate against him for the Democratic gubernatorial nomination in the primary election in March 1976. Walker literally dared Daley to "once again convene his clique of slatemakers to pick their puppet."

So, Walker had thrown down the gauntlet again to Daley, in clearly unmistakable language. Later on, as his political world crashed down around him, Walker would have second thoughts about so directly challenging Daley, thoughts about what might have been if Walker had simply come out for re-election without such deliberate provocation of the mayor, a man every bit as prideful and defiant as the Governor.

Five days after Walker revealed his intention to run again for governor, State Treasurer Dixon ended months of speculation by announcing that he would challenge Walker for the Democratic nomination for governor in 1976.

A Walker-Dixon race could be a dandy, observers quickly predicted, because the Belleville attorney was as much of a scrapper as Walker. And, it was assumed, Dixon would have the support of Daley.

The Walker team was not so sure, though, that Dixon would be the one backed by Daley in the virtually certain move by the mayor to deny the despised Dan Walker another term as governor.

In any case, the Walkerites knew that 1976 was at the doorstep. 〰

 **Defeated**

Just like that, it was over. Not for the spirit of political independence that he had unleashed, but for the man himself. Dan Walker was beaten.

In 1976, for the first time in nearly a half century, an incumbent Illinois governor failed to win his party's renomination for the office.

The last time it had happened was in 1928, when Governor Len Small lost in a bid for renomination to fellow Republican Louis Lincoln Emmerson, then secretary of state.

In the Illinois primary election on March 16, 1976, Governor

Dan Walker's try for renomination also was blocked by the Illinois secretary of state, who at the time was Democrat Michael J. Howlett.

Many Illinoisans could not believe at first that Walker was defeated, especially downstaters who had come to expect political miracles from him. A lot of these persons, miles away from Chicago's media and Democratic machine, took it hard.

Feelings were mixed even in the gaggle of reporters gathered in Chicago the morning after the primary balloting to await an appearance by Walker. More than a few of them had rooted openly for his defeat, daring anyone to say anything positive during the primary campaign about the Governor.

But it also was hitting a number of those journalists that the most exciting political figure in Illinois in many years would now most likely be passing from the scene. In their business, Walker had been great copy, an eighteen-carat headliner.

When an obviously weary Walker finally came before the newspeople, he declared that Mayor Richard J. Daley had drawn even with him in their political slugfests.

"We're tied," the Governor remarked. "Walker one. Daley one." However, almost everybody present sensed that the Walker magic was gone, that there would not be a tiebreaker.

Daley's machine had turned out a huge vote for Chicagoan Howlett, one of the machine's own, a total well beyond what Howlett needed to offset the strong showing by the Governor downstate.

Since the primary was held on the eve of the annual St. Patrick's Day festivities in Chicago, the city's still Irish-heavy Democratic oligarchy had every reason to celebrate with even more gusto than usual. As the St. Pat's parade moved down State Street, Daley and other machine godfathers in the front row had the unmistakable strut of winners.

It would be the proverbial final hurrah for Daley, who would be dead before 1976 was over, a victim of a massive heart attack on Dec. 20.

More than that, the primary defeat of Walker would be the last successful show of muscle by the vaunted machine itself. It was as if the organization summoned its remaining strength for one final great offensive, like the German army in the Battle of the Bulge, before returning to a path leading to an inevitable expiration.

To their dying day, though, the muscle men of the machine could boast that they had steamrolled Dan Walker, the politician who caused the machine its biggest embarrassment and who, more than any other living being, hastened its decline.

The incumbent Governor Dan in the 1976 primary was carrying baggage that brash challenger Dan Walker did not have to bear in his campaign for governor four years earlier.

His constant warfare with all comers had left him worn-out and stretched way too thin. Although Walker always was subject to criticism that he never had stopped campaigning to govern, the reality of it was that masterful campaigner Walker failed to ever get a complete handle on his 1976 primary effort. As he himself admitted, the invigorating spirit of his 1972 political crusade was not visible in 1976.

Nevertheless, he thought he would win the 1976 primary and go on within a few months after that to become a factor in the jockeying for the Democratic Party's nomination for president that year.

More than a few politically savvy Illinoisans did believe that Walker was invincible at the polling booths. In the back of his mind, Walker too may have begun entertaining an idea along this line.

This was why, going into the 1976 primary season, many Walker partisans professed not to care who was tabbed by Daley to run against Walker in the primary. Any challenger would be turned back by the Governor, so went their reasoning. Walker even had invited primary opposition.

He got it all right, but it was Howlett instead of Alan Dixon.

Although Dixon had announced that he would run against Walker, the Illinois Treasurer emerged from the Daley-led Democratic slatemakers' ritual as their choice for the party's nomination for secretary of state in 1976.

To take on Walker, the slatemakers chose Howlett, reportedly because Daley felt the job of ousting Walker was too important to be trusted to a downstater.

Daley hardly could be faulted for going with Howlett, a fellow Irish Catholic. Very popular and gregarious, the 61-year-old Howlett had forged a solid reputation as a politician of consensus in his 15 years in state office, 12 as state auditor of public accounts and three as secretary of state. Howlett also had good rapport with Statehouse reporters, a number of whom recalled that Howlett in his state auditor days seldom hesitated to blow the whistle when records under his control revealed questionable practices by public officials.

An interesting thing about Howlett, he certainly was of the clan that formed the backbone of the Chicago machine. And there was no mistaking his Chicago accent. Yet, Howlett had built a loyal following in many parts of downstate Illinois that transcended the traditional suspicion between Chicago and the rest of the state.

Daley was counting on this as a plus when he persuaded Howlett to challenge Walker for the party's gubernatorial nomination. And the mayor did have to persuade Howlett to do it because Howlett did not volunteer for the task.

As Howlett's running mate on the Daley or so-called regular Democratic ticket, the slatemakers opted for the renomination for lieutenant governor of incumbent Neil Hartigan.

The Walker-Hartigan relationship at the top of Illinois government started off poorly and got considerably worse after that.

In spite of the appearance of cordiality in their infrequent meetings, Walker and Hartigan waged continuous war against each other. Walker excluded Hartigan from policy-making and Hartigan responded with program initiatives independent of the Governor and sometimes counter to what Walker wanted.

Exchanges between Walker and Hartigan could resemble comedy routines.

One day Hartigan, a bright man desperate for things to do, calls for the use of Illinois National Guard troops to renovate the State Fairgrounds at Springfield.

Within hours, Walker shoots back that as long as he is governor, "Guardsmen will not be used as forced labor to displace skilled tradesmen who work to support their families." Anyway, Walker adds, Hartigan knows full well the Governor's administration is already pushing a fairgrounds rehabilitation program.

It was like that between them the whole time.

One of the few things Walker asked of Hartigan was to head the state's effort to land the then proposed new airport for the St. Louis area at an Illinois site. But the pair never got together on, or even discussed to any degree, the steps Illinois should take to win its bid for the airport. A bid that was not successful.

Feeling that he needed help to prevent Howlett, Hartigan and the others on the Democratic ticket endorsed for the 1976 primary by regular party leaders from ganging up on him, Walker raised the stakes in the primary even higher by fielding a primary slate of his own.

For his running mate, the Governor chose Mrs. Joanne H. Alter to oppose Hartigan for the Democratic nomination for lieutenant governor. A 48-year-old mother of four, she was an elected commissioner of the Metropolitan Sanitary District of Greater Chicago.

Challenging Dixon for the nomination for secretary of state on the Governor's ticket was Walker friend Vince Demuzio, the young state senator from Carlinville.

The others on the Walker slate were two members of his cabinet, Roland Burris, director of the Department of General Services, and Ronald E. Stackler, head of the Department of Registration and Education.

Stackler, 36, a Chicago lawyer, ran for the nomination for attorney general against Senator Cecil Partee, the black Chicagoan who was president of the Illinois Senate.

Burris joined the Walker ticket to challenge Michael J. Bakalis for the Democratic nomination for Illinois comptroller. Educator Bakalis was the last elected state superintendent of public instruction.

From the start, nobody on the Walker slate except for the Governor himself was given hardly any chance of victory in the 1976 primary. True to the prediction, each of them, Mrs. Alter, Stackler, Demuzio and Burris, was beaten badly by their better known opponents.

Nevertheless, that quartet running with Walker, dubbed the "expendables" by the press, did all that could be asked to keep the pressure off the Governor by bombarding Howlett with everything that could be dug up on the man. This gave Walker a much freer hand to try to influence the direction of the campaign. Which he was able to do, to some extent.

By all accounts, Walker entered the primary campaign as a definite underdog to Howlett. After all, Howlett had a lot more going for him than just the support of Daley and seemingly every other Democrat in that catchall category of "party regular."

Also behind Howlett were the bulk of Illinois' major labor leaders, a good part of the press, many business bigwigs and even a sizable number of the politically active state employees under Walker's jurisdiction.

Walker anticipated much of this, but that didn't lessen the sting, especially when political two-timing was involved.

A good example was the defection to Howlett of double-crosser Francis Touchette, the veteran Democratic boss of St. Clair County's Centreville Township, a poverty-stricken place that always turned out a huge Democratic vote. Walker had let Touchette handle some gubernatorial patronage, but the Governor knew he should have known better than to trust the guy, the kind of politician Walker originally had campaigned against in the first place.

Another case in point was the back stabbing of Walker by organized labor, for which Walker's governorship had been a godsend. Walker felt labor should be ashamed. So did DuQuoin's Gerald Hawkins.

Hawkins had gone to Springfield for the United Mine Workers of America to promote more positive action for the miners in the Capital, and he scored a bull's-eye with Walker. Dealing personally with the Governor, Hawkins secured Walker's backing for stronger mine safety legislation that would be pushed through the General Assembly in 1975 by the UMWA and signed by Walker.

Looking back years later, Hawkins recalled vividly "how I was so green and young and still fresh out of a coal mine when I got to have breakfast at the Mansion with Governor Walker to map out our plans for passing the safety legislation and to work on his placement of better people on the State Mining Board."

To the tobacco-chewing Hawkins, that breakfast at the Mansion "was probably the first time I had a choice between bacon, sausage or ham."

When the 1976 primary rolled around, the UMWA refused to join most of the other big unions and go for Howlett.

"We stuck with Walker," said Hawkins. "We could not oppose him, Daley or no Daley. Walker was a fantastic governor for labor, but he was not appreciated. The rest of labor lost a lot of credibility by turning its back on Walker."

One of the items stressed by Walker in the primary campaign was his backing of the upgraded mine safety program. He also emphasized his enforcement of personal finance disclosure requirements for state employees, his efforts at criminal justice reform providing for a harder line against offenders and the reduction (at least during his first years as governor) in the number of state workers under his wing. Although acknowledging an increase in state spending during his governorship, he noted that it occurred without any tax increases.

However, as in many Illinois political campaigns, discussion of issues ended up taking a backseat to more titillating subjects—such as attention to imagery. Neither Walker nor Howlett spared any ammunition in trying to impugn the integrity of the other.

Actually, Howlett really wanted to lay low in the campaign, confident that the support of Daley and the other Democratic regulars in itself would carry Howlett to victory. He intended to just ignore Walker and glide through the primary campaign.

For one thing, Howlett refused to debate Walker. The secretary of state may have been unsurpassed on the political dinner circuit in entertaining crowds with jokes and anecdotes, but the plump Howlett was not at ease before cameras. Certainly not like the tall and suave Walker.

The Governor portrayed Howlett's avoidance of him as evidence of Walker's contention that Howlett was a shallow person with little insight into complex issues. But, added Walker, that probably would not matter much if Howlett was governor since he would only be a lackey for Mayor Daley anyway.

Finally, in the last weeks before the primary, Howlett retaliated with a verbal explosion that was most uncharacteristic of the veteran public servant. In an unusual burst of anger, he called Walker an irresponsible "s.o.b." who had "regrettably turned Chicago against downstate, laborer against businessman and so on."

Dan Walker was nothing more than a political con man, Howlett charged in the campaign's final weeks, a flimflammer who had taken the Illinois populace for a ride in order to promote himself.

And so it went, right up to the election. A mudslinging battle focusing on personality traits of these two individuals whose political careers had been framed so differently.

Coming back to Illinois a few days before the primary to endorse Howlett, United States Senator Adlai Stevenson conjectured that if the purpose of a political race was to inform the public, "then the Democratic primary campaign for governor is a failure."

Two days before the primary, the Chicago Sun-Times reported a survey conducted for the newspaper by a Chicago marketing firm showed Walker and Howlett in a neck and neck contest. Even Howlett followers conceded that Walker had outhustled their man on the hustings.

But the Sun-Times survey was wrong.

Michael Howlett won handily, receiving 811,721 votes to 696,380 for Walker. Howlett's total was about 54 percent of the Democratic primary vote for governor. Overall, 43 percent of the state's 5,766,634 registered voters went to the polls in the primary, a high figure.

Cook County clearly dictated the outcome of the Howlett-Walker race.

Sixty percent of those persons taking a Democratic ballot in the primary were from Cook, and 556,397 of them voted for Howlett compared to 327,622 for Walker. This was a plurality of 228,775 for Howlett, the bulk of which he amassed in the city of Chicago, the breadbasket of the Daley machine.

(In Walker's victory over Paul Simon in their race for the Democratic nomination for governor in the 1972 Illinois primary, the Daley-backed Simon emerged from Cook with only a 20,957-vote lead, a far cry from Howlett's showing in 1976.)

As expected, Walker carried the rest of the state, 368,758 to 255,324. However, Walker's plurality of 113,434 in the 101 counties outside of Cook obviously was far short of what he needed to offset Howlett's 228,775-vote margin in Cook. Howlett was left with a statewide victory plurality of 115,341 votes, not exactly a razor-thin margin.

Besides Cook, Howlett carried only 16 other counties, meaning that 85 landed in the Walker column.

The Governor swept all of the heavily populated counties around Cook and in reality lost only two downstate counties with big Democratic votes. One was St. Clair, where Howlett barely edged Walker, 20,144 to 20,062, in spite of the machine mentality long prevalent in that Democratic bastion.

The other county was Sangamon, the home of thousands of state workers, which interestingly went for Howlett, 14,836 to 12,354—a not too subtle indication of Walker's standing with the state bureaucratic community.

It also could be surmised that the result in Sangamon probably underscored quite graphically the difficulties that Walker had encountered in getting his own people inserted into state patronage slots in the Illinois Capital.

Looking at the primary outcome from a statewide viewpoint, it seemed clear that Walker did not get on March 16, 1976, the votes of many who had formed his unofficial coalition in the 1972 primary, namely independents, numerous Republicans, Democratic dissidents and young persons.

Too, Walker had lost the backing of liberals because of his support for restoration of the death penalty and because they realized soon after he took office that he really was quite conservative on numerous issues.

After accepting defeat in the primary, Walker still conjured up a touch of mystery by threatening to run for governor in the fall general election as the candidate of a third party, which was a possibility under state election laws. Consequently, he held off endorsing Howlett. But it was just last-ditch drama that went nowhere.

The rough-and-tumble primary campaign was the political denouement for Dan Walker. There would be no encore. Truthfully, the primary fight also killed Howlett.

Badly bruised by Walker, Howlett was unable to recover to mount a credible campaign for the general election against the attractive Republican candidate for governor, James R. Thompson, the former United States attorney in Chicago.

After Thompson overwhelmed Howlett in every phase of the campaign, Thompson and his running mate for lieutenant governor, Sheriff Dave O'Neal of St. Clair County, clobbered the Howlett-Hartigan ticket by a stunning margin of nearly 1,400,000 votes in the general election.

It was the kickoff for what would be Thompson's 14-year hold on the governor's office. For Howlett, the general election result relegated him to a state of political obscurity lasting until his death in 1992.

Without question, a Thompson-Walker contest would have been a much closer race in the general election of Nov. 2, 1976. No two more exciting campaigners could have been pitted against each other.

That was wishful thinking, though. Just something for the old men who hang around county courthouses to dream about. But never to be. ❧

23

The Presidency, Yachts and Other Memories

January 5, 1988, was extremely cold and gray as Charles Walker, Will Walker and Dan Walker, Jr., drove their father to Duluth, Minnesota, to deliver him at the prison gate as ordered by the federal court. The always-vigilant press wanted to record the event, but the former governor made it difficult by arranging an arrival time apart from what the media expected.

Talking about his time in prison would not be something that Dan Walker would do easily or willingly. He did admit that he was pleased to be given the task of chapel clerk, but not pleased at all when a new warden took away that job and directed him instead to clean toilets.

Many nights, inmate Walker hardly slept at all, finding it impossible to keep his mind from wandering over the past. What had been, what might have been. The glory and the tragedy, all flashing through his head like the frames of a motion picture.

So much of it seemed to have happened yesterday, not years earlier.

A man who could have been president, now languishing in prison. Walker probably should have listened to Dave Green; maybe he should have jumped right into the presidential primaries in 1976 and skipped running again for governor.

He might have been the Democrat elected president in 1976 instead of Jimmy Carter. Walker heard that a lot, and the memories of people telling him that were painful. He often tried to blot out such lofty, dreamy stuff during those sleepless nights at Duluth. It hurt too much.

Rather, his thoughts often ranged over less grandiose topics. Some humorous, others irritating.

Like lawyers in government, one of his pet peeves. Attorney Walker had found the ones who spent their professional lives in government "the worst bureaucrats" because of "their myopic approach to government."

He never ceased to be amazed at their "preoccupation with form over substance, their obsession with regulations, which they loved to write but which usually kept them from contributing in a meaningful way to real programmatic progress."

However, more than lawyers in the bureaucracy frustrated Walker. Time and again, in attempting to deal with issues, even crises, he felt that he could not get the information he needed from the bureaucrats. The biggest challenge in decision-making, Walker came to realize, "was just getting the facts."

But, he found, "many of those bureaucrats frozen into the government establishment stifled facts, making it harder for you to get them. It was obvious the system just influences bureaucrats to tell the boss, the elective person in particular, what they think the boss wants to hear and not what he or she should hear."

With that in mind, Walker often went to meetings with bureaucrats with a certain slip of paper in his pocket. As these sessions progressed, the Governor frequently took the piece of paper out of his pocket to remind himself of its message.

On it he had written: "The bastards are lying."

But thinking about the state bureaucracy on those restless nights in prison only made Walker more depressed. It was better for his spirit to recall the lighter moments, occasions that brought levity to the governorship, that showed he was human.

He could smile inwardly in thinking back to that time—it must have been in 1974—when he agreed to receive in his office state Representative Ralph Dunn, a fine gentleman of a legislator from DuQuoin or Pinckneyville (Walker could never remember) and a group of school youngsters from Marissa.

The kids were in the Capitol lobbying for approval of the opossum as the state animal and they wanted to push their cause with the Governor personally. They had a baby opossum with them and, after being ushered into the presence of Walker, asked him to pose for pictures with the animal on his shoulder.

The Governor obliged, and darned if that little critter did not immediately wet on the suit coat of the great man.

Walker also would lighten up in later years about another incident that was not amusing when it occurred.

The Governor and several other individuals were hunting for doves one day on a farm field west of Springfield where Walker had hunted before. He had noticed that an unusually large number of doves were flying around, but was not sure of the reason.

Suddenly, out of nowhere, three men came striding toward the Walker party. One flipped a badge in the Governor's face, identified himself as a federal game warden, and announced that the Governor was under arrest for shooting over baited ground, an illegality. A quick check revealed that grains of corn were in fact under the dirt where Walker was hunting.

An angry Walker was convinced he was a victim of a setup since he could not have seen the buried corn kernels and because "it was common knowledge in that area that I hunted there." Nevertheless, he paid a $100 fine to get the episode out of the way. Still, the incident was widely reported in downstate newspapers.

Although apprehensive at first that the matter could hurt his image, he discovered that he had nothing to fear.

"After it was over, I even got in the habit when entering a country cafe or tavern to ask if anybody was aware of a good place to go dove hunting. Every time, that got me cheers and good-natured kidding from those on hand. People told me they were sure it was a trap."

Few persons knew it, but Walker did not like to fly any more than he liked women chewing gum or his daughters wearing jeans. This chief executive of Illinois definitely wanted to keep his feet on the ground.

Once at the Illinois State Fair, an annual summer extravaganza in Springfield at which governors generally make a lot of political hay, Walker created a different type of momentary excitement.

By some means, he was coaxed into getting onto a seat of the "sky ride." But when the ride started to propel him skyward, the Governor turned in the seat and frantically shouted back to his always present security chief Pete Wilkes, who was left standing on the ground, to "get me down and out of this thing."

Right pronto, the ride was stopped and put in reverse, and within moments the Governor was back on earth. Meanwhile, fair goers started converging on the scene, anxious to see what the commotion was about.

The State Fair was an ingenious proposition for Walker for

reasons beyond avoiding the sky ride. He wanted the fair to be a celebration of downstate Illinois, but he also sought to curb its constant deficit.

He tried to improve the exposition by reducing the price of admission to attract more people, by permitting the return of beer sales and by introducing bingo. But the red ink continued.

In addition, many aspects of the poor management of the fair that existed prior to Walker persisted during his days in office. At least Illinois Auditor General Robert G. Cronson thought so. In one scathing report, Cronson charged that fiscal supervision of the fair was a disaster under Paul H. King, a former manager of the Milwaukee Summerfest who became director of the Illinois fair under Walker.

However, the big show still went on every year. And while it did, Walker was always around. Nothing seemed too trivial for his attention, not even the entertainment that drew throngs to the nightly shows at the grandstand.

When he became governor, Walker surely had little inkling that he might be dealing with recalcitrant rock groups. But he did one evening when he accompanied his agriculture director, Pud Williams, to the State Fair grandstand show.

The main attraction was a rock outfit which, to the best of anyone's memory, was named ShaNaNa. Thousands had flocked to the grandstand to hear the group. But, ShaNaNa had refused to begin its performance at the scheduled time, complaining that the stage was wet from a rain earlier in the day. As the delay of the start stretched beyond an hour, the crowd began to get restless. That was enough to spur the Governor into action.

Making his way to the dressing room under the grandstand stage, Walker minced no words in confronting the members of ShaNaNa.

"I am Dan Walker. I am the Governor of Illinois. I want to know if you are going to play for us."

Right away, a fellow assumed by Walker to be the leader of ShaNaNa delivered a snappy retort.

"Well, Big Man, did you come down here to lean on us?"

Another chap in the group added quickly that the contract to play at the State Fair gave the performers an out if it was raining.

Unfazed, Walker aimed the gaze on the rockers that he reserved for political enemies and laid down the law in no uncertain terms.

"There are 15,000 people out there who say it's not raining now. If you don't play, we all will be a hell of a lot older before you get any money out of the State of Illinois. I'll be back here in 30 minutes for your answer."

ShaNaNa put on a terrific show.

Yes, Walker could be a tough guy. His brother Lewis (known to family members as Waco) saw it early on. Lewis never forgot that time when his younger brother Dan was 13 or so and the two of them got into a fight, a really hard-hitting encounter, in one of those arid canyons behind their San Diego home.

"I was on top of him, beating him up pretty badly," Waco recalled. "I kept asking him to give up. But, he refused even though he was taking quite a licking. So I finally just quit and let him up.

"Dan just would not surrender. He was so stubborn."

During those interminable hours in prison when his mind roamed wildly, sometimes almost crazily from subject to subject, Walker would be momentarily back in that canyon with his brother on top of him.

Then, a second later, Walker would be walking again through southern Illinois, parched from the sun and praying for a cold drink from Steve Senderowitz, a young campaign worker assigned to the walk who later in life would be a successful Chicago attorney.

The next second, though, Walker would be huddling in his mind once again with Harold (Hal) Shapiro, a close friend and fellow Chicago lawyer who was instrumental in handling finances in the early part of Walker's drive for the governorship—when hardly anybody wanted to contribute to a candidate going nowhere.

However, with the passing of another second, Walker would be reflecting on that comment once by Vic de Grazia that some persons viewed the Walker administration as an employment agency for Chicago's liberal Hyde Park neighborhood. Well, perhaps it did look that way, Walker thought.

So many out of Hyde Park had played key roles. One coming to mind might be Louis Silverman, a Walkerite from start to finish who was the administration's Capital Development Board chairman. Or maybe Olga Corey, who had handled public relations for the Chicago Urban League and Roosevelt University before Walker sent her to Washington to direct the state's office on the Potomac, to run interference for him with the Illinois congressional delegation.

It was incredible the way Walker's mind raced over these things. If he dwelled on anything, it would be the time between the governor's office and prison.

Nothing was more glamorous in Walker's life after the governorship than his new wife and his yachts.

Walker bought the first one, a 48-foot Hatteras powerboat, for $350,000 from a Little Rock, Arkansas, businessman late in 1983. Dan and Roberta II viewed the purchase as an investment, with the yacht to be available for chartering for private parties or other purposes.

The twin-engine diesel motor cruiser, which had two cabins that slept four, had been used as a party boat. One bedroom was glass-mirrored. Walker berthed the yacht at Fort Lauderdale, where he kept it less than a year before "trading up" for the second yacht.

The second one, also named The Governor's Lady, was the

most prized possession he ever had. It contributed greatly to his financial downfall.

The $850,000 cruiser, which remained in Walker's hands for two years, was a custom-built oceangoing vessel, 76 feet in length, that contained three staterooms. The gracefully-lined boat, which Walker purchased from its designer, had a four-foot draft. This meant it could be maneuvered into even the smallest of the Bahama islands, which is just what Walker did.

Capable of a 1,500-mile range, the second yacht offered Walker and Roberta II a life-style beyond even the wildest dreams of most Illinoisans.

Dan Walker, who had shunned so many of the perks available to him when governor, now owned a yacht with a crew of three persons—a captain, a mate and a part-time chef. The cost of operating and maintaining the ship, including debt service, was hitting $30,000 a month. The outstanding loan on the boat remained close to $850,000.

Financially, this was more than the former governor could handle. It was great fun while it lasted, though.

Although the second yacht also was berthed at Fort Lauderdale, Dan piloted it up through the inland waterway system to Chicago two summers in a row. There, at anchor in Burnham harbor, where the yacht was among the biggest, the boat was at the center of a social whirl that more than made up for the sparsity in Walker's social life in his earlier days.

Dan and Roberta were toasts of the town. They made the good life look easy, this former governor and old Navy man turned yacht skipper and the striking woman by his side. She certainly had journeyed far from the days when she was Roberta Estelle Martin growing up on New York's Long Island, where her father was an employee of the shipbuilding industry.

A specialty of Dan and Roberta were cruise parties on Lake Michigan, occasions at which many in Chicago's smart set were present. Not always for purely personal pleasure, some of the cruises were for charity fund-raising while others served the business entertainment needs of Walker and his wife.

Going back to the original investment angle concerning the yachts, Walker did try with both boats to defray the heavy costs involved by renting them for private parties. This generated, with the second yacht at least, about $125,000 a year in charter fees. The income was far short, though, of the money necessary to make ends meet with the yachts.

Not all fairy tales have happy endings, and this one did not. Walker was having a devilish time coming up with the money needed to cover the operating bills, to meet the loan purchase payments, to handle huge outlays for repairing and redecorating the second yacht. Repair bills alone added up to $150,000 annually.

Consequently, when he fell two months behind in paying off the loan, the savings and loan firm in Florida that had financed the Walker loan to buy the yacht foreclosed on it, secured the title to the boat and took possession of it in Florida without even telling Walker. Dan learned of this only when he flew to Florida to get the yacht ready for a charter and found it in the possession of marshals pursuant to a court order.

To those persons who had suspected Walker was living beyond his means, the loss of the second yacht was hardly a surprise. The only part that mystified Walker watchers was the motive for his involvement in such an expensive venture in the first place.

The reason was at least partially traceable, Roberta II later felt upon reflection, to circumstances unfolding in the time leading up to the purchase of the first yacht.

When Walker was still contemplating the initial yacht purchase, he suffered what he and medical authorities believed to be three heart attacks.

This led her husband, said Roberta II, "to really come to think that he was not going to be around long enough to ever enjoy life the way he had dreamed. He really thought there was no longer any reason to hold back."

As it turned out, a well-known cardiologist determined after coronary angiography that Walker had not been a heart attack victim, but that his symptoms (the same as those associated with heart attacks) actually were caused by reflex esophagitis—acid reflexing from the stomach back into the esophagus, a situation causing prolonged and often severe heartburn.

Nevertheless, while still under the belief that he was suffering heart attacks, Walker had verbally committed to buy the first yacht. And he went ahead and did it, even after being told that his painful medical problem was not his heart.

As governor, Walker hesitated to go near horse racing tracks, fearful of the stigma from the racing stock scandals that had tarnished so many other Illinois politicians. Indeed, reform of the state's regulation of racing made considerable headway under Anthony Scariano, the onetime state legislator named by Walker to chair the Illinois Racing Board.

But that hardly meant Walker disliked horses. To the contrary, his more affluent way of life with Roberta II included frequent visits to the Oak Brook Polo Club, which was not far from their home in the tony Chicago suburb of Oak Brook.

The former governor owned no horses, but that did not deter he and his wife from watching the private club's matches at the beautiful village-owned polo grounds, where the steeds were quite a sight galloping up and down the fields of the old-fashioned country English setting.

Of course, the history of the polo club was tied closely to the much talked-about Butler family that in turn was linked to Walker in the business world after his departure from the governorship.

Although Walker's attempt after leaving office to run a successful statewide law firm fell short, he did much better with the speedy oil change venture established across the country by Butler-Walker, Inc., a corporation set up by himself, Roberta II and Paul Butler of the Oak Brook polo family—a man whose name was synonymous with the founding of the community of Oak Brook.

However, after the death of Paul Butler, his share of the business was taken over by Frank Butler, one of his sons. Frank Butler and Walker did not hit it off, leading to irreparable conflicts and court encounters between the two. In the end, the business was sold at a greatly reduced price in 1984 to Jiffy Lube, a large national firm.

In 1983, two years after founding the oil change business, Walker and Roberta II got into the field of thrifts with the purchase of the First American Savings and Loan Association in the southern Illinois town of Benton.

Between them, Walker and Roberta II bought all of the stock in First American. They proceeded to open a branch of the thrift in Oak Brook, and it would become the headquarters of the operation. The Benton end of it became a branch.

Among other things, Dan and Roberta created a subsidiary of the savings and loan association to participate in development of the oil change business, especially the franchising of it.

Still, making money with the savings and loan was another task that Walker and his wife found daunting. Too, federal regulators of the savings and loan industry opposed the couple's control of the thrift and the rapid lubrication business at the same time, meaning that Dan and Roberta were under the gun to divest themselves of one or the other holding. In view of the problems with Frank Butler, the sale of the oil change business seemed the logical way to go.

However, the savings and loan, which was continuing to lose

money, would not remain in the hands of Dan and Roberta that much longer. Federal officials took over First American in 1986, contending after a disagreement with Walker and Roberta over the value of the firm's assets that the thrift was insolvent.

More to the point, First American was placed in conservatorship by the Federal Home Loan Bank Board and the Walker management was terminated. The Federal Savings and Loan Insurance Corporation was named the conservator of First American and authorized to run the business.

However, setbacks like the loss of the savings and loan would pale in comparison to the depth of Walker's plunge in life by the end of the following year, 1987, as he was starting his prison phase.

By then, Walker appeared to be merely a shadow of the person who once was governor of his state and more recently a possessor of luxury boats, a savings and loan and a share of the good life tasted by very few but the truly rich and famous.

He was a beaten man. His pride and honor crushed, his professional life extinguished, his finances in a shambles, his reputation soiled by the tag of convicted felon.

Many of the individuals with whom he had contact in the period leading up to prison also noticed he was drinking heavily, a situation that would not be reversed until his incarceration at Duluth.

Actually, as time would show, many of Walker's business concepts were positive, judging by the success of others who would undertake similar ventures.

However, in the words of Thomas Foran, the attorney defending Walker against the federal charges, the former governor ended up "out of his depth as a businessman."

Added Foran: "Walker's ideas were mostly good but he ran too fast and fell on his face."

In the words of Roberta Nelson-Walker, the former governor she had married in 1978 turned out to be "a man very idealistic about life but very unrealistic about money.

"We did not see eye to eye on finances all the time, but Dan was so aggressively optimistic in always looking at life and financial situations as a glass half full rather than half empty."

The heavy borrowing by Walker from a variety of sources— for a wide array of business and other purposes besides yacht financing—triggered the charges that landed him in prison.

Specifically, Walker pleaded guilty to three offenses: obtaining benefits (worth about $250,000) from funds loaned by First American to other individuals (including Dan Walker, Jr.); committing perjury in stating that he, Dan Walker, had not received any financial benefit from money borrowed by Dan Walker, Jr., from First American; and signing false personal financial statements with financial institutions other than First American (documents that overstated income and omitted certain contingent liabilities).

As a business partner of her husband, Roberta II was a cosignatory on a number of the loans or loan guaranties tied to her husband in the couple's halcyon days. In the financial debacle that followed, she was hard pressed to pay off the debts on which she was a cosigner. However, she had succeeded in largely doing so by the early 1990s.

In 1988, while Walker was imprisoned, Roberta II obtained a divorce from him, ending a marriage that lasted 10 years.

However, the divorce did not end the torment of it all for her. While Walker was behind bars, Roberta II found herself besieged by creditors as well as by auditors from the Internal Revenue Service and the Illinois Department of Revenue still prying into the financial dealings of herself and Walker.

Back on that November day in 1987 in Chicago when Federal District Court Judge Ann Williams imposed a seven-year prison sentence on Walker for his crimes, the former governor sat through the proceeding with his head erect and his hands in his lap. Afterward, he walked quickly from the courtroom without comment, flanked by his lawyer Foran and Dan Walker, Jr.

Disgraced and embittered, Walker appeared almost oblivious to those seeking one more look at this man of stature suddenly shorn of seemingly everything, not the least of which was his dignity.

And, quite literally, Walker was unmindful of the noisy excitement following his sentencing.

Before exiting that courtroom he already had turned to the state of introversion, to the exclusion of all else, that he well knew would be necessary to survive this upcoming nadir of his tumultuous life—every up-and-down stage of which he had entered with his eyes wide open. ❧

Hard to Forget

Illinois has long been in the fast lane of American life.

Hardly a backwater among the states, Illinois has been propelled through its history by unusually strong energy in every kind of endeavor. In its culture, literature, gangsterism, the making of its heroes, in the explosive mix of its diverse population and in the changing face of its once mainly agrarian landscape.

Often beautiful, sometimes ugly. But never boring in Illinois. Never. Politics included.

The raucous tradition of Illinois' political world, the progenitor of Lincoln and also sleazy ward heelers, was just right for Dan Walker.

Really, Illinoisans expected a person such as Walker to come along every now and then, to shake up things, to serve as a reminder that Illinois still was Illinois and not Kansas.

Whether people cottoned to him or not, Walker got their attention. From the small town gang huddling in the homey warmth of Alongi's restaurant in DuQuoin to University of Chicago students hanging out at the venerable C Shop grill. All of them knew who was governor.

Understanding him was another matter. Compared to many others in Illinois public life, Walker was a political comet that burned out rather quickly—maybe not fast enough for a lot of individuals but far too soon for those who had pinned on him their hopes for a better Illinois.

Numerous Walker detractors even reluctantly acknowledge that he revitalized the Illinois political process in a period when the nation was undergoing a spiritually renewing catharsis in its own political and social fabrics.

Yet, Walker seemed strangely unable to capitalize on the opportunities for change presented by the political revolution he had wrought, his critics were quick to add. More than a few Walker partisans nodded in accord.

Bill O'Daniel, whom Walker helped elect to the General Assembly in 1974, considered himself a close friend of Walker. Nevertheless, southern Illinoisan O'Daniel could not help but lament in later years that "Dan was not as politically astute in the end as he should have been.

"He was just so headstrong. He just destroyed himself. It was a damn shame because he had everything it took to work out his differences."

As time moved on after Walker's departure from office, many members of the political science community were not finding it easy to come up with a snug interpretation of the Walker era, which some likened to a flash fire on the Illinois political scene.

Of the state's more recent governors, none may have been a more ripe subject for psychoanalysis than Walker in the view of Jack Van Der Slik, a professor of political studies at Sangamon State University at Springfield.

"What a story," said Van Der Slik of Walker.

"It was the classic man against the hostile world tale. It was the underlying characteristic of Walker's whole career, the poor boy who comes up from nothing to make good. It was the forging experience of his personality, the kind of thing that makes some people indomitable.

"He (Walker) got to be a more than $100,000-a-year man in the business world. But that wasn't good enough for him. He had to climb the public mountain to get approval of a large mass of people. He seemed to need this; corporate life just could not give it to him.

"He beat the political system in a big way to get the recognition he needed. But once on top, he made a strategic mistake in shunning conventional political tactics of negotiation and compromise. Instead, he seemed to insist on the antithesis. I am going to win or going to lose, but I will not accommodate.

"A question, of course, was whether this was still a sign of insecurity associated with this man who came up from nothing."

Intriguingly, in rising from his humble beginning, observed Van Der Slik, "Walker developed incredible personal magnetism, a great ability to move relatively anonymous sets of people. He could capture attention, and obviously loved to do it."

Those once "anonymous" people who Walker brought into play in life would be the core of his legacy. The years after his governorship saw the ascendancy of Walker proteges in many places in Illinois.

Even though organized labor abandoned Walker in his bid in 1976 to retain the governor's office, by the 1990s the Illinois AFL-CIO was being run by Richard Walsh as president and Don

Johnson as secretary-treasurer. In the Walker administration, Johnson was director of the Department of Labor and Walsh was a key assistant to Johnson. The communications director for the labor department in Walker's time was Sue Kolker Altman, who had worked for Walker's election to the governorship back in her East St. Louis days. Later, she surfaced with Walsh and Johnson at the AFL-CIO as director of communications.

If anything, this was a commonplace turn of events. Many veterans of the army of fresh political faces spawned by Dan Walker did not fade from the public spotlight like the general.

Some of them took to glossing over their early days with Walker after he went to prison. Plenty of others, though, would recall with pride the allegiance and sweat and blood they gave to the Walker movement. They were not going to apologize to anybody.

One who remained steadfast about this was Toby Olszewski, a tireless campaigner for Walker in Kankakee County in 1976 as well as in 1972 (and a person who never accepted a state job when Walker was governor).

Speaking years later from her newspaper publishing office, she insisted that Walker "made it less scornful to be associated with Illinois politics or government.

"He undid the traditional party patronage stuff. He opened the political door to a whole new legion of people, and that was really something in those times—when Illinois politics had gotten low and dirty and just plain tiresome to people.

"Let's face it, the political parties have just not been the same since Walker."

Sharing that sentiment was the feisty Alice Josephine Marks, whose energetic assistance to Walker in the 1972 campaign earned her a gubernatorial appointment when Walker was in office to a $15,000-a-year seat on the Illinois Toll Road Highway Authority.

"Sure," Alice Marks said later in life, "we all felt let down when Dan went to jail."

Still, she insisted, "history will show that the whole Walker thing was a great chapter in Illinois politics. All of us who were part of it believe that he was an excellent governor whose presence made for a better Illinois."

On the other hand, there were Walkerites who gave his governorship a mixed review. Their number included the late John Forbes, the Blackburn College political science professor whose relationship with Walker went back to the 1950s.

Although Forbes awarded Walker high marks for spurring a needed shake-up of the Illinois political structure, he hesitated to give Walker much more than an average grade as governor.

Forbes, a political idealist to his dying day, had hoped that Walker would resurrect in Illinois the enlightened brand of leadership that the state had received in the eyes of Forbes from Governor Adlai Stevenson, the political icon of both Forbes and Walker.

However, Forbes failed to detect the further growth in Walker as governor that Forbes deemed to be necessary for Walker to earn the mantle of greatness.

Conversing with a reporter shortly before Walker left office, Forbes voiced disappointment that Walker had not risen above "the mundane fighting day after day on issues, big or small, that finally overwhelmed the spirit and soul of what Dan Walker was really supposed to be about."

The image of Walker after taking office was felt by Forbes to have fallen "from a very promising guiding light in the Stevensonian tradition to a largely confusing mishmash."

Patrick Quinn would not go that far, but he too was not satisfied that the full potential of Walker's governorship was being fulfilled when the young political activist left Walker in 1975 after holding a series of posts in the administration.

After experiencing the excitement of Walker's 1972 campaign and his own much-lauded organizing role in it, Quinn admittedly found it difficult to adjust to the daily tedium ingrained in most government jobs. He even had to begin wearing a tie (but still no suit coat) after Walker entered office.

Quinn actually had more interesting assignments than most. At first, he was Walker's personal ombudsman, a role that afforded him valuable insight into the working of government as he sought to resolve complaints to the Governor's office about the quality of agencies' services and other doings. In that and subsequent positions, Quinn got a taste of handling patronage, although the Walker crowd was always loath to use that word in describing job-dispensing by the administration.

No matter what, though, Quinn found that being a government insider was too tame for him at that stage of his life. He was itching to hit the streets again, eager to resume raising cain with the political establishment, to further nurture the spirit of political mutiny at the grass roots unleashed by Walker.

To Quinn, Walker's campaign for governor in 1972 "was entrepreneurial in every way. It changed the way candidates ran for office. The citizens' coalition that it flowered was a truly unique happening, a rare moment in history for the iconoclasts, the mavericks and the independent thinkers to bloom."

Once in office, Quinn said, Walker "fostered a lot of experimentation that saw unusual flexibility in programs that were being driven by many unconventional persons."

Nevertheless, continued Quinn, "the energy and enthusiasm of the administration was obviously beginning to wane after several years in office." By that time, Quinn added, "Walker was no longer enough of a populist for me...his administration had stopped being a vehicle for organizing citizens."

Consequently, Quinn walked away from the administration, telling Walker that "it was time for me to hit the road again, time for me to do what I did best—which was organizing people to bring about change. There were no hard feelings with Walker. I just told him I was a better outsider than insider."

Fifteen years after leaving Walker, Quinn was elected state treasurer. During that decade and a half, Quinn became an incredible thorn in the side of the politically entrenched through the Oak Park-based Coalition for Political Honesty that he established and through other volunteer groups.

Quinn spearheaded a drive that led to the creation of the Citizens Utility Board, to the horror of the utilities, and he was the main mover behind a state constitutional amendment—the first change in the 1970 document approved by voters—that reduced the size of the General Assembly.

Debate over whether the so-called Cutback Amendment did indeed improve legislative accountability went on long after its ratification in 1980, but nobody disputed the impact on Illinois public life of self-styled populist Quinn.

Predictably, in winning his state office in 1990, Quinn had to circumvent the regulars in his own Democratic Party, which made him a chip off the old block in respect to the person who had brought Quinn onto the state political scene.

If Quinn endured frustration in trying to function as a government insider while a member of the Walker administration, he was not alone. The same was even true for some of those higher up.

As counsel to Governor Walker, attorney William Ira Goldberg normally followed his early morning tennis match against Walker with frequent consultation with his boss during the day. Goldberg was involved in most of the innumerable issues facing Illinois government.

"Believe me, many persons in government get frustrated. Nobody who went to work or serve with Dan thought it would be easy. And it was not."

Those were the words of Goldberg to a person who visited him in 1992 at his office with the Chicago law firm of Holleb & Coff.

When Walker was governor, Illinois state government was spending close to $30 million in taxpayers' funds every working day. Trying to keep on top of the problems and challenges posed by an operation of that magnitude turned out to be a task beyond anything Goldberg ever imagined.

On the positive side, though, Goldberg was convinced that Walker brought renewed accountability to Illinois government in both its programs and fiscal policies—partly because of his persistence on his personal hands-on approach to governmental management.

"And, of course, we also tried to make things better by raising the ethical level of government," said Goldberg.

"That meant change, especially when we insisted on standing up for what we thought was right. That also meant we made enemies. You always do when you push change."

Yet, observed Goldberg, "Dan might have been much more popular when we were in Springfield if we had agreed to govern just 101 counties (leaving the running of Cook County entirely to the Daley machine)."

The Daley factor again. It would never be far beneath the surface in any discourse about the political life of Dan Walker, from its infancy to the postmortems.

"You are asking me again if we could have worked things out with Mayor Daley," Victor de Grazia said to a questioner many years after his friend Walker was finished politically.

"That was always the question.

"The answer is probably not. It was a classic confrontation between the two. Daley was a traditional Irish politician, authentic in every way, and Dan was his Protestant antagonist."

Walker himself went into more detail on the subject in a guest column that he penned for *Illinois Issues* magazine in 1980. He called it one more try at explaining his side of the frequent charge that his political career was impeded by his refusal to stop fighting with the Chicago mayor and countless others.

"I start with the premise that the (confrontationist) label has been used in a pejorative sense," wrote Walker, "depicting a man who would rather fight than lead, either because he liked to fight for the sake of fighting or he did not know how to lead without fighting."

He would not argue, Walker went on, that he "did have to fight to get attention" in order to win the governorship against great odds.

"I will also agree that I had a deep philosophical difference with the 'club' brand of politics that pervaded both parties and continually affected government, and that I never was and never wanted to be a member of that 'club'."

Furthermore, Walker said, "I will also agree that there could never have been a total rapport...between me and Mayor Daley, simply because we had such a wide divergence of views as to how the Democratic Party should operate and be structured and as to certain key governmental issues."

In conclusion, he wrote that "all I'm trying to say is that there is a much deeper story behind the so-called 'confrontation' image than has been portrayed. Sure, some part was political fighting. But another part was an attempt to change the way politics and government have traditionally been practiced in Illinois."

Walker also referred in the column to the numerous investigations of his political fund-raising that were conducted both during and after his governorship.

At one point or another, federal and state prosecutors, the United States Department of Justice, the Illinois Board of Elections and investigative journalists scrutinized contributions to Walker from firms doing business with the state. Also looked into were various allegations such as the one that individuals bought state jobs with political contributions during the Walker years.

At least eight grand jury investigations delved into one or more aspects of Walker's fund-raising. Walker himself testified before two of them, refusing each time to hide behind the Fifth Amendment prohibiting self-incrimination on a ground that, in his words, he "had nothing to hide."

As he saw it, Walker would say later, "it apparently did not occur to those behind the grand jury investigations that if I had been willing to take what amounted to bribes I never would have had the fund-raising problems and political debts that I did."

None of the inquiries resulted in any indictment of or charge against Walker.

This led him to conclude that the investigations were motivated by two reasons. One was to inflict revenge on Walker for upstaging the Illinois political establishment. The other motive, he suspected, was to damage his image so as to discourage his chances for a political comeback.

Following Walker's years at the helm of Illinois, prosecutors and other investigators did appear to take little interest as the amount of state contracts awarded to campaign contributors by Governor Jim Thompson and other state officials soared to levels far beyond the scope of the practice under Walker.

Dubbed pin-striped patronage, leaders of both parties were quick to note that it was not illegal if the state's purchasing rules were followed—irrespective of the raised eyebrows of many governmental watchdogs.

Whether it was accurate or not that the repeated investigations of Walker's political money-raising were intended to hamper his future electability, it was certainly true that most in the Illinois political world fully expected to see the defeated Walker make a serious bid again for high office.

His last Statehouse press conference as Illinois governor, on cold and snowy January 6, 1977, was not regarded at the time as a swan song.

Laughter greeted his observation that he had "created a little news now and then." And nobody took him lightly when he depicted the event as his "final opportunity to meet with all of you—at least this time."

Sure enough, in ensuing years, Walker would make several abortive moves toward another run for the Governor's Mansion. But they would be false starts by a man whose real interests had turned from politics to his business ventures and his new wife and the glamorous existence the two were building early in the 1980s. The direction of the epilogue of his life clearly was taking shape, the final chapter and a wonderful one at that.

But there would be more to it than he anticipated.

For the record, when Dan Walker observed his seventieth birthday August 6, 1992, he was more than half way through his five-year probation period following his release from prison in June 1989. He served a year and a half of his seven-year sentence.

For the record, after Walker left prison he lived with his brother for six months in Virginia Beach, Virginia. During that time, he completed 500 hours of community service, which was required as part of his sentence, by helping to start and staff without pay an outreach program for persons without homes.

For the record, Walker then returned to his boyhood home of San Diego, where he worked full-time for more than a year as a $250-a-week special assistant to the Rev. Joe Carroll, the head of the St. Vincent de Paul complex for the homeless at San Diego. Walker subsequently obtained a job as a legal assistant in a San Diego law firm, while continuing to work part-time for Father Joe.

For the record, as Walker reached seventy years of age he had written a cookbook and finished drafting the manuscript for a book exploring and interpreting the life and times of Jesus from a historical standpoint. Walker was searching for a publisher.

For the record, CBS News producer David Caravello had a simple comment when informed in 1992 that former Illinois Governor Dan Walker—whom Caravello once served as an advance man and then legislative assistant—was putting his life back together in San Diego.

"He is an unbelievable person," said Caravello. "I only hope that he has at last found peace in his life." ஐ

Index

A

Accardo, Tony, 171
Adams, Donald G., 231
Allen, Richard, 41
Allphin, Robert H., 223
Alter, Joanne H., 330
Altgeld, John P., 161
Amberg, Thomas, 244
Angelos, Anthony G., 198
Arndt, Dorothy G., 24
Arndt, Samuel, 25
Arrington, W. Russell, 206
Austin, Richard B., 37

B

Bagley, James, 114
Bakalis, Michael J., 331
Barnhart, William, 260
Barringer, Dean, 231
Barry, Tobias, 210
Bartulis, A. C. (Junie), 314
Beeler, B.I., 294
Bensinger, Peter B., 197
Bernstein, Carl, 243
Bertinetti, C. F., 298
Bird, Fred, 28
Blair, W. Robert, 205
Blau, Sandra, 253
Block, Rich, 89
Bond, Langhorne, 223
Boyle, Ken, 299
Briceland, Richard H., 277
Brooks, Gwendolyn, 189
Broz, Elmer, 153
Brunner, J. Terrence, 242
Bundesen, Herman, 117

Burris, Roland W., 231
Butler, Frank, 7
Butler, Paul, 347
Byers, Harold D., 313

C

Callahan, Francis, 143
Callahan, Gene, 57
Calley, William, Jr., 112
Camille, George J., 141
Camper, John, 244
Caravello, Dave, 74
Carter, Jimmy, 4
Carroll, Joe, 361
Castellano, Tony, 273
Chancey, Ray, 144
Chapman, Eugenia, 210
Chapman, Lee (Mrs.), 47
Chiles, Lawton, 54
Choate, Clyde, 208
Clark, Mark, 246
Clarke, Terrel, 206
Clayton, Pete, 55
Clement, Jim, 35
Cleverdon, David, 79
Cobb, Irvin, 45
Cody, John Cardinal, 202
Colson, William P., 127
Conn, M. L. (Mr. and Mrs.), 50
Connelly, Joe T., 141
Cooke, Alistair, 36
Corcoran, Thomas J., 174
Corey, Olga, 343
Cox, Ferne, 50
Cronson, Robert G., 341
Curran, Duke, 317
Curran, Mark, 317
Curran, Michael, 317